高等职业教育"十三五"创新型规划教材

外贸单证实务

胡越明 编著

北京理工大学出版社
BEIJING INSTITUTE OF TECHNOLOGY PRESS

版权专有　侵权必究

图书在版编目（CIP）数据

外贸单证实务：英文/胡越明编著．—北京：北京理工大学出版社，2018.5（2018.6 重印）
ISBN 978－7－5682－5653－7

Ⅰ.①外…　Ⅱ.①胡…　Ⅲ.①进出口贸易－原始凭证－高等学校－教材－英文　Ⅳ.①F740.44

中国版本图书馆 CIP 数据核字（2018）第 104316 号

出版发行 / 北京理工大学出版社有限责任公司	
社　　址 / 北京市海淀区中关村南大街 5 号	
邮　　编 / 100081	
电　　话 /（010）68914775（总编室）	
（010）82562903（教材售后服务热线）	
（010）68948351（其他图书服务热线）	
网　　址 / http：//www.bitpress.com.cn	
经　　销 / 全国各地新华书店	
印　　刷 / 山东临沂新华印刷物流集团有限责任公司	
开　　本 / 787 毫米×1092 毫米　1/16	
印　　张 / 14	责任编辑 / 梁铜华
字　　数 / 330 千字	文案编辑 / 梁铜华
版　　次 / 2018 年 5 月第 1 版　2018 年 6 月第 2 次印刷	责任校对 / 周瑞红
定　　价 / 38.00 元	责任印制 / 李　洋

图书出现印装质量问题，请拨打售后服务热线，本社负责调换

前　言

"外贸单证实务"直接对应外贸公司单证员工作岗位，也是培养外贸公司业务员和跟单员必需的技能课程。该课程的主要功能是使学生能承担外贸企业单证员所从事的工作内容：能在不同时段与业务关系方进行沟通协调，顺利获得制单所需的数据；熟练完成外贸业务进程中不同时段各种单据的制作，理解制作的技巧及其不同时段单据制作的差异性；了解各类单据移交所规定的时间，及时正确递交各时段的单据，指引业务关系方（部门）工作的顺利开展；培养严谨、忠诚、负责的职业操守，提高语言表达能力、沟通协调能力和现代化办公设备的运用能力。

该课程的前置课程包括：国际贸易基础、国际贸易实务、外贸英语函电等岗位基础课程。同步或后续课程包括：外贸客户开发与管理、外贸洽谈与签约、外贸订单管理、进出口货物托运与通关等岗位核心技术课程。

本书的编著过程历时2年，编著思路体现为以下五点。

1. 充分体现外贸单证员岗位工作的任务引领、工作过程导向的设计思想。

2. 将外贸单证业务工作，按照工作过程或工作内容的逻辑顺序分解成典型的工作项目，按完成工作项目的需要和现行岗位操作规程，结合外贸单证员资格考试标准组织教材内容，并将相关的国际惯例知识和业务理论分解到相应的操作中。

3. 以完成任务的典型活动项目来驱动，通过实际案例、情景模拟和课后拓展作业等多种手段，使学生能够获得职业认知和职业技能。

4. 体现先进性、通用性、实用性，将单证员业务领域最新操作规范和行业动态及时地纳入教材，内容包括外贸公司单证员岗位的主要业务，贴近国际商务行业发展的实际需要。

5. 活动设计内容具体，尽可能与外贸公司业务活动相同，并在实训室环境下进行，具有可操作性。

本书的内容共十章，每章下有若干小节。每小节主要有四个部分。其中："教学目标"给出了最基本的教学要求，供任课教师参考；"情景案例"给出了典型业务举例；"相关知识"给出了完成本任务所需的基础知识；"实训练习题"给出了更多的工作任务，使学习者在反复操作的过程中，达到技能的强化和加深。

本书专门针对外贸单证学习者和教师设计，可作为大中专院校国际贸易、国际商务、跨境电商专业的教材，也可作为外贸行业单证岗位培训之用，以及有志从事外贸单证工作的人士自学之用。

本书的编著，得到了浙江工商职业技术学院各位同人、有关专家和多家外贸公司的热心帮助——大量外贸单证材料以及他们的许多宝贵意见，特此表示衷心的感谢。在编著过程中，我们参阅和引用了国内外有关论著的资料和观点，部分参考资料来源于网络，书中未一一列出，在此一并向有关作者致谢。

受编著者的学识水平和能力所限，书中的谬误及疏漏之处在所难免，敬请广大读者批评指正。

编著者

目 录

前　言 ………………………………………………………………………… (1)

第一章　开证和审证 …………………………………………………… (1)
　　第一节　结算方式概述 ……………………………………………… (1)
　　第二节　开立信用证 ………………………………………………… (16)
　　第三节　审核并修改信用证 ………………………………………… (23)

第二章　制作发票和装箱单 …………………………………………… (39)
　　第一节　制作商业发票 ……………………………………………… (39)
　　第二节　制作装箱单 ………………………………………………… (46)

第三章　托运和提单 …………………………………………………… (53)
　　第一节　托运操作 …………………………………………………… (53)
　　第二节　提单操作 …………………………………………………… (59)

第四章　报检 …………………………………………………………… (68)
　　第一节　报检操作 …………………………………………………… (68)

第五章　报关 …………………………………………………………… (80)
　　第一节　出口报关操作 ……………………………………………… (80)
　　第二节　进口报关操作 ……………………………………………… (92)

第六章　申请产地证 …………………………………………………… (102)
　　第一节　一般原产地证 ……………………………………………… (102)
　　第二节　普惠制产地证 ……………………………………………… (110)

第七章　投保 …………………………………………………………… (118)
　　第一节　投保单和保险单 …………………………………………… (118)

第八章　制作其他单据 …………………………………………………（130）
　第一节　装船通知和受益人证明 ………………………………………（130）
　第二节　汇票 ……………………………………………………………（151）

第九章　寄单和交单议付 ………………………………………………（155）
　第一节　电汇方式下单据的寄送 ………………………………………（155）
　第二节　托收方式下的结汇 ……………………………………………（162）
　第三节　信用证方式下交单议付 ………………………………………（171）
　第四节　审单 ……………………………………………………………（184）

第十章　跨境电商单据 …………………………………………………（212）
　第一节　快递面单和"三单合一" ……………………………………（212）

第一章

开证和审证

第一节 结算方式概述

教学目标

最终目标：理解合同条款与结算方式。

促成目标：
1. 熟悉外贸合同的条款构成。
2. 熟悉翻译、审核合同的基本技巧。
3. 熟悉不同结算方式的流程和风险特点。

情景案例

机构：
外贸企业：宁波欧胜塑化有限公司（OCEAN PLASTIC & CHEMICAL PRODUCTS CO., LTD）。

人物：
小余：宁波欧胜塑化有限公司单证员。
张经理：宁波欧胜塑化有限公司业务经理。

背景资料：
（1）2016年3月27日，宁波欧胜塑化有限公司外贸业务部张经理以业务员的身份与荷兰公司TONNY PRODUCTS PLC签订一份2 040套运动装（Jogging Suit）的出口合同，合同号为OPCP08008。

（2）单证员小余在办公室接到外贸业务部张经理的电话：小余，出货明细单邮件明后天就会发过来，我先把合同副本传真给你。

小余马上接收传真，下面是合同的具体内容。

外贸合同：

SALES CONTRACT

1. THE SELLERS	S/C NO. OPCP08008
OCEAN PLASTIC & CHEMICAL PRODUCTS CO., LTD	DATE: MAR. 27 2016

2. ADDRESS

#1926 CANGHAI RD., NINGBO, 315041, CHINA

TEL: 0574 - ××××××××   FAX: 0574 - ××××××××

E - MAIL: Christina@163.com

3. THE BUYERS

TONNY PRODUCTS PLC

4. ADDRESS

BERSTOFSGADE 48, ROTTERDAM, THE NETHERLANDS

TEL: + (31) 74 12 37 08   FAX: + (31) 74 12 37 09

E - MAIL: chila@tvl.com.ntl

THE SELLERS AGREE TO SELL AND THE BUYERS AGREE TO BUY THE UNDERMENTIONED GOODS ACCORDING TO THE TERMS AND CONDITIONS AS STIPULATED BELOW

NAME OF COMMODITY & SPECIFICATION	QUANTITY	UNIT PRICE	TOTAL VALUE
JOGGING SUIT			CFRC 3% AMSTERDAM
Art. No. KB5200	840 sets	EUR 15.20	EUR 12,768.00
Art. No. KP6300	600 sets	EUR 12.50	EUR 7,500.00
Art. No. KY5200	600 sets	EUR 10.60	EUR 6,360.00
TOTAL	2,040 sets		EUR 26 628.00

5. PACKING

PACKED IN CARTONS OF 12 SETS

6. SHIPPING MARKS

TONNY/XD06008/AMSTERDAM/NO. 1 - UP

7. PORT OF SHIPMENT

ANY CHINESE PORT

8. PORT OF DESTINATION

AMSTERDAM

9. TIME OF SHIPMENT

NOT LATER THAN MAY 31ST, 2016

10. TERMS OF PAYMENT

30% T/T IN ADVANCE, THE OTHERS 70% T/T AFTER SHIPMENT

11. FORCE MAJEURE

The Sellers shall not be held responsible if they, owing to Force Majeure causes, fail to make delivery within the time stipulated in the contract or can't deliver the goods. However, in such a case the Sellers shall inform the Buyers immediately by cable. The Sellers shall send to the Buyers by registered letter at the request of the

Buyers a certificate attesting the existence of such a cause or causes issued by China Council for the Promotion of International Trade or by a competent Authority

12. DISCREPANCY AND CLAIM

In case discrepancy on the quality of the goods is found by the Buyers after arrival of the goods at the port of destination, claim may be lodged within 30 days after arrival of the goods at the port of destination. While for quantity discrepancy, claim may be lodged within 15 days after arrival of the goods at the port of destination, being supported by an inspection certificate issued by a reputable public surveyor agreed upon by both party. The Sellers shall, then, consider the claim in the light of actual circumstances. For the losses due to natural cause or causes falling within the responsibilities of the ship-owners or the underwriters, the sellers shall not consider any claim for compensation. In case the Letter of Credit does not reach the Sellers within the time stipulated in the Contract, or under FOB price terms Buyers do not send any vessel to appointed ports or the Letter of Credit opened by the Buyers does not correspond to the Contract terms and the Buyers fail to amend thereafter its terms by telegraph within the time limit after receipt of notification by the Sellers, the Sellers shall have right to cancel the contract or to delay the delivery of the goods and shall have also the right to lodge claims for compensation of losses

13. ARBITRATION

All disputes in connection with the contract or the execution thereof, shall be settled amicably by negotiation. In case no settlement can be reached, the case under dispute may then be submitted to the "China International Economic and Trade Arbitration Commission" for arbitration. The arbitration shall take place in China and shall be executed in accordance with the provisional rules of Procedure of the said Commission and the decision made by the Commission shall be accepted as final and binding upon both parties for setting the disputes. The fees for arbitration shall be borne by the losing party unless otherwise awarded

THE SELLERS:
OCEAN PLASTIC & CHEMICAL
PRODUCTS CO., LTD

THE BUYERS:
TONNY PRODUCTS PLC
ROTTERDAM THE NETHERLAND

参考译文(例):

售货合同

(1) 卖方:
宁波欧胜塑化有限公司

合同编号 OPCP08008

(2) 地址:
中国宁波沧海路1926号

合同日期 2016 年 3 月 27 日

(3) 买方:
TONNY PRODUCTS PLC

(4) 地址:
BERSTOFSGADE 48, ROTTERDAM, THE NETHERLANDS

电话: + (31) 74 12 37 08　　传真: + (31) 74 12 37 09　　电子邮箱: chila@ tvl. com. mtl

买卖双方同意按下列条件购进、售出下列商品:

商品名称及规格	数量/套	单价/EUR	总值/EUR
运动套装 商品编号 KB5200	840	15.20	(CFRC3% 阿姆斯特丹) 12 768.00

续表

商品名称及规格	数量/套	单价/EUR	总值/EUR
商品编号 KP6300	600	12.50	7 500.00
商品编号 KY5200	600	10.60	6 360.00
合计	2 040		26 628.00

(5) 包装：
12 套/纸箱
(6) 唛头：
TONNY/XD06008/AMSTERDAM/NO. 1 – UP
(7) 装船港口：
任何中国港口
(8) 目的港口：
阿姆斯特丹
(9) 装船期限：
不迟于 2016 年 5 月 31 日
(10) 付款条件：
30% 电汇方式预付，剩余 70% 装运后电汇支付
(11) 不可抗力：
因人力不可抗拒事故，使卖方不能在合同规定期限内交货或不能交货，卖方不负责任，但是卖方必须立即以电报通知买方。如果买方提出要求，卖方应以挂号函向买方提供由中国国际贸易促进会或有关机构出具的证明，证明事故的存在
(12) 异议索赔：
品质异议须于货到目的口岸之日起 30 天内提出，数量异议须于货到目的口岸之日起 15 天内提出，买方须同时提供双方同意的公证行的检验证明。卖方将根据具体情况解决异议。由自然原因或船方、保险商责任造成的损失，卖方将不予考虑任何索赔。信用证未在合同指定日期内到达卖方，或 FOB 条款下，买方未按时派船到指定港口，或信用证与合同条款不符，买方未在接到卖方通知所规定的期限内电改有关条款时，卖方有权撤销合同或延迟交货，并有权提出索赔
(13) 仲裁：
凡因执行本合同所发生的或与合同有关的一切争议，双方应友好协商解决。如果协商不能解决，应提交中国国际经济贸易仲裁委员会，根据该委员会的有关仲裁程序暂行规定在中国进行仲裁的，仲裁裁决是终局的，对双方都有约束力。仲裁费用除另有裁决外由败诉一方承担

卖方：
欧胜塑化有限公司

买方：
TONNY PRODUCTS PLC
ROTTERDAM THE NETHERLAND

相关知识

一、国际货物销售合同的条款构成

国际货物销售合同，是地处不同国家的当事人双方买卖一定货物达成的协议，是当事人各自履行约定义务的依据；也是发生违约行为时，进行补救、处理争议的依据。为此，一项

有效的国际货物销售合同,必须具备必要的内容,否则会使当事人在履行义务、进行违约补救或处理争议时遇到困难。一般来说,国际货物销售合同应包括以下七个方面的基本内容:

(1) 品质条款(Quality Clause)。
(2) 数量条款(Quantity Clause)。
(3) 包装条款(Packing Clause)。
(4) 价格条款(Price Clause)。
(5) 支付条款(Terms of Payment)。
(6) 违约条款(Breach Clause)。
(7) 不可抗力条款(Force Majeure Clause)。

二、贸易术语的国际惯例

国际贸易术语又称价格术语。

有关贸易术语的国际惯例,主要有三种。

1) 1932年《华沙—牛津规则》由国际法协会制定,本规则共21条,主要说明CIF买卖合同性质,具体规定了买卖双方所承担的费用、风险和责任。

2) 1941年《美国对外贸易定义修正本》由美国九大商业团体制定,对以下六种术语作了解释:

(1) EX(point of origin)——产地交货价。
(2) FOB——运输工具上交货价。FOB又分为六种,其中第五种为装运港船上交货——FOB vessel(named port of shipment)。
(3) FAS——船边交货价。
(4) C&F——成本加运费(目的港)价。
(5) CIF——成本加保险费、运费〔目的港〕价。
(6) EX DOCK——目的港码头交货价。

该惯例在美洲国家影响较大。在与采用该惯例的国家贸易时,要特别注意与其他惯例的差别,双方应在合同中明确规定贸易术语所依据的惯例。

3) 2010年《国际贸易术语解释通则》由国际商会制定,国际商会于2010年9月通过了该通则,并规定该版本于2011年1月1日生效,它是迄今为止关于贸易术语含义的国际惯例的最新版本。该通则考虑了免税贸易区的不断增加,电子沟通在商务中的不断增多,以及被更加重视的货物运输中的安全和变化等问题。它更新并加强了交货规则,将规则总量从13条减少到了11条,并且使所有规则的表述更加简洁明确。

该通则共包含11种贸易术语,见下表。

适用于任何运输方式类		
EXW	Ex Works	工厂交货
FCA	Free Carrier	货交承运人
CPT	Carriage Paid to	运费付至
CIP	Carriage and Insurance Paid to	运保费付至
DAT	Delivered at Terminal	指定终端交货
DAP	Delivered at Place	指定目的地交货

续表

DDP	Delivered Duty Paid	完税后交货
仅适用于水运类		
FAS	Free Alongside Ship	装运港船边交货
FOB	Free on Board	装运港船上交货
CFR	Cost and Freight	成本加运费
CIF	Cost, Insurance and Freight	成本加运保费

三、三种主要结算方式的操作流程

（一）汇款（又称汇付）

1. 汇款的概念

国际汇款有动态和静态两种含义。

国际汇款的静态含义是指外汇，它是一国以外币表示的、用于国际结算的支付手段的总称。国际汇款的动态含义，即通过银行的汇兑来实现国与国之间债权债务的清偿和国际资金的转移。通常所指的汇款都是指它的动态含义，因此，国际汇款又被称作国际汇兑。

2. 基本当事人

（1）汇款人；

（2）收款人或受益人；

（3）汇出行；

（4）汇入行或解付行。

3. 汇款种类

（1）电汇。电汇汇款（T/T），是汇款人委托银行以电报、电传、环球银行间金融电信网络方式，指示出口地某银行作为汇入行，解付一定金额给收款人的汇款方式。

电汇工具一般包括：电报（Cable）、电传（Telex）、SWIFT、CHIPS 等。一般采用密押证实。

（2）信汇。信汇汇款（M/T），是汇出行应汇款人申请，将信汇委托书或支付委托书邮寄给汇入行，授权其解付一定金额给收款人的一种汇款方式。

信汇工具：邮寄支付凭证。一般采用签字证实。

（3）票汇。票汇汇款（D/D），是汇出行应汇款人申请，代汇款人开立以其分行或代理行为解付行的银行即期汇票，支付一定金额给收款人的汇款方式。

票汇工具：银行即期汇票。一般采用签字证实。

4. 汇款的解付与偿付

（1）汇款的解付。它是汇入行向收款人付款的行为。

为了保证付款的正确，解付行往往都很慎重，特别是当汇出行的汇出汇款还未到达汇入行的账户时，解付行就相当于垫付了货款，因而更加慎重。

为了正确验定每笔汇款的真实性，解付行根据每种汇款的特点，采取不同的查验方法。

（2）汇款的偿付俗称拨头寸，是指汇出行在办理汇出汇款业务时，应及时将汇款金额拨交给其委托解付汇款的汇入行的行为。

5. 汇款在国际贸易中的运用

（1）预付货款。预付货款是进口商（付款人）在出口商（收款人）将货物或货运单据交付以前将货款的全部或者一部分通过银行付给出口商，出口商收到货款后，再根据约定发运货物。

（2）货到付款。货到付款与预付货款相反，它是进口商在收到货物以后，立即或一定时期以后再付款给出口商的一种结算方式。也被称为延期付款，或赊销。

货到付款包括售定和寄售两种。

售定是进出口商达成协议，规定出口商先发货，再由进口商按合同规定的货物售价和付款时间进行汇款的一种结算方式，即"先出后结"。

寄售是指出口方将货物运往国外，委托国外商人按照事先商定的条件在当地市场上代为销售，待货物售出以后，国外商人将扣除佣金和有关费用的货款再汇给出口商的结算方法。

（3）凭单付汇。凭单付汇是进口商通过银行将款项汇给出口商所在地银行（汇入行），并指示该行凭出口商提供的某些商业单据或某种装运证明即可付款给出口商。

因为汇款是可以撤销的，在汇款尚未被支取之时，汇款人随时可以通知汇款行将汇款退回，所以出口商在收到银行的汇款通知后，应尽快发货，尽快交单，尽快收汇。

（二）托收

1. 定义及当事人

托收（Collection）是出口方委托本地银行根据其要求通过进口地银行向进口方提示单据，收取货款的结算方式。

托收当事人包括：

（1）委托方（Principal）。

（2）托收行（Remitting Bank）。

（3）代收行（Collecting Bank）。

（4）付款人（Payer 或 Drawee）。

另外，提示行（Presenting Bank）是向付款人提示单据的代收银行。

再者，如果发生拒付的情况，委托人就可能需要有一个代理人为其办理在货物运出目的港时所有有关货物存仓、保险、重新议价、转售或运回等事宜。这个代理人必须由委托人在委托书中写明，称作"需要时的代理"（a representative to act as case-of-need）。

2. 托收种类及交单条件

（1）跟单托收（Documentary Collection）。跟单托收是指附有商业单据的托收。卖方开具托收汇票，连同商业单据（主要指货物装运单据）一起委托给托收行。跟单托收也包括不使用汇票的情况。

托收的交单条件有即期付款交单（D/P at sight）、远期付款交单（D/P at…days after sight）、承兑交单（D/A at…days after sight）等。按具体的交单条件不同分为以下三种。

a. 即期付款交单。

即期付款交单是指代收行凭进口商的即期付款而交单。

b. 远期付款交单。

远期付款交单是指代收行凭进口商的远期付款而交单。

在远期付款交单条件下，如果付款期限较长，在货物到达港口后，进口商可凭信托收据先借出单据去处理货物，待汇票到期时再付款。这被称为凭信托收据借单（Document against Trust Receipt，D/P. T/R）。注意：假如托收指示中允许凭信托收据借单，则由此产生的风险由委托人自负；假如托收指示中未提到允许凭信托收据借单，由代收行自行决定借出单据，由此而产生的一切风险由代收行承担。

c. 承兑交单。

承兑交单是指代收行凭进口商承兑而交出商业单据。

（2）光票托收（Clean Collection）。光票托收是指出口商仅开具汇票而不附商业单据（主要指货运单据）的托收。光票托收并不一定不附带任何单据，有时也附有一些非货运单据，如发票、垫款清单等，这种情况仍被视为光票托收。

（3）直接托收（Direct Collection）。银行办理的托收也包括卖方/委托人使用自己银行的托收格式，以此作为向买方银行寄单的托收指示，同时向自己的银行提交一份副本。

（三）信用证

1. 信用证的概念和流程

信用证（letter of credit，L/C）根据国际商会第 600 号出版物《跟单信用证统一惯例》第 2 条规定："信用证是指一项不可撤销的安排，无论其名称或描述如何，该项安排构成开证行对相符交单予以承付的确定承诺。"

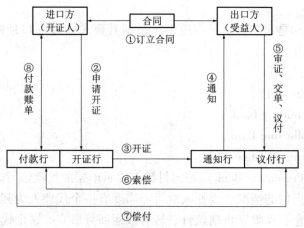

信用证业务流程

2. 信用证业务中存在的契约关系

（1）在开证申请人（进口商）和信用证受益人（出口商）之间存在一份贸易合同。由这份贸易合同带来了对支付信用的需要。

（2）在开证申请人和开证银行之间存在一份开证申请书。由这份开证申请书保证了信用证下收进的单据和付出的款项将由开证申请人赎还。

（3）开证银行与信用证受益人之间的关系由信用证锁定。信用证保证了信用证受益人交到银行的符合规定的单据将必定得到支付。

3. 信用证业务的特点

（1）信用证是一项自足文件（self-sufficient instrument）。信用证不依附于买卖合同，银行在审单时强调的是信用证与基础贸易相分离的书面形式上的认证；

（2）信用证方式是纯单据业务（pure documentary transaction）。信用证是凭单付款，不以货物为准。只要单据相符，开证行就应无条件付款；

（3）开证银行负首要付款责任（primary liabilities for payment）。信用证是一种银行信用，它是银行的一种担保文件，开证银行对支付有首要付款的责任。

4. 信用证的当事人

（1）开证申请人。在国际贸易中，信用证的开证申请人是进口商或买方。有时开证申请人也称开证人，他还是运输单据的收货人。进口商根据贸易合同的规定到其有业务往来的银行申请开立信用证。

（2）开证行。接受开证申请人委托开立信用证的银行即开证行。

开证行也被称作开证人、授予人。开证行是以自己的名义对信用证下的义务负责的。虽然开证行同时受到开证申请书和信用证本身两个契约约束，但是根据 UCP 500 第三条规定，开证行依信用证所承担的付款、承兑汇票或议付或履行信用证项下的其他义务的责任，不受开证行与申请人或申请人与受益人之间产生纠纷的约束。开证行在验单付款之后无权向受益人或其他前手追索。

（3）受益人。国际贸易中，信用证的受益人是出口商或卖方。受益人同时还是信用证汇票的出票人、货物运输单据的托运人。受益人与开证申请人之间存在一份贸易合同，而与开证行之间存在一份信用证。受益人有权依照信用证条款和条件提交汇票及/或单据要求取得信用证的款项。受益人交单后，如遇开证行倒闭，信用证无法兑现，则受益人有权向进口商提出付款要求，进口商仍应负责付款。这时，受益人应将符合原信用证要求的单据通过银行寄交进口商进行托收索款。如果开证行并未倒闭，却无理拒收，受益人或议付行可以进行诉讼，也有权向进口商提出付款要求。

（4）通知行。通知行是开证行在出口国的代理人。通知行的责任是及时通知或转递信用证，证明信用证的真实性并及时澄清疑点。如通知行不能确定信用证的表面真实性，即无法核对信用证的签署或密押，则应毫不延误地告知从其收到指示的银行，说明其不能确定信用证的真实性。如通知行仍决定通知该信用证，则必须告知受益人它不能核对信用证的真实性。通知行对信用证内容不承担责任。

（5）保兑行。保兑行是应开证行的要求在不可撤销信用证上加具保兑的银行。通常由通知行做保兑行。但是，保兑行有权做出是否加保的选择。保兑行承担与开证行相同的责任。保兑行一旦对该信用证加具了保兑，就对信用证负独立的确定的付款责任。如果遇到开证行无法履行付款的情况，则保兑行履行验单付款的责任。保兑行付款后只能向开证行索偿，因为它是为开证行加保兑的。保兑行付款后无权向受益人或其他前手追索票款。

（6）付款行。付款行是开证行的付款代理人。开证行在信用证中指定另一家银行为信用证项下汇票上的付款人，这银行就是付款行。它可以是通知行或其他银行。如果开证行资信不佳，付款行有权拒绝代为付款。但是，付款行一旦付款，即不得向受益人追索，而只能向开证行索偿。

（7）承兑行。远期信用证如果要求受益人出具远期汇票，则应指定一家银行作为受票行，由它对远期汇票做出承兑，这就是承兑行。如果承兑行不是开证行，承兑后又最后不能履行付款，开证行应负最后付款的责任。若单证相符，而承兑行不承兑汇票，开证行可指示受益人另开具以开证行为受票人的远期汇票,由开证行承兑并到期付款。承兑行付款后向开证行要求偿付。

(8) 议付行。议付是信用证的一种使用方法。它是指由一家信用证允许的银行买入该信用证项下的汇票和单据,向受益人提供资金融通。议付又可称作"买单"或"押汇"。买入单据的银行就是议付银行。具体做法是,议付行审单相符后买入单据垫付货款,即按票面金额扣除从议付日到汇票到期之日的利息,将净款付给出口商。在信用证业务中,议付行是接受开证行在信用证中的邀请并且信任信用证中的付款担保,凭出口商提交的包括有代表货权的提单在内的全套出口单证的抵押,而买下单据的。议付行议付后,向开证行寄单索偿。如果开证行发现单据有不符合信用证要求的情况存在,拒绝偿付,则议付行有向受益人或其他前手进行追索的权利。

(9) 偿付行。偿付行是开证行指定的对议付行或付款行、承兑行进行偿付的代理人。为了方便结算,开证行有时委托另一家有账户关系的银行代其向议付行、付款行或承兑行偿付,偿付行只有在开证行存有足够的款项并受到开证行的偿付指示时才付款。偿付行偿付后再向开证行索偿。偿付行的费用以及利息损失一般由开证行承担。偿付行不受单和审单,因此如事后开证行发现单证不符,只能向索偿行追索而不能向偿付行追索。如果偿付行没有对索偿行履行付款义务,开证行有责任付款。

四、信用证的开立形式和内容

(一) 信用证的开立形式

开证行可以用电报、电传、信函等方式开立信用证,因此,根据信用证的开立方式及记载内容的不同,常见的信用证形式可分为信开本信用证和电开本信用证。

1. 信开本信用证

信开本信用证是指开证行用书信格式编制并通过邮寄方式送达通知行的信用证,目前这种开证方式较少使用。

2. 电开本信用证

电开本信用证是指开证行以电子文本形式开立信用证的有效文本,并用电报、电传或SWIFT系统传送给通知行的开证方式。通知行收到电开本信用证后,需复制一份作为副本存档备查。由于电信技术的发展,特别是各国从事国际结算的中等以上的商业银行基本上都参加了SWIFT,为了节省时间和费用,银行做全电本开证时大多采用SWIFT方式开证。使用SWIFT开证,克服了全电本开证各国标准不统一、条款和格式不相同及文字烦琐等缺陷,使信用证具有了标准化、固定化统一格式的特征,而且传递速度快、安全性高、成本低,当前被全球大多数国家和地区的银行广泛使用。

电开本信用证又可以分为以下两种。

(1) 简电本信用证 (Brief Cable of Credit),是指仅记载信用证号码、受益人名称和地址、开证行名称、金额、货物名称、数量、价格、装运期及有效期等主要内容,用电文预先通知通知行,但详细条款将另行通知。简电本的内容比较简单,它不是有效的信用证,一般注明"详情后告",借以表明该简电仅做预先通知之用,而不是信用证或信用证修改的有效文本。

(2) 全电本信用证 (Full Cable of Credit),是指开证行以电文形式开出的内容完整的信用证。开证行一般会在电文中注明"This is an operative instrument no airmail confirmation to follow. 后面没有随寄证实书"字样。全电本信用证包含信用证的全部条款,是可以用来交单议付的信用证。

(二)信用证的内容和 SWIFT 信用证的格式

以跟单信用证 MT700 报文格式为例:

必选,20,DOCUMENTARY CREDIT NUMBER(信用证号码)。

可选,23,REFERENCE TO PRE – ADVICE(预先通知号码),如果信用证是采取预先通知的方式,该项目内应该填入"PREADV/",再加上预先通知的编号或日期。

必选,27,SEQUENCE OF TOTAL(电文页次)。

可选,31C,DATE OF ISSUE(开证日期),如果这项没有填,则开证日期为电文的发送日期。

必选,31D,DATE AND PLACE OF EXPIRY(信用证有效期和有效地点),该日期为最后交单的日期。

必选,32B,CURRENCY CODE,AMOUNT(信用证结算的货币和金额)。

可选,39A,PERCENTAGE CREDIT AMOUNT TOLERANCE(信用证金额上下浮动允许的最大范围),该项目的表示方法较为特殊,数值表示百分比的数值,如:5/5,表示上下浮动最大为5%。39B 与 39A 不能同时出现。

可选,39B,MAXIMUM CREDIT AMOUNT(信用证最大限制金额),39B 与 39A 不能同时出现。

可选,39C,ADDITIONAL AMOUNTS COVERED(额外金额),表示信用证所涉及的保险费、利息、运费等金额。

必选,40A,FORM OF DOCUMENTARY CREDIT(跟单信用证形式)。

必选,41A,AVAILABLE WITH...BY...(指定的有关银行及信用证兑付的方式)。① 指定银行作为付款、承兑、议付。② 兑付的方式有 5 种:BY PAYMENT(即期付款);BY ACCEPTANCE(远期承兑);BY NEGOTIATION(议付);BY DEF PAYMENT(迟期付款);BY MIXED PAYMENT(混合付款)。③ 如果是自由议付信用证,则对该信用证的议付地点不做限制,该项目代号为:41D,内容为:ANY BANK IN。

可选,42A,DRAWEE(汇票付款人),必须与42C 同时出现。

可选,42C,DRAFTS AT(汇票付款日期)必须与42A 同时出现。

可选,42M,MIXED PAYMENT DETAILS(混合付款条款)。

可选,42P,DEFERRED PAYMENT DETAILS(迟期付款条款)。

可选,43P,PARTIAL SHIPMENTS(分装条款),表示该信用证的货物是否可以分批装运。

可选,43T,TRANSSHIPMENT(转运条款),表示该信用证是直接到达,还是通过转运到达。

可选,44A,LOADING ON BOARD/DISPATCH/TAKING IN CHARGE AT/FROM(装船、发运和接收监管的地点)。

可选,44B,FOR TRANSPORTATION TO(货物发运的最终地)。

可选,44C,LATEST DATE OF SHIPMENT(最后装船期),装船的最迟的日期。44D 与

44C不能同时出现。

可选，44D，SHIPMENT PERIOD（船期），44C与44D不能同时出现。

可选，45A，DESCRIPTION OF GOODS AND/OR SERVICES（货物描述），货物的情况、价格条款。

可选，46A，DOCUMENTS REQUIRED（单据要求），各种单据的要求。

可选，47A，ADDITIONAL CONDITIONS（特别条款）。

可选，48，PERIOD FOR PRESENTATION（交单期限），表明开立运输单据后多少天内交单。

必选，49，CONFIRMATION INSTRUCTIONS（保兑指示）。

其中，CONFIRM：要求保兑行保兑该信用证；MAY ADD：收报行可以对该信用证加具保兑；WITHOUT：不要求收报行保兑该信用证。

必选，50，APPLICANT（信用证开证申请人），一般为进口商。

可选，51A，APPLICANT BANK（信用证开证的银行）。

可选，53A，REIMBURSEMENT BANK（偿付行）。

可选，57A，"ADVISE THROUGH" BANK（通知行）。

必选，59，BENEFICIARY（信用证的受益人），一般为出口商。

可选，71B，CHARGES（费用情况），表明费用是否由受益人（出口商）出，如果没有这一条，表示除了议付费、转让费以外，其他各种费用由开出信用证的申请人（进口商）出。

可选，72，SENDER TO RECEIVER INFORMATION（附言）。

可选，78，INSTRUCTION TO THE PAYING/ACCEPTING/NEGOTIATING BANK（给付款行、承兑行、议付行的指示）。

实训练习题

请阅读给定信用证,并进行翻译和解释

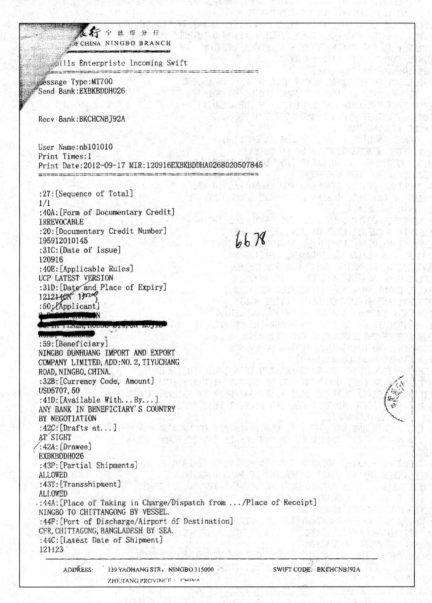

OF CHINA NINGBO BRANCH

:[Description of Goods and/or Services]
ERING : AUTOMOTIVE SUSPENSION PARTS.
ESCRIPTION OF GOODS, UNIT PRICE, QUALITY, QUANTITY, PACKING, NET
WEIGHT, MARKING AND ALL OTHER SPECIFICATION OF MERCHANDISE ARE
STRICTLY AS PER BENEFICIARY'S PROFORMA INVOICE
NO. SPD. EXP. 07. 2012, DATE:03.09.2012.)
:46A:[Documents Required]
A) FULL SET OF ORIGINAL OCEAN BILL OF LADING ISSUED
(TO THE ORDER OF LC ISSUING BANK) AND (DATED NOT
LATER THAN THE SHIPMENT VALIDITY OF THE CREDIT)
SHOWING FREIGHT PREPAID AND NOTIFY APPLICANT
AND LC ISSUING BANK.
B) SIGNED INVOICE 6 (SIX) FOLDS IN ENGLISH
(CERTIFYING MERCHANDISE TO BE OF CHINA)
(ORIGIN QUOTING IRC NO. BA0181789, LCA NO. EBL091303
UNDER CFER HS CODE 87089900.)
C) PACKING: (EXPORT STANDARD WOODEN BOX) AND 6 (SIX)
COPIES OF DETAILS PACKING LIST MUST ACCOMPANY THE
ORIGINAL DOCUMENTS.
D) INSURANCE COVERED BY THE APPLICANT. ALL SHIPMENT
UNDER THIS CREDIT MUST BE ADVISED BY THE
BENEFICIARY DIRECTLY TO M/S REPUBLIC INSURANCE
COMPANY LTD, LALADIGHI BRANCH, CHITTAGONG,
BANGLADESH, REFERING THEIR COVER NOTE NO.
RICL/LDG/MC-584/09/2012, DATED-16/09/2012,
MARINE COVER NOTE NO GIVING FULL DETAILS OF
SHIPMENT AND A COPY OF SUCH ADVICE MUST
ACCOMPANY THE ORIGINALLY SHIPPING DOCUMENTS.
E) CERTIFICATE OF ORIGIN ISSUED BY THE CHAMBER OF
COMMERCE OF THE EXPORTING COUNTRY MUST
ACCOMPANY THE ORIGINAL SHIPPING DOCUMENTS.
:47A:[Additional Conditions]
A) SHIPMENT MUST NOT BE MADE EARLIER THAN THE CREDIT ISSUING
DATE. A SET OF COPY DOCUMENTS TO BE SENT TO THE APPLICANT
WITHIN 05 (FIVE) WORKING DAYS AFTER SHIPMENT BY INTERNATIONAL
COURIER SERVICES AND THAT COURIER RECEIPT MUST ACCOMPANY
THE ORIGINAL DOCUMENTS.
B) L/C NUMBER AND DATE MUST BE QUOTED ON ALL DOCUMENTS.
C) TIN NO. 313-107-7319 MUST APPEAR ON ALL INVOICE AND PACKING
LIST.
D) IMPORTER'S NAME, ADDRESS AND TIN NO. MUST BE PRINTED BY
IRREMOVABLE INK AT LEAST 2 PERCENT OF EACH PACKING. A
CERTIFICATE IN THIS REGARD MUST ACCOMPAN SHIPPING DOCUMENTS.
E) FCR, THIRD PARTY, CHARTED PARTY, SHORT FORM, STALE AND BLANK
BACKED B/L ARE NOT ACCEPTABLE.
F) SHIPMENT, TRANSHIPMENT BY ISRAELI FLAG CARRIER ARE STRICTLY
PROHIBITED AND CERTIFICATE TO THIS EFFECT MUST ACCOMPANY THE
ORGINAL SHIPPING DOCUMENT.
G) COUNTRY OF ORIGIN OF THE GOODS MUST BE MENTIONED IN EACH
PACKAGES. A CERTIFICATE TO THIS EFFECT FROM BENEFICIARY
REQUIRED.
H) ON THE DATE OF NEGOTIATION, NEGOTIATING BANK MUST INFORM
OPENING BANK REGARDING BILL OF LADING NO. DATE, QUANTITY, SHIPPED

ADDRESS: 139 YAOHANG STR. NINGBO 315000   SWIFT CODE: BKCHCNBJ92A
ZHEJIANG PROVINCE

INVOICE VALUE/NEGOTIATING AMOUNT BY SWIFT-EXBKBDDH026 OR FAX-
031-653026 AND COPY OF THE SAME MUST ACCOMPANY SHIPPING
DOCUMENTS. PAYMENT AGAINST DISCREPANT DOCUMENTS MUST NOT BE MADE
UNDER RESERVE OR GUARANTEE WITHOUT OUR PRIOR APPROVAL.
:71B:[Charges]
ALL BANKING CHARGES OUTSIDE
BANGLADESH ARE ON
BENEFICIARY'S ACCOUNT WHETHER L/C
UTILIZED OR NOT.
:48:[Period for Presentation]
21 DAYS FROM THE DATE OF SHIPMENT
BUT NOT LATER THAN THE CREDIT
VALIDITY.
:49:[Confirmation Instructions]
WITHOUT
:78:[Instructions to the Paying/Accepting/Negotiating Bank]
A. DISCREPANT DOCUMENTS MUST NOT BE NEGOTIATED WITHOUT OUR PRIOR
APPROVAL.
B. DOCUMENTS SHOULD BE MAILED BY COURIER IN ONE/TWO LOT
TO EXPORT IMPORT BANK OF BANGLADESH LTD., CDA AVENUE BRANCH,
COMMERCE VIEW COMPLEX, 191, CDA AVENUE, CHITTAGONG, BANGLADESH.
C. AMOUNT OF THE DRAFT(S) AS NEGOTIATED SHOULD BE ENDORSED ON
THE REVERSE OF THIS CREDIT.
D. WE SHALL ARRANGE PAYMENT OF THE
BILL AS PER NEGOTIATING BANK INSTRUCTION ONLY ON RECEIPT OF
CREDIT CONFORM DOCUMENTS AT OUR COUNTER.
:72:[Sender to Receiver Information]
EXCEPT SO FAR AS OTHERWISE
EXPRESSLY STATED THIS CREDIT IS
SUBJECT TO UNIFORM CUSTOMS AND
PRACTICE FOR DOCUMENTARY CREDITS
(2007 REVISION) ICC PUBLICATION NO
600.
-}{5:{MAC:50D9AB22}{CHK:84AAEB85CA11}}

ADDRESS: 139 YAOHANG STR., NINGBO 315000   SWIFT CODE: BKCHCNBJ92A
            ZHEJIANG PROVINCE   CHINA

第二节　开立信用证

教学目标

最终目标：能熟练填写开证申请书。

促成目标：
1. 熟悉开证申请书的一般格式。
2. 能根据合同和其他信息，在开证申请书上找到相应空格。
3. 能进行规范化的填写。

情景案例

机构：
外贸企业：宁波宏基对外贸易发展有限公司（Ningbo Hongji Foreign Trade Development Co., Ltd.）。
银行：中国工商银行宁波分行（ICBC NINGBO BR.）。
人物：
小沈：宁波宏基对外贸易发展有限公司单证员。
王经理：宁波宏基对外贸易发展有限公司业务经理。
小周：中国工商银行宁波分行单证中心进口业务部职员。
背景资料：
（1）2016年10月11日宁波宏基对外贸易发展有限公司外贸业务部王经理与新加坡的公司General Trading Company 签订一份300吨聚乙烯的进口合同，合同号为GTC/PE5765。
（2）2016年10月12日单证员小沈在办公室接到王经理的电话：小沈，进口合同副本现在传真给你，你马上联系工商银行小周，这星期之内把信用证开出去。
（3）小沈立刻接收传真，填写开证申请书，并随后联系小周。下面是合同的内容和一份空白开证申请书。

形式发票/合同（例）：

Sales Confirmation
销售确认书

号码：GTC/PE5765
日期、地点：2016年10月11日于新加坡
卖方（Seller）：新加坡通用贸易公司
　　　　　　　（General Trading Company, Singapore）
买方（Buyer）：宁波宏基对外贸易发展有限公司
　　　　　　　（Ningbo Hongji Foreign Trade Development Co., Ltd.）
商品名称（Commodity）：聚乙烯（Polyethylene）
规格（Specification）/数量（Quantity）/单价（Unit Price）：
（1）高密度聚乙烯（high density polyethylene, HDPE），200 MT, USD631/MT CIF NINGBO
（2）低密度聚乙烯（low density polyethylene, LDPE），100 MT, USD579/MT CIF NINGBO

总值（Value）：USD184,100.00
　　SAY U.S. DOLLARS ONE HUNDRED EIGHTY FOUR THOUSAND ONE HUNDRED ONLY
装运期：
　　2016年12月31日前自新加坡至中国港口，允许分装运和转船
付款条件：
　　凭不可撤销即期信用证付款，于装运期前一个月开到卖方，并于上述装运期后十五天内在新加坡议付有效
保险：
　　由卖方按发票金额的110%投保一切险和战争险

The Buyer:	The Seller:
宁波宏基对外贸易发展有限公司	新加坡通用贸易公司
×××	×××
————————————	————————————
Authorized Signature	Authorized Signature

开证申请书（例）：

不可撤销跟单信用证申请书
APPLICATION FOR IRREVOCABLE DOCUMENTARY CREDIT

TO: INDUSTRIAL AND COMMERCIAL BANK OF CHINA _____ BRANCH　　Date:
Please establish by □SWIFT □ brief cable □ airmail an Irrevocable Credit as follows:

Advising Bank: (to be left for bank to fill in)	(20) Irrevocable Documentary Credit No. (31D) Expiry Date and Place
(50) Applicant: (Full name & detailed address)	(59) Beneficiary: (Full name & detailed address)
(32B) Currency code, amount (in words and figures) (39A) Quantity and credit amount tolerance _____%	
(41A) Credit available with □ any bank □ issuing bank □ other (pl. indicate) By □ negotiation □ acceptance □ sight payment □ deferred payment at _____	
(42C) Draft at _____ for _____ % of invoice value	
(42A) Draw on _____	
(43P) Partial shipment □ allowed □ not allowed	(43T) Transshipment □ allowed □ not allowed
(44A) Loading on board from	(44B) for transportation to
(44C) Latest shipment date	

(45A) Description of goods

Price term：
Packing：

(46A) Documents required：(marked with X)
( ) Signed Commercial Invoice in _____ indicating L/C No. and Contract No.
( ) _____ set of clean on board ocean Bills of Lading made out to order and blank endorsed marked " freight _____ "
  ☐ notifying ☐ applicant
( ) Air Waybills showing "freight ☐ to collect ☐ prepaid" indicating freight amount and consigned to
  ☐ applicant ☐ issuing bank
( ) Forwarding agent's Cargo Receipt
( ) Insurance Policy/Certificate in _____ for _____ % of the invoice value showing claims payable in China in currency of the draft
  blank endorsed, covering (☐ Ocean Marine Transportation ☐ Air Transportation ☐ Over Land Transportation) All Risks, War Risks, including _____ as per _____ Clause
( ) Packing List / Weight Memo in _____ indicating quantity / gross and net weights of each package and packing conditions as called for by the L/C
( ) Certificate of Quantity / Weight in _____
( ) Certificate of Quality in _____ issued by ☐ beneficiary ☐ public recognized surveyor ☐ manufacturer
( ) Beneficiary's certified copy of fax / telex dispatched to the accountees within _____ hours after shipment advising ☐ name of vessel ☐ B/L No. ☐ flight No. ☐ wagon No. ☐ shipping date ☐ contract No. ☐ L/C No., commodity, quantity, weight and value of shipment

(47A) Additional conditions：(Marked with ×)
( ) Documents issued earlier than L/C issuing date are not acceptable
( ) All documents to be forwarded in one cover, unless otherwise stated
( ) The remaining _____ % of invoice value
( ) Third party as shipper ☐ is ☐ is not acceptable

(71B) All banking charges and interest if any outside opening bank are for account of ☐ beneficiary ☐ other (pl. indicate)

(48) Documents to be presented within _____ days after the date of issuance of the transport document (s) but within the validity of the credit

依照国际商会《跟单信用证统一惯例》第600号出版物

相关知识

一、申请开立信用证的具体手续

1. 递交有关合同的副本及附件

进口商在向银行申请开证时，要向银行递交进口合同的副本以及所需附件，如进口许可证、进口配额证、某些部门的审批文件等。

2. 填写开证申请书

进口商根据银行规定的统一开证申请书格式进行填写，一式三份，一份留业务部门；一份留财务部门；一份交银行。填写开证申请书，必须按合同条款的具体规定，写明信用证的各项要求，内容要明确、完整，无词义不清的记载。

3. 缴纳保证金

按照国际贸易的习惯做法，进口商向银行开立信用证，应向银行缴付一定比例的保证金，其金额一般为信用证金额的百分之几到百分之几十，一般根据进口商的资信情况而定。在我国的进口业务中，开证行根据不同企业和交易情况，要求开证申请人缴付一定比例的人民币保证金，然后银行才可以开证。

二、进口开证申请书的填制

(1) DATE（申请开证日期）。在申请书右上角填写实际申请日期。

(2) TO（致）。银行印制的申请书上事先都会印有开证银行的名称、地址，银行的 SWIFT CODE、TELEX NO 等也可同时显示。

(3) PLEASE ISSUE ON OUR BEHALF AND/OR FOR OUR ACCOUNT THE FOLLOWING IRREVOABLE LETTER OF CREDIT（请开列以下不可撤销信用证）。如果信用证是保兑或可转让的，则应在此加注有关字样。开证方式多为电开（BY TELEX），也可以是信开、快递、简电开立。

(4) L/C NUMBER（信用证号码）。此栏由银行填写。

(5) APPLICANT（申请人）。填写申请人的全称及详细地址，有的要求注明联系电话、传真号码等。

(6) BENEFICIARY（受益人）。填写受益人的全称及详细地址。

(7) ADVISING BANK（通知行）。由开证行填写。

(8) AMOUNT（信用证金额）。分别用数字和文字两种形式表示，并且表明币制。如果允许有一定比率的上下浮动，要在信用证中明确表示出来。

(9) EXPIRY DATE AND PLACE（到期日期和地点）。填写信用证的有效期及到期地点。

(10) PARTIAL SHIPMENT（分批装运）、TRANSHIPMENT（转运）。根据合同的实际规定打"×"进行选择。

(11) LOADING IN CHARGE、FOR TRANSPORT TO、LATEST DATE OF SHIPMENT（装运地/港、目的地/港的名称、最迟装运日期）。按实际填写，如允许有转运地/港，也应清楚标明。

(12) CREDIT AVAILABLE WITH/BY（付款方式）。在所提供的即期、承兑、议付和延期付款四种信用证有效兑付方式中选择与合同要求一致的类型。

(13) BENEFICIARY'S DRAFT（汇票要求）。金额应根据合同规定填写为：发票金额的一定百分比；发票金额的 100%（全部货款都用信用证支付）；如是部分信用证，部分托收的情况，则按信用证下的金额比例填写。付款期限可根据实际填写即期或远期，如属后者，则必须填写具体的天数。信用证条件下的付款人通常是开证行，也可能是开证行指定的另外一家银行。

(14) DOCUMENTS REQUIRED（单据条款）。各银行提供的申请书中已印就的单据条款通常为十几条，从上至下一般为发票、运输单据（提单、空运单、铁路运输单据及运输备忘录等）、保险单、装箱单、质量证书、装运通知和受益人证明等。最后一条是 OTHER DOCUMENTS, IF ANY（其他单据），如要求提交超过上述所列范围的单据，就可以在此栏填写，比如有的合同要求 CERTIFICATE OF NO SOLID WOOD PACKING MATERIAL（无实木包装材料证明）、CERTIFICATE OF FREE SALE（自由销售证明书）、CERTIFICATE OF CONFORMITY（合格证明书）等。申请人填制这部分内容时应依据合同规定，不能随意增加或减少。选中某单据后对该单据的具体要求（如一式几份、要否签字、正副本的份数、单据中应标明的内容等）也应如实填写，如申请书印制好的要求不完整，则应在其后予以补足。

(15) COVERING/EVIDENCING SHIPMENT OF（商品描述）。所有内容（品名、规格、包装、单价、唛头）都必须与合同内容相一致，价格条款里附带"AS PER INCOTERMS 2010"、数量条款中规定"MORE OR LESS"或"ABOUT"、使用某种特定包装物等特殊要求必须清楚列明。

(16) ADDITIONAL INSTRUCTIONS（附加指示）。该栏通常体现为以下一些印就的条款：

+ ALL DOCUMENTS MUST INDICATE CONTRACT NUMBER（所有单据加列合同号码）。

+ ALL BANKING CHARGES OUTSIDE THE OPENING BANK ARE FOR BENEFICIARY'S ACCOUNT（所有开证行以外的银行费用由受益人承担）。

+ BOTH QUANTITY AND AMOUNT FOR EACH ITEM % MORE OR LESS ALLOWED（每项数量与金额允许%增减）。

+ THIRD PARTY AS SHIPPER IS NOT ACCEPTABLE（第三方作为托运人是不能接受的）。

+ DOCUMENTS MUST BE PRESENTED WITHIN ××× DAYS AFTER THE DATE OF ISSUANCE OF THE TRANSPORT DOCUMENTS BUT WITHIN THE VALIDITY OF THIS CREDIT（单据必须在提单日后×××天送达银行并且不超过信用证有效期）。

+ SHORT FORM/BLANK BACK/CLAUSED/CHARTER PARTY B/L IS UNACCEPTABLE（银行不接受略式/不清洁/租船提单）。

+ ALL DOCMENTS TO BE FORWARDED IN ONE COVER, UNLESS OTHERWISE STATED ABOVE（除非有相反规定，所有单据应一次提交）。

+ PREPAID FREIGHT DRAWN IN EXCESS OF L/C AMOUNT IS ACCEPTABLE AGAINST PRESENTATION OF ORIGINAL CHARGES VOUCHER ISSUED BY SHIPPING CO./AIR LINE OR ITS AGENT（银行接受凭船公司/航空公司或其代理人签发的正本运费收据索要超过信用证金额的预付运费）。

+ DOCUMENT ISSUED PRIOR TO THE DATE OF ISSUANCE OF CREDIT NOT ACCEPTABLE（不接受早于开证日出具的单据）。

如需要已印就的上述条款，可在条款前打"×"，对合同涉及但未印就的条款还可以做补充填写。

(17) NAME, SIGNATURE OF AUTHORISED PERSON, TEL NO., FAX, ACCOUNT

NO.（授权人名称、签字、电话、传真、账号等内容）。

三、开证行可能面对的信用证欺诈

（一）开证申请人欺诈开证行

开证申请人为了套取银行资金，通过与受益人签订不存在的买卖合同（受益人并不知情），开立无贸易背景的远期信用证。当信用证受益人提交单据后，开证申请人只要交纳少量的保证金或者出具信托收据（T/R TRUSTRE CEIPT）做担保就可以取得货物的物权凭证，随后在到期付款日故意制造破产的假象，甚至在拿到货物变卖后，就卷款而逃，以此来欺诈开证行；这时开证行已经丧失货物的所有权，并且将承担到期向持票人垫付货款的责任。

（二）受益人欺诈开证行

1. 受益人不履行交货义务，通过伪造信用证项下所要求的全套单据来骗取贷款

受益人在货物根本不存在的情况下，通过欺诈手段与进口商订立货物买卖合同，让后者通过开证行开出以其自己为受益人的不可撤销信用证，并伪造与信用证表面所要求完全相符的单据，使银行无条件付款或承兑，从而诈取开证行资金，这种情况往往也不能获得开证申请人的赎单。

2. 受益人在单据中做欺骗性陈述

此种行为是卖方往往通过倒签、预借、保函清洁提单的方式在没有装货，或没有及时装货，或所交付货物表面不符合信用证的规定时篡改提单的内容，同时受益人还可能以另外一种货物或残、次货物代替信用证所要求的货物而伪造单据的信用证欺诈。此种欺诈方式，单据是真的，货物也存在，但装运期不符合规定，或装运的货物不是信用证所要求的货物，而是残、次品或废物。

3. 受益人伪造、变造信用证的信用证欺诈

伪造信用证是指行为人未经国家有关部门的批准，采用描绘、复制、印刷等方式，仿照信用证的格式制造假信用证的行为或以其编造、冒用某银行的名义开出的假信用证。变造信用证是指行为在真实、合法的银行信用证结算凭证的基础上或以真实的银行信用证结算凭证为基本材料，通过剪接、挖补、涂改等手段改变银行信用证结算凭证的内容和主要条款，使其成为虚假的信用证的行为。

（三）开证申请人和受益人共同欺诈开证行

此种欺诈表现为开证申请人与受益人相互勾结，编造虚假或根本不存在的买卖方关系，由所谓的买方申请开立远期信用证，所谓的卖方向开证行提交伪造的单据骗取开证行的贷款。我国的开证行在开展信用证业务时，往往将受益人提交的单据直接交给开证申请人审单，询问开证申请人是否存在不符合点以及是否接受单据或对外付款，这样受益人提交的伪造的单据很容易就被开证行接受。当开证行对汇票承兑后，卖方就把汇票贴现出去，随后双方消失或宣布破产。而开证行还需要对该信用证项下的善意持票人承担付款责任，且大多数国家规定只要开证行对汇票进行了承兑，即使发现卖方所提交的单据是伪造的，也不能动用例外原则进行止付。

（四）利用信用证打包放款欺诈开证行

打包放款（PACKINGLOAN）又称信用证抵押贷款，是指出口商收到境外开来的信用证后，在采购这笔与信用证有关的出口商品或生产出口商品时，资金出现短缺，用该信用证作为抵押，向银行申请本、外币流动资金贷款，用于出口货物进行加工、包装及运输过程出现的资金缺口，出口方银行给其发放贷款的融资行为。如果在无贸易背景且开证保证金较低的情况下开立的信用证被用来进行打包放款，则打包放款银行所抵押的不过是废纸一张。贷款银行到期收不回资金时，就会来找开证行，追究开证行没有尽到审单和调查买卖双方资信情况的责任，迫使开证行对自己开出的信用证承担偿还责任。

实训练习题

请根据下列合同填写开证申请书

Purchase Contract

S/C No.：RT05342
DATE：MAR. 20, 2016
SIGNED AT：BARCELONA

SELLERS：MAMUT ENTERPRISESAV
　　　　　TARRAGONA75－3ER, BARCELONA, SPAIN
BUYERS：NINGBO HAIWEN IMP&EXP. CORP. , LTD
　　　　　9FL, NO. 428, ZHONGSHAN EAST ROAD, NINGBO

Dear Sirs,
　We hereby confirm having sold to you the following goods on terms and conditions as specified below：

DESCRIPTIONS	QUANTITY	U/PRICE	AMOUNT
HAND TOOLS		CIF NINGBO	
(1) 9 pc Extra Long Hex Key Set	1,200 SETS	USD 1.76	USD 2,112.00
(2) 8 pc Double Offset Ring Spanner	1,200 SETS	USD 3.10	USD 3,720.00
(3) 12 pc Double Offset Ring Spanner	800 SETS	USD 7.50	USD 6,000.00
(4) 12 pc Combination Spanner	1,200 SETS	USD 3.55	USD 4,260.00
(5) 10 pc Combination Spanner	1,000 SETS	USD 5.80	USD 5,800.00
	5,400 SETS		USD 21,892.00

PACKING：　　Packed in three 40′ container.
Delivery from　BARCELONA, SPAIN　　to　NINGBO, CHINA
Shipping marks　　　HAIWEN
　　　　　　　　　　NINGBO
　　　　　　　　　　C/No. 1－UP
Time of shipment：Latest date of shipment May. 10, 2016
Partial shipment：Not allowed
Transshipment：Allowed

Terms of payment: By 100% confirmed irrevocable letter of credit to be available at 30 days after sight draft to be opened by the sellers.

L/C must mention this contract number. L/C advised by Bank of China Barcelona Branch. All banking charges outside China (the mainland of China) are for account of Seller.

Arbitration: All dispute arising from the execution of or in connection with this contract shall be settled amicably by negotiation. In case no settlement can be reached through negotiation the case may then be submitted to China International Economic & Trade Arbitration Commission in Shanghai (or in Beijing) for arbitration in accordance with its procedures. The arbitral award is final and binding upon both parties for setting the dispute. The fee for arbitration shall be borne by the losing party unless otherwise awarded.

THE BUYER: THE SELLER:
NINGBO HAIWEN IMP&EXP. CORP., LTD MAMUT ENTERPRISESAV

第三节　审核并修改信用证

教学目标

最终目标：理解信用证条款，能熟练写作改证函。

促成目标：

1. 能根据合同审核信用证，写出审证意见。
2. 能进行规范化的改证函写作。

情景案例

机构：
外贸企业：宁波欧胜塑化有限公司（OCEAN PLASTIC & CHEMICAL PRODUCTS CO., LTD）。
银行：上海浦东发展银行（SHANGHAI PUDONG DEVELOPMENT BANK）。

人物：
小余：宁波欧胜塑化有限公司单证员
张经理：宁波欧胜塑化有限公司业务经理
小黄：上海浦东发展银行宁波分行国际业务部职员

背景资料：
（1）2016年11月6日，宁波欧胜塑化有限公司外贸业务部张经理与阿拉伯联合酋长国的公司ABC TRADING CO., LLC签订一份36 800支唇膏（LIP BALM）的出口合同，合同号为081106。

（2）2016年12月9日，单证员小余在办公室接到上海浦东发展银行宁波分行小黄打来的电话："小余，你们有一票信用证开到了，赶紧来拿。""好的。我需要交什么费用吗？""如果在我行议付，就可以免去通知费。不过，正本信用证必须留在我行，你可以拿副本去备货。""谢谢！"

（3）拿回信用证副本以后，小余向外贸业务部张经理索取相应的外贸合同，具体了解这笔交易的成交细节。下面是合同和信用证的内容。

形式发票/合同（例）：

OCEAN PLASTIC & CHEMICAL PRODUCTS CO., LTD
PROFORMA INVOICE（R）

Cont. No.：081106	Add：Rm1105, Building#2, Shangdong
P. I. NO.：081106	Nationals, #1926 Canghai rd.
Date：Nov. 06, 2016	Ningbo, 315040, China
Signed at：Ningbo	Fax：86-574-87665377
The Buyer：ABC TRADING CO., LLC	
P. O. BOX 13087 DUBAI, UAE	

This contract is made by and between the Buyer and Seller according to the terms and conditions stipulated below:

1. Commodity and Specification	2. Qty.	3. U-price	4. Amount
			CIF JEBEL ALI, UAE
Lip balm	36,800pcs	US $ 0.30	US $ 11,040.00

（1）500pcs display stand（32pcs/display stand）of lip balm and each display stand include in equal qty of flavours-Blueberry, Vanilla, Mint and Cinnamon.

（2）Following qty will be in loose packaging in 64pcs/box, each box should be one type of flavour.

    Blueberry：100 box

    Vanilla：75 box

    Mint：75 box

    Cinnamon：75 box

5. More or less：With 0 % More or Less both in amount & qty. Allowed at the seller's opinion.

6. Time of shipment：Will confirm later.

7. Loading port & destination：From Ningbo Port by sea.

8. Insurance：To be effected by the seller.

9. Terms of payment：By 100% irrevocable letter of credit to be available with drafts at sight to be opened by the seller.

10. Special clause

THE SELLER	THE BUYER
MANAGER（OR REPRESENTATIVE）	MANAGER（OR REPRESENTATIVE）

信用证（例）：

From		
HSBC BANK, DUBAI, UAE		
To		
SHANGHAI PUDONG DEVELOPMENT BANK		
15F, DONGYIN MANSION, NO. 689 BEIJING DONG ROAD, SHANGHAI, 200001, CHINA		
Sequence of Total	27:	1/1
Form of Documentary Credit	40A:	IRREVOCABLE
Documentary Credit Number	20:	HSBC657708467464
Date of Issue	31C:	161208
Date and Place of Expiry	31D:	Date 170105 Place CHINA
Applicant	50:	ABC TRADING CO., LLC
		P. O. BOX 13087 DUBAI, UAE
Beneficiary	59:	OCEAN PLASTIC & CHEMICAL PRODUCTS CO., LTD
		1101 - 1105 SHANGDONG NATIONALS, #1926 CANG-HAI RD., NINGBO, 315041, CHINA
Currency Code, Amount	32B:	Currency USD Amount 11,040.00
Available with…by…	41D:	ANY BANK
		BY NEGOTIATION
Drafts at…	42C:	SIGHT
Drawee	42D:	HSBC BANK, DUBAI, UAE
Partial Shipment	43P:	NOT ALLOWED
Transshipment	43T:	NOT ALLOWED
Loading/Dispatch/Taking in Charge/Fm	44A:	NINGBO, CHINA
For Transportation to…	44B:	JEBEL ALI, UAE
Latest Date of Shipment	44C:	161231
Description of Goods/Services	45A:	

　　36,800 PCS OF LIP BALM,
　　USD 0.30 / PC CIF JEBEL ALI, UAE

Documents Required: 　　　　　　　　46A:
　　+ SIGNED COMMERCIAL INVOICE IN TRIPLICATE
　　+ FULL SET OF CLEAN ON BOARD OCEAN BILLS OF LADING CONSIGNED TO THE ORDER OF ABC TRADING CO., LLC P. O. BOX 13087 DUBAI, UAE MARKED FREIGHT PREPAID NOTIFYING APPLICANT
　　+ PACKING LIST IN TRIPLICATE
　　+ INSURANCE POLICY/CERTIFICATE BLANK ENDORSED COVERING ALL RISKS FOR 10 PER CENT ABOVE THE CIF VALUE
　　+ CERTIFICATE OF CHINA ORIGIN ISSUED BY A RELEVANT AUTHORITY

Additional Conditions 　　　　　　　　47A:
　　+ DRAFTS ARE TO BE MARKED AS DRAWN UNDER THIS DOCUMENTARY CREDIT
　　+ T/T REIMBURSEMENT IS NOT ALLOWED

		+ A USD50.00 (OR EQUIVALENT) FEE SHOULD BE DEDUCTED FROM THE REIMBURSEMENT CLAIM FOR EACH PRESENTATION OF DISCREPANT DOCUMENTS UNDER THIS DOCUMENTARY CREDIT NOTWITHSTANDING ANY INSTRUCTIONS TO THE CONTRARY, THIS CHARGE SHALL BE FOR THE ACCOUNT OF THE BENEFICIARY.
Details of Charges	71B:	ALL BANKING CHARGES OUTSIDE ISSUING BANK ARE FOR BENEFICIARY'S ACCOUNT
Presentation Period	48:	DOCUMENTS MUST BE PRESENTED FOR NEGOTIATION WITHIN 5 DAYS AFTER BILL OF LADING DATE, BUT WITHIN THE VALIDITY OF THIS CREDIT
Confirmation	49:	WITHOUT
Instructions	78:	
		+ WE UNDERTAKE TO HONOUR ALL DRAFTS DRAWN IN STRICT COMPLIANCE WITH THE TERMS OF THIS CREDIT
		+ PLEASE FORWARD TO US THE ORIGINAL SET OF DOCUMENTS BY REGISTERED AIRMAIL AND THE DUPLICATES BY SUBSEQUENT AIRMAIL
Sender to Receiver info	72:	THIS LC IS SUBJECT TO UCP 2007 ICC PUB. NO. 600. THIS IS OPERATIVE INSTRUMENT AND NO MAIL CONFIRMATION WILL FOLLOW
Trailer		Order is <MAC:> <PAC:> <ENC:> <CHK:> <TNG:> <PDE:> MAC: BA00E6EA CHK: 9E5503EE1810

相关知识

一、信用证的种类

（一）以信用证项下的汇票是否附有货运单据划分

（1）跟单信用证（Documentary Credit）。是凭跟单汇票或仅凭单据付款的信用证。此处的单据指代表货物所有权的单据（如海运提单等），或证明货物已交运的单据（如铁路运单、航空运单、邮包收据）。

（2）光票信用证（Clean Credit）。是凭不随附货运单据的光票（Clean Draft）付款的信用证。银行凭光票信用证付款，也可要求受益人附交一些非货运单据，如发票、垫款清单等。

在国际贸易的货款结算中，绝大部分使用跟单信用证。

（二）以开证行所负的责任为标准划分。

（1）不可撤销信用证（Irrevocable L/C）。指信用证一经开出，在有效期内，未经受益人及有关当事人的同意，开证行不能片面修改和撤销，只要受益人提供的单据符合信用证规定，开证行必须履行付款义务。

（2）可撤销信用证（Revocable L/C）。开证行不必征得受益人或有关当事人同意，即有权随时撤销的信用证，应在信用证上注明"可撤销"字样。

《UCP600》规定银行不可开立可撤销信用证。

（三）以有无另一银行加以保证兑付为依据划分

（1）保兑信用证（Confirmed L/C）。指开证行开出的信用证，由另一银行保证对符合信用证条款规定的单据履行付款义务。对信用证加以保兑的银行，称为保兑行。

（2）不保兑信用证（Unconfirmed L/C）。开证行开出的信用证没有经另一家银行保兑。

（四）以付款时间不同划分

（1）即期信用证（Sight L/C）。指开证行或付款行收到符合信用证条款的跟单汇票或装运单据后，立即履行付款义务的信用证。

（2）远期信用证（Usance L/C）。指开证行或付款行收到信用证的单据时，在规定期限内履行付款义务的信用证。

（3）假远期信用证（Usance Credit Payable at Sight）。信用证规定受益人开立远期汇票，由付款行负责贴现，并规定一切利息和费用由开证人承担。这种信用证对受益人来讲，实际上仍属即期收款，在信用证中有"假远期"（usance L/C payable at sight）条款。

（五）以受益人对信用证的权利可否转让划分

（1）可转让信用证（Transferable L/C）。指信用证的受益人（第一受益人）可以要求授权付款、承担延期付款责任，承兑或议付的银行（统称"转让行"），或当信用证是自由议付时，可以要求信用证中特别授权的转让银行，将信用证全部或部分转让给一个或数个受益人（第二受益人）使用的信用证。开证行在信用证中要明确注明"可转让"（transferable），且只能转让一次。

（2）不可转让信用证。指受益人不能将信用证的权利转让给他人的信用证。凡未注明"可转让"的信用证即为不可转让信用证。

（六）循环信用证（Revolving L/C）

这种信用证是指被全部或部分使用后，它的金额又恢复到原金额，可再次使用，直至达到规定的次数或规定的总金额为止。它通常在分批均匀交货情况下使用。在按金额循环的信用证条件下，恢复到原金额的具体做法有：

（1）自动式循环。每期用完一定金额，不需等待开证行的通知，即可自动恢复到原金额。

（2）非自动循环。每期用完一定金额后，必须等待开证行通知到达，信用证才能恢复到原金额使用。

（3）半自动循环。即每次用完一定金额后若干天内，开证行未提出停止循环使用的通知，自第×天起即可自动恢复至原金额。

（七）对开信用证（Reciprocal L/C）

这种信用证是指两张信用证的申请人互以对方为受益人而开立的信用证。两张信用证的金额相等或大体相等，可同时互开，也可先后开立。它多用于易货贸易或来料加工和补偿贸易业务。

（八）背对背信用证（Back to Back L/C）

背对背信用证又称转开信用证，指受益人要求原证的通知行或其他银行以原证为基础，另开一张内容相似的新信用证，对背信用证的开证行只能根据不可撤销信用证来开立。对背信用证的开立通常是中间商转售他人货物，或两国不能直接办理进出口贸易时，通过第三者以此种办法来沟通贸易。原信用证的金额（单价）应高于对背信用证的金额（单价），对背信用证的装运期应早于原信用证的规定。

（九）预支信用证/打包信用证（Anticipatory Credit/Packing Credit）

这种信用证是指开证行授权代付行（通知行）向受益人预付信用证金额的全部或一部分，由开证行保证偿还并负担利息，即开证行付款在前，受益人交单在后，与远期信用证相反。预支信用证凭出口人的光票付款，也有要求受益人附一份负责补交信用证规定单据的说明书，当货运单据交到后，付款行在付给剩余货款时，将扣除预支货款的利息。

（十）备用信用证（Standby Credit）

备用信用证又称商业票据信用证（Commercial paper credit）、担保信用证，它是指开证行根据开证申请人的请求，对受益人开立的承诺承担某项义务的凭证。即开证行保证在开证申请人未能履行其义务时，受益人只要凭备用信用证的规定并提交开证人违约证明，即可取得开证行的偿付。它是银行信用，对受益人来说是备用于开证人违约时，取得补偿的一种方式。

二、受益人要求通知行尽到的责任

1. **审查开证行资信**

开证行的政治背景、资信状况是否可靠，有否无理拒付的不良记录。

2. **审查信用证的有效性**

信用证印鉴、密押是否相符，条款是否完整清晰。

3. **审查信用证的责任条款**

开证行付款义务有否附加不利于出口商或背离国际惯例的条件。

4. **索汇路线和索汇方式的审查**

索汇路线是否直接，索汇方式是否正确，是否符合支付协定。

5. **费用问题**

费用承担方式是否合理，有无转嫁费用的现象。

三、信用证的审核方法和要点

1. **审证第一步**

将信用证与买卖合同进行核对，审查信用证与合同的一致性。

2. **审证第二步**

（1）价格条款的完整性，例如：

FOB 的特征：不要求保单，运费未付。

CFR 的特征：不要求保单，运费已付。

CIF 的特征：要求保单，运费已付。

（2）信用证的有效期和装运期是否足够。如离最后装运日太近，应要求展延装期、效期；信用证的装期和效期为同一天即"双到期"时，须自行将装期提前 10 天办理托运；如信用证规定向银行交单的日期不得迟于装运日期若干天，要注意该期限是否合理，能否办到。

(3) 信用证的到期日和到期地点是否合理。凡未注明到期日的信用证应视作无效；规定的到期地点应在出口国。

(4) 对信用证里的模糊用语的理解。《UCP600》第三条对某些用语做了一些解释，就惯例而言：

如情形适用，单数词形包含复数含义，复数词形包含单数含义。

信用证是不可撤销的，即使未如此标明。

单据签字可用手签、摹样签字、穿孔签字、印戳、符号或任何其他机械或电子的证实方法为之。

诸如单据须履行法定手续、签证、证明等类似要求，可由单据上任何看似满足该要求的签字、标记、印戳或标签来满足。

一家银行在不同国家的分支机构被视为不同的银行。

用诸如"第一流的"、"著名的"、"合格的"、"独立的"、"正式的"、"有资格的"或"本地的"等词语描述单据的出单人时，允许除受益人之外的任何人出具该单据。

除非要求在单据中使用，否则诸如"迅速地"、"立刻地"或"尽快地"等词语将不予理会。

"在或大概在（on or about）"或类似用语将被视为规定事件发生在指定日期的前后五个日历日之间，起讫日期计算在内。

"至（to）"、"直至（until、till）"、"从……开始（from）"及"在……之间（between）"等词用于确定发运日期时包含提及的日期，使用"在……之前（before）"及"在……之后（after）"时则不包含提及的日期。

"从……开始（from）"及"在……之后（after）"等词用于确定到期日时不包含提及的日期。

"前半月"及"后半月"分别指一个月的第一日到第十五日及第十六日到该月的最后一日，起讫日期计算在内。

一个月的"开始（beginning）"、"中间（middle）"及"末尾（end）"分别指第一到第十日、第十一日到第二十日及第二十一日到该月的最后一日，起讫日期计算在内。

3. 审证第三步

(1) 货物的控制权。下列情况是出口人在收到信用证时必须注意的。

信用证规定提单应以进口人作为收货人；

信用证要求空运单或邮包收据，并以进口人为收货人；

信用证规定出口人在货物装运后将部分提单或全套提单直接寄给进口人。

(2) 审查信用证条款的可接受性。即审核信用证中是否存在"软条款"。

最常见的软条款有：

限制信用证生效的条款，如："本证生效须由开证行以修改书形式另行通知"；"本证是否生效依进口人是否能取得进口许可证"；

限制出口人装运的条款，如："货物只能待收到申请人指定船名的装运通知后装运，而该装运通知将由开证行随后以信用证修改书的方式发出。受益人应将该修改书包括在每套单据中议付"。

限制出口人单据的条款，如："受益人所交单据中应包括：由开证申请人或其代表签署的检验证书一份";"受益人所交单据中应包括：由开证申请人手签的说明运输船名的信函一封"。

限制出口人交单的条款，如："船样寄开证申请人确认后受益人才可交单"。

开证行有条件付款责任的条款，如："开证行在货到目的港后通过进口商品检验后才付款";"在货物清关或由主管当局批准进口后才支付货款"。

四、信用证的修改

在任何情况下，不可撤销信用证的修改应由开证申请人提出，由开证行修改，并经开证行、保兑行（如已保兑）和受益人的同意，才能生效。

改证函一般格式如下：

Dear Sir：

While we thank you for your L/C No. L-1234, we regret to inform you that we have found some discrepancies. You are requested to make the following amendments：

1. …should be amended as…
2. …should read…
3. …should be…instead of …
4. …should be amended to read "…"
5. Delete the term "…" or change the term into "…"

We look forward to receiving your amendment to the L/C at an early date and thank you in advance.

Sincerely yours

商务函电的作用：一是索取信息或传递信息；二是处理商务交流中有关事宜；三是联络与沟通感情。

商务函电的写作应掌握7C原则，即：完整（complete）、正确（correctness）、清楚（clearness）、简洁（conciseness）、具体（concreteness）、礼貌（courtesy）、体谅（consideration）。

完整原则：商务函电应完整表达所包含的内容和意思，何人、何时、何地、何事、何种原因、何种方式等。

正确原则：表达的用词用语及标点符号应正确无误，因为商务函电的内容大多涉及商业交往中双方的权利、义务以及利害关系，如果出错，势必会造成不必要的麻烦。

清楚原则：所有的词句都应该能够非常清晰明确地表现真实的意图，避免双重意义的表示或者模棱两可。用最简单普通的词句来直截了当地告诉对方。

简洁原则：在无损于礼貌的前提下，用尽可能少的文字清楚表达真实的意思。清楚和简洁经常相辅相成，摒弃函电中的陈词滥调和俗套，可以使交流变得更加容易和方便。一事一段则会使函电清楚易读和富有吸引力。

具体原则：内容当然要具体而且明确，尤其是要求对方答复或者对之后的交往产生影响的函电。

礼貌原则：文字表达的语气上应表现出一个人的职业修养，客气而且得体。最重要的礼貌是及时回复对方，最感人的礼貌是从不怀疑甚至计较对方的坦诚。商务交往中肯定会发生意见分歧，但礼貌和沟通可能化解分歧而不影响双方的良好关系。

体谅原则：这是拟定商务函电时一直强调的原则：为对方着想，站在对方立场。在起草商务函电时，始终应该以对方的观点来看问题，根据对方的思维方式来表达自己的意思，只有这样，与对方的沟通才会有成效。

五、《UCP600》和《ISBP》

《跟单信用证统一惯例》（Uniform Customs and Practice for Documentary Credits, UCP），是一套适用于跟单信用证业务，国际银行界、律师界、学术界自觉遵守的国际惯例。

2006年10月25日，在巴黎举行的ICC银行技术与惯例委员会2006年秋季例会上，以点名（Roll Call）形式，经71个国家和地区ICC委员会投票，《UCP600》最终得以通过。2007年7月1日正式运行。

《关于审核跟单信用证项下单据的国际标准银行实务》（International Standard Banking Practice for the Examination of Documents under Documentary Credits, ISBP），包括引言及200个条文，它不仅规定了信用证单据制作和审核所应该遵循的一般原则，而且对跟单信用证的常见条款和单据都作出了具体的规定。

《ISBP》引言主要对ISBP的产生、作用、范围等问题作了说明。ISBP的200个条文共分为11部分，包括先期问题，一般原则，汇票与到期日的计算，发票，海洋/海运提单（港到港运输），租船合约提单，多式联运单据，空运单据，公路、铁路或内河运输单据，保险单据和原产地证明。ISBP较UCP增加了许多新的内容，例如原产地证明、缩略语、未定义的用语、语言、数学计算、拼写错误及/或打印错误、多页单据的附件或附文、唛头等。

实训练习题

请根据下列合同审核信用证，写出审证意见

形式发票/合同：

```
            OCEAN PLASTIC & CHEMICAL PRODUCTS CO., LTD
                         SALES      CONFIRMATION

Rm 1105, Building #2, Shangdong
Nationals, #1926 Canghai Rd.
Ningbo, 315041, China
Fax: 86-574-87665377
TO: CONSOLIDATORS LIMITED                        NO: OPCP08253
RM. 13001-13007E, 13/F,                          DATE: Sept. 15, 2016
ASUA TERMINALS CENTER B.
BERTH 3, KWAI CHUNG, N.T., HONGKONG
P.O. Box 531 HONGKONG
We hereby confirm having sold to you the following goods on terms and conditions as stated below:
NAME OF COMMODITY: Butterfly Brand Sewing Machine
SPECIFICATION:      JA-115 3 Drawers Folding Cover
```

PACKING:	Packed in wooden cases of one set each
QUANTITY:	Total 5,500sets
UNIT PRICE:	US $ 64.00 per set CIFC 3% H.K.
TOTAL AMOUNT:	US $ 352,000.00
	(Say U.S. dollars three hundred and fifty two thousand only.)
SHIPMENT:	During Oct./Nov. 2016 from Ningbo to H.K. with partial shipments and transshipment permitted
INSURANCE:	To be covered by the seller for 110% of total invoice value against All Risks and War Risks as per the relevant ocean marine cargo clauses of the People's Insurance Company of China dated January 1st, 1981
PAYMENT:	The buyer should open through a bank acceptable to the seller an Irrevocable Letter of Credit at 30 days after sight to reach the Seller 30 days before the month of shipment valid for negotiation in China until the 15th day after the date of shipment
REMARKS:	Please sign and return one copy for our file

The Buyer: The Seller:
CONSOLIDATORS LIMITED   OCEAN PLASTIC & CHEMICAL PRODUCTS CO., LTD

信用证:

HONGKONG & SHANGHAI BANKING CORPORATION
QUEEN'S ROAD CENTERAL, P.O. BOX 64, H.K.
TEL: 822-1111   FAX: 810-1112

Advised through: Bank of China,   NO: CN3099/714
                 Ningbo Branch   DATE: Oct. 2, 2016 H.K.

To: OCEAN PLASTIC & CHEMICAL PRODUCTS CO., LTD
Rm1105, Building#2, Shangdong
Nationals, #1926 Canghai rd.
Ningbo, 315041, China

Dear Sirs:

We are pleased to advise that for account of Consolidators Limited, H.K., we hereby open our L/C No. CN3099/714 in your favour for a sum not exceeding about US $ 330,000.00 (Say US Dollars Three Hundred Thirty Thousand only) available by your drafts on HSBC at 30 days after date accompanied by the following documents:

1. Signed commercial invoice in 6 copies.

2. Packing List in quadruplicate.

3. Full set of (3/3) clean on board Bs/L issued to our order notify the above mentioned buyer and marked "Freight Collect" dated not later than October 31, 2016. From Shanghai to Hongkong, partial shipment is not permitted and trans-shipment is not permitted.

4. Insurance policy in 2 copies covering C.I.C for 150% invoice value against All Risks and War Risks as per the relevant ocean marine cargo clauses of the People's Insurance Company of China dated January 1st, 1981.

5. Certificate of Origin issued by China Council for the Promotion of International Trade.

Description of Goods:

5,500 sets Sewing Machine Art. No. JA – 115 packed in wooden cases or cartons each at US $ 64.00 CIF H. K.

Drafts drawn under this credit must be marked "drawn under HSBC, H. K.," bearing the number and date of this credit.

We undertake to honour all the drafts drawn in compliance with the terms of this credit if such drafts are to be presented at our counter on or before Oct. 31, 2016.

SPECIAL INSTRUCTIONS:

(1) Shipment advice to be sent by telefax to the applicant immediately after the shipment stating our L/C No., shipping marks, name of the vessel, goods description and amount as well as the bill of lading No. and date. A copy of such advice must accompany the original documents presented for negotiation.

(2) The negotiating bank is kindly requested to forward all documents to us (HONGKONG & SHANGHAI BANKING CORPORATION QUEEN'S ROAD CENTERAL, P. O. BOX 64, H. K.) in one lot by airmail.

It is subject to the Uniform Customs and Practice for Documentary Credits, International Chamber of Commerce Publication No. 600.

Yours faithfully

For HONGKONG & SHANGHAI BANKING CORPORATION

二、请根据下列合同审核信用证，写出审证意见

合同：

SALES CONFIRMATION

S/C NO: 954361

DATE: June 15, 2016

THE BUYER: The Eastern Trading Company, Osaka, Japan

THE SELLER: Shanghai Donghai Garments Imp. & Exp. Corp., Shanghai, China

NAME OF COMMODITY AND SPECIFICTION:

   Pure Cotton Men's Shirts

   Art. No. 9 – 71323

   Size Assortment S/3 M/6 and L/3 per dozens

QUANTITY: 5,000 dozens 3% more or less at the seller's option

PACKING: Each piece in a polybag, half a dozen to a paper box, 10 dozens to a carton

UNIT PRICE: US $ 120.00 per doz. CIFC 5% Kobe/Osaka

SHIPMENT: During Aug./Sept 2016 in two equal shipments

INSURANCE: To be covered by the seller for 110% of invoice value against all Risks as per China Insurance Clause dated Jan. 1st, 1981

PAYMENT: By irrevocable letter of credit payable at sight, to reach the seller not later than July 20, 2016 and remain valid for negotiation in China until the 15th days after the date of shipment

信用证：

IRREVOCABLE DOCUMENTARY LETTER OF CREDIT

FUJI BANK, LTD.
1 – CHOME, CHIYODA – KU
C. P. O. BOX 148 , TOKYO, JAPAN

L/C NO: 219307
July 15th, 2016

Advising Bank:
Bank of China, Shanghai

Beneficiary:
Shanghai Donghai Carments Imp. & Exp. Corp.
Shanghai China

Amount: not exceeding
US $ 600, 000. 00

Dear Sir:

At the request of THE EASTERN TRADING COMPANY , Osaka, Japan. We here issue in your favour this irrevocable documentary credit No. 219307 which is available by acceptance of your draft at 30 days after sight for full invoice value drawn on Fuji Bank Ltd. New York Branch, New York , N. Y. U. S. A. bearing this clause:
"Drawn under documentary credit No. 219307 of Fuji Bank Ltd. " accompanied by the following documents:

(1) Signed commercial invoice in four copies.
(2) Full set clean on board Bills of Lading made out to order and blank endorsed marked "freight collect" and notify applicant.
(3) Insurance Policy for full invoice value of 150% covering all Risks as per ICC dated Jan. 1st, 1981.
(4) Certificate of Origin issued by China Exit and Entry Inspection and Quarantine Bureau.
(5) Inspection Certificate issued by applicant.

Covering: 5, 000 dozens pure cotton men's shirts
  Art. No. 9 – 71323
  Size Assortment: S/3、M/6、L/3 per dozen
  At US $ 120 CIFC 5% Kobe/Osaka, packed in cartons of 10 dozens each.

Shipment from Chinese Port to Yokohama at buyer's option not later than Sept. 30, 2016.

Transshipment is prohibited, partial shipments are allowed.

The credit is valid in Shanghai, China.

Special conditions: Documents must be presented within 15 days after the date of the issuance of the Bills of Lading, but in any event within this credit validity.

We hereby undertake to honor all drafts drawn in accordance with the terms of this credit.

For Fuji Bank Ltd.

– signed –

三、根据合同审核信用证，并拟定改证函

SALES CONTRACT

(1) THE SELLERS: S/C NO: HYMA 401747
P. CO., LTD., DATE: OCT. 21, 2012
ADDRESS: FENGTING BUILDING, HEFENG CREATIVE PLAZA, NO. 375, JIANGDONG ROAD (NORTH), NINGBO, P. R. CHINA, 315040

(2) THE BUYERS: MAXIMA LT UAB
ADDRESS: SAVANORIU AVE. 247 LT-02300 VILNIUS-53 LITHUANIA

THE SELLERS AGREE TO SELL AND THE BUYERS AGREE TO BUY THE UNDERMENTIONED GOODS ACCORDING TO THE TERMS AND CONDITIONS AS STIPULATED BELOW.

(3) COMMODITY:
STATIONERY
ACCORDING TO THE PURCHASE ORDER NO.: 401747, DATED 10.17, 2012 C26

(4) AMOUNT:
USD21, 127.33 FOB NINGBO, CHINA AS PER INCOTERMS 2010

(5) PACKING:
PACKED IN CARTONS

(6) SHIPPING MARKS:
MAXIMA LT UAB /401747/KLAIPEDA, LITHUANIA/NO. 1-UP

(7) PORT OF SHIPMENT:
ANY CHINESE PORT

(8) PORT OF DESTINATION:
KLAIPEDA, LITHUANIA

(9) TIME OF SHIPMENT:
NOT LATER THAN 12.30, 2012
PARTIAL SHIPMENT AND TRANSHIPMENT ALLOWED

(10) TERMS OF PAYMENT:
THE BUYER SHOULD OPEN THROUGH A BANK ACCEPTABLE TO THE SELLER AN IRREVOCABLE LETTER OF CREDIT AT SIGHT TO REACH THE SELLER 30 DAYS BEFORE SHIPMENT, VALID FOR NEGOTIATION IN CHINA UNTIL THE 21ST DAY AFTER THE DATE OF SHIPMENT.
CERTIFICATE OF ORIGIN GSP FORM A IS ACCEPTABLE.
10 PERCENT MORE OR LESS IN L/C AMOUNT AND QUANTITY ALLOWED.

(11) FORCE MAJEURE:

(12) DISCREPANCY AND CLAIM:

(13) ARBITRATION:

THE SELLERS: THE BUYERS:
P. CO., LTD. MAXIMA LT UAB
　STIVEN　　　　　　　　　　　　　　　　　　　　JAMSON

信用证（例）：

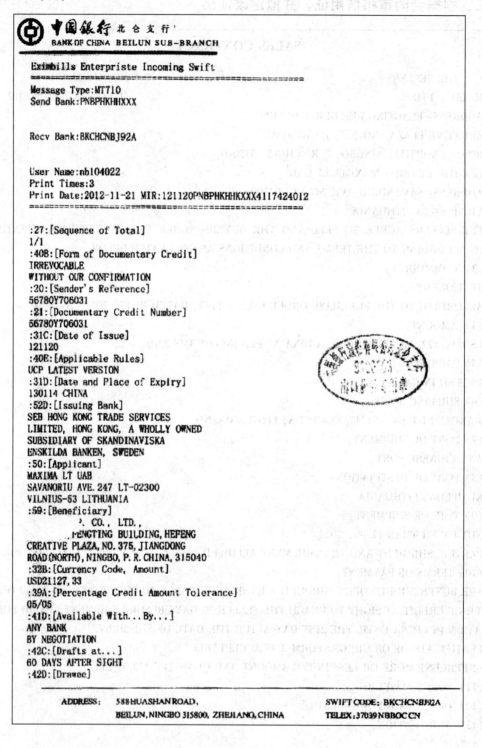

BANK OF CHINA BEILUN SUB-BRANCH

SEB HONG KONG TRADE SERVICES LTD.,
HONG KONG.
:43P:[Partial Shipments]
NOT ALLOWED
:43T:[Transshipment]
ALLOWED
:44E:[Port of Loading/Airport of Departure]
NINGBO, CHINA
:44F:[Port of Discharge/Airport of Destination]
KLAIPEDA, LITHUANIA
:44D:[Shipment Period]
GOODS MUST BE LOADED AND SHIPPED NOT EARLIER THAN 2012.12.15 AND NOT LATER THAN 2012.12.30
:45A:[Description of Goods and/or Services]
STATIONERY ACCORDING TO THE PURCHASE ORDER NO.: 401747, DATED 2012.10.19. C26.
...
TERMS OF DELIVERY: FOB NINGBO, CHINA AS PER INCOTERMS 2010
:46A:[Documents Required]
1) FULL SET CLEAN ON-BOARD MARINE/OCEAN BILL OF LADING CONSIGNED TO ORDER, BLANK ENDORSED, NOTIFY THE APPLICANT, MARKED 'FREIGHT COLLECT'.
2) SIGNED COMMERCIAL INVOICE ISSUED BY THE BENEFICIARY IN THE NAME OF THE APPLICANT SHOWING DATE, NUMBER, PURCHASE ORDER NO., CONTAINER NO., DELIVERY TERMS ACCORDING TO INCOTERMS 2010, GOODS DESCRIPTION, BARCODE NUMBER, GOODS QUANTITY, UNIT PRICE, CURRENCY, AMOUNT IN DIGITS AND WORDS, IN THREE ORIGINALS.
3) PACKING LIST ISSUED BY THE BENEFICIARY IN THE NAME OF THE APPLICANT SHOWING INVOICE DATE, INVOICE NUMBER, PURCHASE ORDER NO., CONTAINER NO., BARCODE NUMBER, NUMBER OF CARTONS OF EACH ITEM, NETT WEIGHT OF EACH ITEM, GROSS WEIGHT OF EACH ITEM, CBM (MEASUREMENT) OF EACH ITEM IN THREE ORIGINALS.
4) CERTIFICATE OF ORIGIN INDICATING ORIGIN OF THE GOODS CHINA, ISSUED BY AUTHORITATIVE INSTITUTION IN ONE FOLD.
:47A:[Additional Conditions]
THE AMOUNT OF ANY PRESENTATION UNDER THIS CREDIT MUST BE ENDORSED BY THE BENEFICIARY'S BANK. THE PRESENTING BANK SIGNIFIES THAT THE ENDORSEMENT HAS BEEN MADE BY MAKING A PRESENTATION.
DOCUMENTS PRESENTED WITH DISCREPANCY(IES) WILL BE SUBJECT TO A DISCREPANCY FEE OF FLAT RATE OF USD80.00 OR EQUIVALENT WILL BE DEDUCTED FROM THE AMOUNT CLAIMED.
IF THE DOCUMENTS ARE PRESENTED FOR NEGOTIATION/PAYMENT/ACCEPTANCE 15 DAYS AFTER THE EXPIRATION OF THE CREDIT, THIS WILL BE SUBJECT TO A POST EXPIRATION CHARGES OF USD75.00 OR EQUIVALENT AND THIS AMOUNT WILL BE DEDUCTED FROM THE AMOUNT CLAIMED.
5 PERCENT MORE OR LESS IN L/C AMOUNT AND QUANTITY ALLOWED.
AT MATURITY WE SHALL REIMBURSE THE NEGOTIATING BANK (IN THE CURRENCY OF THE L/C) AS PER THEIR INSTRUCTIONS.
1) ALL DOCUMENTS MUST BE ISSUED IN ENGLISH.
2) CERTIFICATE OF ORIGIN GSP FORM A IS NOT ACCEPTABLE.
3) SEPARATE SET OF DOCUMENTS MUST BE PRESENTED FOR EACH CONTAINER.

ADDRESS: 588 HUASHAN ROAD, BEILUN, NINGBO 315800, ZHEJIANG, CHINA
SWIFT CODE: BKCHCNBJ92A
TELEX: 37039 NBBOCCN

4) INVOICE AND PACKING LIST MUST SHOW 14 POSITIONS OF GOODS.
5) EXTRA COPIES OF DOCUMENTS MENTIONED UNDER THE FIELD '46A' FOR ISSUING BANK FILES.
:71B:[Charges]
ALL BANK CHARGES OTHER THAN
ISSUING COMMISSION AND DOCUMENTARY
COMMISSION INCURRED IN LITHUANIA
ARE FOR A/C OF BENEFICIARY.
:48:[Period for Presentation]
DOCUMENTS MUST BE PRESENTED WITHIN
15 DAYS AFTER THE DATE OF SHIPMENT,
BUT WITHIN THE VALIDITY OF THE L/C
:49:[Confirmation Instructions]
WITHOUT
:78:[Instructions to the Paying/Accepting/Negotiating Bank]
IF WE OBTAIN THE APPLICANT'S WAIVER AND DECIDE TO ACCEPT
DISCREPANCY(IES), IF ANY, WE SHALL SURRENDER THE
DOCUMENTS TO THE APPLICANT WITHOUT OBTAINING YOUR PRIOR APPROVAL.
THIS L/C WAS ISSUED BY SEB HONG KONG TRADE SERVICES LIMITED, HONG
KONG, A WHOLLY OWNED SUBSIDIARY OF SKANDINAVISKA ENSKILDA BANKEN,
SWEDEN.
THIS L/C IS CONFIRMED BY SKANDINAVISKA ENSKILDA BANKEN, LITHUANIA
ALL DOCUMENTS TOGETHER WITH DRAFT(S) ARE TO BE SENT BY COURIER
SERVICES OR REGISTERED AIRMAIL TO SEB HONG KONG TRADE SERVICES
LIMITED, 7/F, CITYPLAZA FOUR, 12 TAIKOO WAN ROAD, TAIKOO SHING,
ISLAND EAST HONG KONG ATTN : LC PROCESSING CENTRE IN ONE LOT.
:57D:["Advise through" Bank]
YOUR BEILUN SUB BRANCH
NO.245 HUASHAN ROAD, BEILUN,
NINGBO, CHINA
:72:[Sender to Receiver Information]
ALL SWIFT COMMUNICATIONS TO SEB
HONG KONG TRADE SERVICES LIMITED
MUST BE SENT TO PNBPHKHH
ATTN LC PROCESSING CENTRE OF SEB
HONG KONG TRADE SERVICES LIMTIED
-}{5:{MAC:E6C1A88F}{CHK:4506C681890B}}

ADDRESS: 588 HUASHAN ROAD,
BEILUN, NINGBO 315800, ZHEJIANG, CHINA
SWIFT CODE: BKCHCNBJ92A
TELEX: 37039 NBBOC CN

第二章

制作发票和装箱单

第一节 制作商业发票

教学目标

最终目标:制作商业发票。

促成目标:

1. 理解发票的分类、作用、内容。
2. 熟悉 UCP600 中关于商业发票的条款。
3. 能够手工制作发票。

情景案例

机构:
外贸企业:宁波欧胜塑化有限公司(OCEAN PLASTIC & CHEMICAL PRODUCTS CO., LTD)
人物:
小余:宁波欧胜塑化有限公司单证员
张经理:宁波欧胜塑化有限公司业务经理
背景资料:
(1) 2016 年 11 月 6 日,宁波欧胜塑化有限公司外贸业务部张经理与阿拉伯联合酋长国的公司 ABC TRADING CO., LLC 签订一份 36 800 支唇膏(LIP BALM)的出口合同,合同号为 081106。
(2) 单证员小余在办公室接到外贸业务部张经理的电话:小余,出货明细单邮件发过来了,查收下,请安排商检和订仓。小余马上接收邮件,下载明细单,阅读明细单。
(3) 制备报检基本文件:12 月 20 日,单证员根据明细单信息在办公室制作用于报检和报关的发票、装箱单。

货物明细表（例）：

OCEAN PLASTIC & CHEMICAL PRODUCTION CO., LTD

Rm 1105, Building#2, Shangdong Nationals, #1926 Canghai Rd., 315041, Ningbo, China

出 口 货 物 明 细 单

1. PO#：<u>081106</u>   L/C NO. HSBC657708467464   Customer：ABC TRADING CO., LLC
   P. O. BOX 13087 DUBAI, UAE
2. FROM：Ningbo   TO：JEBEL ALI, UAE   Shipment：By <u>sea</u>
3. Freight：Prepaid
4. Trade terms：CIF JEBEL ALI, UAE
5. Goods ready date：2016-12-31

   佳隆跟单：小朱
   TEL：87092188   FAX：87097215
6. Consignee：To the order of ABC TRADING CO., LLC, P. O. BOX 13087 DUBAI, UAE
7. Notify party：ABC TRADING CO., LLC
   P. O. BOX 13087 DUBAI, UAE
8. Forwarder：
   AFS – VISA INTERNATIONAL (HK) LTD.
   Attn：Charles Lau, charles@afs-int.com.hk
   Phone：0852-2368 5288
   Fax：00852-2724 8878
9. Goods details：

Desc.	QTY.	UNIT	U-PRICE	AMOUNT	CTN	MEAS.	G.W.	N.W.
LIP BALM	36,800	PCS	US$0.30	US$11,040.00	825	27.62	3,300	2,475
	36,800			11,040.00	825	27.62	3,300	2,475

10. 唛头如下
    PRITTY
    FRUITFULLY YOURS
    LIP BALM
11. Payment：
    By 100% irrevocable letter of credit to be available with drafts at sight to be opened by the seller
12. Insurance：
    COVERING ALL RISKS FOR 10 PER CENT ABOVE THE CIF VALUE
13. 特别指示：做商检, C/O, 提单正本
    Transparent red, transparent purple, transparent green, transparent blue, transparent orange, transparent yellow

商业发票（例）：

```
OCEAN PLASTIC AND CHEMICAL PRODUCTS CO., LTD.
       1101-1105 ShangDong Nationals,#1926 CangHai Rd.,NingBo,315040,China
                              COMMERCIAL  INVOICE
L/C NO.:        HSBC657708467464            INV.NO.:    09OS002
CONTRACT NO.:   081106                      DATE:       JAN.04,2017
FROM:           NINGBO,CHINA                TO:         JEBEL ALI,UAE
MESSRS:         ABC
   MARKS              QTY. & DESC.                      AMOUNT
                                                    CIF JEBEL ALI
                PO#081106
                LIP BALM           36800 PCS    US$0.300   US$11,040.00
                HS CODE :3304100000
PRITTY
FRUITFULLY YOURS
LIP BALM

                       TTL PACKED:825CTNS
                       TTL G.W. :3300.00KGS
                       TTL N.W. 2475.00KGS


                BANK INFORMATION:
                Intermediary Bank:   HSBC BANK NEW YORK
                Swift BIC:           MRMDUS33
                Beneficiary Bank:    SHANGHAI PUDONG DEVELOPMENT
                                     BANK, OFFSHORE BANKING UNIT
                Swift BIC:           SPDBCNSHOSA
                FAX:                 021-63522801
                ADD:                 15F, DONGYIN MANSION, NO.689 BEIJING
                                     DONG ROAD, SHANGHAI,200001,CHINA
                Beneficiary Name:    OCEAN PLASTIC &CHEMICAL PRODUCTS CO., LTD
                Account No.:         OSA11443630248709
                TEL.:                + 86 574 8766 3877   13867865787


                        For and on behalf of
                    OCEAN PLASTIC & CHEMICAL PRODUCTS CO., LIMITED

                                                Authorized Signature(s)
```

相关知识

一、发票分类

发票（Invoice）是进出口贸易结算中使用的最主要的单据之一。我国进出口贸易中使用的发票主要有：

（1）商业发票（Commercial Invoice）。是卖方向买方开立的，对所装运货物的全面、详细说明，并凭以向买方收取货款的货款价目总清单；是进出口贸易结算中使用的最主要的单据之一。商业发票是全套进出口单据的核心，其他单据均以其为中心来缮制。

（2）海关发票（Customs Invoice）。由出口商填制，供进口商凭以报关用的特定格式的发票。

（3）形式发票（Proforma Invoice）。进口商要求出口商制作的包括货物名称、规格、单价等内容的，非正式的参考性发票，供其向本国的贸易或外汇管理等当局申请进口或批准给予支付外汇之用。它是一种简式合同，不能用于托收和议付。但若信用证上有"依××形式发票"的规定，则出口商交单时须附上形式发票，否则银行不予审核单据内容。

（4）领事发票（Consular Invoice）。有些进口国为了解进口货物的原产地、货物有无倾销等情况，规定进口货物必须领取进口国驻出口国的领事签证的发票，作为征收有关货物进口关税的前提条件，同时也作为领事馆的经费来源。

（5）厂商发票（Manufacturer's Invoice）。进口国为确定出口商有无倾销行为，以及为了进行海关估价、核税和征收反倾销税之用，而由出口货物的制造厂商所出具的、以本国货币计算的、用来证明出口国国内市场的出厂价的发票。

二、商业发票作用

（1）核对卖方履约情况是否符合合同规定。
（2）进、出口商收付货款和记账的凭证。
（3）进口商通关纳税的依据。
（4）在不使用汇票的交易中，可替代汇票作为付款依据。

三、商业发票制作要点

商业发票一般无统一格式，由出口商自行设计，但内容必须符合信用证或合同的要求。其基本内容及制单要点如下：

（1）出口商名称及地址：信用证中一般表示为"BENEFICIARY：×××"。通常出口商名称及地址都已事先印好。

（2）单据名称：商业发票上应明确标明"INVOICE"（发票）或"COMMERCIAL INVOICE"（商业发票）字样。

（3）发票抬头（TO：…）：除信用证有其他要求外，发票抬头一般缮制为开证申请人（APPLICANT）。信用证中一般表示为"FOR ACCOUNT OF×××"或"TO THE ORDER OF×××"中"×××"部分。

（4）发票号码（INVOICE NO.）：发票号码一般由出口商按统一规律自定。

（5）发票日期（INVOICE DATE）：发票日期最好不要晚于提单的出具日期。

（6）合同及信用证号码（S/C NO.，L/C NO.）：根据实际填写。

（7）装运港和目的港：一般只简单地标明运输路线及运输方式，如FROM×× TO×× BY SEA/AIR。

（8）唛头（SHIPPING MARKS）：一般由卖方自行设计，但若合同或信用证规定了唛头，则须按规定。若无唛头，则应注明 N/M。

（9）货物描述（DESCRIPTION）：必须与信用证中的货物描述（DESCRIPTION OF GOODS）完全一致，必要时要照信用证原样打印，不得随意减少内容，否则有可能被银行视为不符点。但有时信用证货物描述的表述非常简单，此时按信用证打印完毕后，再按合同要求列明货物具体内容。

（10）数量（QUANTITY）：按合同标明装运货物数量，必须标明数量单位如 PIECE、SET、KG 或 METER 等。

（11）单价（UNIT PRICE）、总价（AMOUNT）：对应不同货物标明相应单价，注意货币单位及数量单位。总价即实际发货金额，应与信用证规定一致，同时还应注明贸易术语。

（12）签字盖章：若信用证要求 SIGNED INVOICE，就要求出口商签字或加盖图章。

（13）其他：有些国家对商业发票有特殊要求，如必须在商业发票上注明船名、重量、"无木制包装"等字样，需根据具体业务及信用证要求具体对待。

四、信用证发票条款示例

（1）MANUALLY SIGNED COMMERCIAL INVOICE IN SIX COPIES QUOTING ORDER NO. MADE OUT IN NAME OF CONSIGNEE.

（2）SIGNED INVOICE IN ONE ORIGINAL AND NINE COPIES.
ALL DOCUMENTS MUST BESTATED L/C NO.

（3）THE ORIGINAL INVOICE IS TO BE DULY CERTIFIED BY THE CCIC.

（4）5% COMMISION SHOULD BE DEDUCTED FROM TOTAL AMOUNT OF THE COMMERCIAL INVOICE.

实训练习题

根据交易信息制作商业发票

ALAHLI BANK OF KUWAIT	
ISSUE OF A DOCUMENTARY CREDIT	
SEQUENCE OF TOTAL	27：1/1
FORM OF DOCUMENTARY CREDIT	40A：IRREVOCABLE
DOCUMENTARY CREDIT NUMBER	20：609/23262
DATE OF ISSUE	31C：160505
DATE AND PLACE OF EXPIRY	31D：160715 CHINA
APPLICANT	50：SAMIEH TEXTLE & BLANKET CO. LTD
	P. O. BOX 299934, SAFAT, KUWAIT
BENEFICIARY	59：SHANDONG IMPORT & EXPORT CORP.
	7 ZHANSHAN ROAD, QINGDAO, CHINA
CURRENCY CODE, AMOUNT	32B：USD7,200.00
AVAILABLE WITH…BY…	41D：ADVISING BANK
	BY NEGOTIATION
DRAFTS AT…	42C：SIGHT
DRAWEE	42D：DRAWN ON US

PARTIAL SHIPMENT	43P: PERMITTED
TRANSHIPMENT	43T: PERMITTED
LOADING/DISPATCH/TAKING IN CHARGE/FM	44A: CHINA
FOR TRANSPORTATION TO…	44B: KUWAIT
LATEST DATE OF SHIPMENT	44C: 160630 BY VESSEL
DESCRIPTION OF GOODS/SERVICES	45A:

  ABOUT 6,000 YARDS ART 032, 65% POLYESTER 35% VISCOSE MIXED SUITING FABRICS WEIGHT: ABT. 250 GRAMS PER METER.

  SIZE: 58″ X ABT. 25 YARDS PIECES @ USD1. 20 PER YARD CFR KUWAIT

  SHIPPING MARKS: ABUZIAD – KUWAIT

       CTT/CH – 33/93

        MADE IN CHINA

       NO. 1 – 12

DOCUMENTS REQUIRED: 46A:

  1. SIGNED COMMERCIAL INVOICE IN QUINTUPLICATES CERTIFYING THAT EACH PIECE CARTON/ CASE OF THE GOODS CARRIES THE NAME OF COUNTRY OF ORIGIN IN NON – DETACHABLE OF NON – ALTERABLE WAY.

  CERTIFIED ON INVOICES THAT ALL OTHER DETAILS OF THE GOODS SHIPPED ARE AS PER INDENT NO. CTT/CH – 33/93 S/C: 00JUN30.

  2. CERTIFICATE OF ORIGIN IN ORIGINAL AND AT LEAST ONE COPY SHOWING BENEFICIARIES AS MANUFACTURERS.

  3. PACKING LIST IN TRIPLICATE SHOWING DESCRIPTION OF GOODS ITEM NO. AS PER HARMONIC SYSTEM NO. OF PACKAGES, KIND OF PACKAGE, CONTENTS OF PACKAGE, GROSS WEIGHT, NET WEIGHT AND TOTAL COST OF EACH ITEM.

  4. COMPLETE SET OF AT LEAST 3/3 CLEAN "ON BOARD" MARINE BILLS OF LADING ISSUED TO THE ORDER OF ALAHLI BANK OF KUWAIT. K. S. C. NOTIFYING OPENERS AND EVIDENCING "FREIGHT PREPAID."

ADDITIONAL CONDITIONS   47A:

  + CERTIFICATE OF ORIGIN MUST SHOW NAME AND ADDRESS OF MANUFACTURERS AND NAME OF EXPORTING COUNTRY/IES

  + AT THE TIME OF NEGOTIATION, PLEASE DEDUCT FROM YOUR PAYMENTS TO THE BENEFICIARIES 3% OF INVOICE VALUE OUT OF WHICH 1% DUE TO SAMIEH BASHEER NESWETH KUWAIT AND THE BALANCE 2 & DUE TO ACHIM TEXTILES CO. LTD. KUWAIT AS COMMISSION WHICH WILL BE PAID BY US LOCALLY

  + TRANSHIPMENT AT ISRAEL IS PROHIBITED.

  +5 PCT MORE OR LESS BOTH IN QUANTITY AND AMOUNT ARE ALLOWED.

CHARGES   71B: ALL BANKING CHARGES OUTSIDE ISSUING BANK
              ARE FOR BENEFICIARY'S ACCOUNT

INSTR. TO PAY/ACPT/NGG BANK   78:

  + WE UNDERTAKE TO HONOUR ALL DRAFTS DRAWN IN STRICT COMPLIANCE WITH THE TERMS OF THIS CREDIT.

+ PLEASE FORWARD TO US THE ORIGINAL SET OF DOCUMENTS BY REGISTERED AIRMAIL AND THE DUPLICATES BY SUBSEQUENT AIRMAIL.
SENDER TO RECEIVER INFO   72: THIS LC IS SUBJECT TO UCP 2007 ICC PUB. NO. 600. THIS IS OPERATIVE INSTRUMENT AND NO MAIL CONFIRMATION WILL FOLLOW.

其他资料:

(1) Packed in cartons of 22 pieces each (No. 1 – 10) 10 piece each (11 – 12), total: 240 pieces.

(2) Gross weight: 1,398kg;

    Net weight: 1,370kg;

    Measurement: 42.505m^3.

(3) Shipped per M/V "Maria" B/L No. 275.

(4) Invoice No. 20MSF43.

商业发票

ISSUER		COMMERCIAL INVOICE	
TO			
		NO.	DATE
TRANSPORT DETAILS		S/C NO.	L/C NO.
		TERMS OF PAYMENT	
Marks and Numbers	Number and kind of package Description of goods	Quantity	Unit Price	Amount
	Total:			
SAY TOTAL:				

第二节　制作装箱单

教学目标

最终目标：制作出口报检装箱单。
促成目标：
1. 理解装箱单的分类、作用、内容。
2. 熟悉《UCP600》中关于装箱单的条款。
3. 能够手工制作装箱单。

情景案例

机构：
外贸企业：宁波欧胜塑化有限公司（OCEAN PLASTIC & CHEMICAL PRODUCTS CO., LTD）
人物：
小余：宁波欧胜塑化有限公司单证员
张经理：宁波欧胜塑化有限公司业务经理
背景资料：
（1）2016年11月6日宁波欧胜塑化有限公司外贸业务部张经理与阿拉伯联合酋长国的公司ABC TRADING CO., LLC 签订一份36 800支唇膏（LIP BALM）的出口合同，合同号为081106。
（2）单证员小余在办公室接到外贸业务部张经理的电话：小余，出货明细单邮件发过来了，查收下，请安排商检和订仓。小余马上接收邮件，下载明细单，阅读明细单。
（3）制备报检基本文件：12月20日单证员根据明细单信息在办公室制作用于报检和报关的发票、装箱单。

装箱单（例）：

```
           OCEAN PLASTIC AND CHEMICAL PRODUCTS CO., LTD.
        Room1101-1105, Building#2, ShangDong Nationals,#1926 CangHai Rd.,NingBo,315040,China
                              PACKING LIST
   L/C NO.:    HSBC657708467464           INV.NO.:  09OS002
   CONTRACT NO.:  081106                  DATE:     JAN.04,2017
   FROM:       NINGBO,CHINA               TO:       JEBEL ALI,UAE
   MESSRS:     ABC
   SHIPPING MARKS: AS PER INVOICE NO.
       DESC.        CTNS    QTY.      TTL.G.W.   TTL.N.W.   MEAS.
                            (PCS)     (KGS)      (KGS)      M3
   PO#081106
   LIP BALM          825    36800     3300.00    2475.00    27.62
   HS CODE :3304100000


                                    TTL PACKED:825CTNS
                                    TTL G.W. :3300.00KGS
                                    TTL N.W.:2475.00KGS


                    For and on behalf of
                    OCEAN PLASTIC & CHEMICAL PRODUCTS CO., LIMITED
                    
                                      Authorized Signature(s)
```

相关知识

一、装箱单（尺码单、重量单）的类别和作用

出口商品在运输过程中，除散装货（In Bulk）如谷物、煤炭、矿砂等商品不需包装外，大多数商品为了避免在搬运、装卸和运输途中发生碰撞、振动或受外界其他影响而损伤货物，必须经过适当的包装才能装运出口。

包装单据（Packing Documents）是指一切记载或描述商品包装情况的单据，是商业发票内容的补充。海关、进口商为了了解包装情况和核验货物，或为便于对货物进行分拨转售，往往要求包装单据。

常见的包装单据有：

1. 装箱单/包装单（Packing List）

重点说明包装情况、包装条件和每件的毛重、净重等方面的内容。

2. **规格单（Specification List）**

内容与 Packing List 基本一致，名称上要与规定相符，重点说明包装的规格。

3. **重量单/磅码单（Weight List/Memo）**

一般以重量计价的商品，或当商品的重量对其质量能有一定的反映时，收货人对商品的重量比较重视，往往要求重量单。重量单重点说明商品的重量，包括单件包装的毛、净重等。

4. **尺码单（Measurement List）**

偏重于说明所装运货物的体积，即每件商品的包装尺码以及总尺码。

5. **中性包装单（Neutral Packing List）**

不表明出具单位和收货人的名称，也不盖章、不签字。

6. **包装声明（Packing Declaration）**

出口至澳大利亚、新西兰等地的商品，不论是否使用了木质包装材料，均需声明。

除上述情况外，还有：包装说明（Packing Specification）、包装提要（Packing Summary）、重量证书（Weight Certificate）、花色搭配单（Assortment List）。

二、包装类单据的缮制要点

（一）装箱单名称（Packing List）

应按照信用证规定使用。通常用"Packing List""Packing Specification""Detailed Packing List"。如果来证要求用中性包装单（Neutral Packing List），则包装单名称打"Packing List"，但包装单内不打卖方名称，不能签章。

常见的单据名称有：

Packing List（Note）装箱单

Weight List（Note）重量单

Measurement List 尺码单

Packing List and Weight List 装箱单/重量单

Packing Note and Weight Note 装箱单/重量单

Packing List and Weight List and Measurement 装箱单/重量单/尺码单

Packing Note and Weight Note and Measurement 装箱单/重量单/尺码单

Weight and Measurement List 重量单/尺码单

Weight and Measurement Note 重量单/尺码单

Packing and Measurement List 装箱单/尺码单

Packing and Measurement Nite 装箱单/尺码单

（二）编号（No.）

编号与发票号码一致。

（三）合同号或销售确认书号（Contract No. / Sales Confirmation No.）

注明此批货的合同号或者销售合同书号。

（四）唛头（Shipping Mark）

与发票一致，有的注实际唛头，有时也可以只注"as per invoice No. ×××"。唛头的具体写法请参见发票制单第七点。

（五）箱号（Case No.）

箱号又称包装件号码。在单位包装货量或品种不固定的情况下，需注明每个包装件内的包装情况，因此包装件应编号。

例如：Carton No. 1 – 5…
Carton No. 6 – 10…

有的来证要求此处注明"CASE NO. 1—UP"，UP 是指总箱数。

（六）货号（Name of Commodity）

货号按照发票填写，与发票内容一致。

（七）货描（Description of Goods；Specification）

货描要求与发票一致。

货名如有总称，应先注总称，然后逐项列明详细货名。与前5、6栏对应逐一注明每一包装件的货名、规格、品种。

（八）数量（Quantity）

应注明此箱内每件货物的包装件数。

例如"bag 10"、"drum 20"、"bale 50"，合同栏同时注明合计件数。

（九）毛重（Gr. Weight）

注明每个包装件的毛重和此包装件内不同规格、品种、花色货物各自的总毛重（sub total），最后在合计栏处注总货量。信用证或合同未要求，不注亦可。如为"Detailed Packing List"，则此处应逐项列明。

（十）净重（Net Weight）

注明每个包装件的净重和此包装件内不同规格、品种、花色货物各自的总净重（sub total），最后在合计栏处注总货量。信用证或合同未要求，不注亦可。如为"Detailed Packing List"，则此处应逐项列明。

（十一）箱外尺寸（Measurement）

注明每个包装件的尺寸。

（十二）合计（Total）

此栏对5、8、9、10栏合计。

（十三）出票人签章（Signature）

应与发票相同，如信用证规定包装单为"中性"，则在包装单内不应出现买卖双方的名称，不能签章。

三、装箱单缮制中的注意事项

（1）有的出口公司将两种单据的名称印在一起，当来证仅要求出具其中一种时，应将另外一种单据的名称删去。单据的名称，必须与来证要求相符。如信用证规定为"Weight Memo"，则单据名称不能用"Weight List"。

（2）两种单据的各项内容，应与发票和其他单据的内容一致。如装箱单上的总件数和重量单上的总重量，应与发票、提单上的总件数或总重量相一致。

（3）包装单所列的情况，应与货物的包装内容完全相符，例如，货物用纸箱装，每箱200盒，每盒4打。

（4）如来证要求这两种单据分别开列，则应按来证办理，提供两套单据。

（5）如来证要求在这两种单据（或其中一种）上注明总尺码，则应照办，此单据上的尺码应与提单上注明的尺码一致。

（6）如来证要求提供"中性包装清单"（Neutral Packing List），则应由第三方填制，不要注明受益人的名称。这是由于进口商在转让单据时，不愿将原始出口者暴露给其买主，故才要求出口商出具中性单据。如来证要求用"空白纸张"（Plain Paper）填制这两种单据，在单据内一般不要表现出受益人及开证行名称，也不要加盖任何签章。

实训练习题

请根据给定业务信息，制作一份装箱单

```
08AUG08              14：10：38                    LOGICAL TERMINAL P005
MT S700              ISSUE OF DOCUMENTARY CREDIT
                                                         PAGE 00001
                                                         FUNC SWPR3
MSGACK DWS765I AUTHENTICATION SUCCESSFUL WITH PRIMARY KEY
BASIC HEADER         F 01 BKCHCNBJA300        5976 662401
                     O 700 1530 030807  MITKJPJTA×××  1368 960990
APPLICATION HEADER   080808
                              *SAKURA BANK, LTD. , THE (FORMERLY
                              *MITSUI TAIYO KOBE)
                              *TOKYO
USER HEADER          BANK, PRIORITY       113：
                     MSG USER REF         108：
SEQUENCE OF TOTAL    *27      ：1/1
FORM OF DOC. CREDIT  *40 A : IRREVOCABLE
DOC. CREDIT NUMBER   *20     : 090 – 3001573
DATE OF ISSUE        *31 C : 080804
EXPIRY               *31 D : DATE 080915 PLACE IN THE COUNTRY OF BENEFICIARY
APPLICANT            *50 : TIANJIN – DAIAI CO. , LTD, SHIBADAIMON
                              MF BLOG, 2 – 1 – 16, SHIBADAIMON,
                              MINATO – KU, TOKYO, 105 JAPAN
BENEFICIARY          *59 : NINGBO HAIWEN IMP&EXP. CORP. , LTD
                              9FL, NO. 428, ZHONGSHAN EAST ROAD, NINGBO
AMOUNT               *32 B : CURRENCY USD AMOUNT 74, 157.00
ADD. AMOUNT COVERED   39 C : FULL CIF INVOICE VALUE
AVAILABLE WITH/BY    *41 D : BANK OF CHINA
                              BY NEGOTIATION
```

DRAFTS AT...	42 C:	DRAFT (S) AT SIGHT
DRAWEE	42 A:	CHEMUS33
		*CHEMICAL BANK
		*NEW YORK, NY
PARTIAL SHIPMENT	43 P:	PARTIAL SHIPMENTS ARE ALLOWED
TRANSSHIPMENT	43 T:	TRANSHIPMENT IS NOT ALLOWED
LOADING IN CHARGE	44 A:	NINGBO, CHINA
FOR TRANSPORT TO...	44 B:	KOBE/OSAKA, JAPAN
LATEST DATE OF SHIP.	44 C:	080831
DESCRIPTION OF GOODS	45 A:	

    GIRL'S T/R VEST SUITS

       ST/NO. 353713   6,000 SETS.   USD6.27/SET   USD37,620.00

               353714   5,700 SETS.   USD6.41/SET   USD36,537.00

       TOTAL: 11,700 SETS.   USD74,157.00

PRESENTATION PERIOD	48:	DOCUMENTS MUST BE PRESENTED WITHIN 15 DAYS AFTER THE DATE OF SHIPMENT
CONFIRMATION	*49:	WITHOUT
REIMBURSEMENT BANK	53A:	CHEMUS33
		*CHEMICAL BANK
		*NEW YORK, NY
INSTRUCTIONS	78:	

    IN REIMBURSEMENT, NEGOTIATING BANK SHOULD SEND THE BENEFICIARY'S DRAFT TO THE DRAWEE BANK FOR OBTAINING THE PROCEED, NEGOTIATING BANK SHOULD FORWARD THE DOCUMENTS DIRECT TO THE SAKURA BANK, LTD., TOKYO INTL OPERATIONS CENTER P.O. BOX 766, TOKYO, JAPAN BY TWO CONSECUTIVE REGISTERED AIRMAILS

DOCUMENTS REQUIRED   46B:

    + SIGNED COMMERCIAL INVOICE IN 5 COPIES INDICATING IMPORT ORDER NO. 131283 AND CONTRACT NO. 08-09-403 DATED JUL. 12, 2003 AND L/C NO.

    + FULL SET OF 3/3 CLEAN ON BOARD OCEAN BILLS OF LADING MADE OUT TO ORDER OF SHIPPER AND BLANK ENDORSED AND MARKED "FREIGHT PREPAID" NOTIFY TIANJIN-DAIEI CO., LTD 6F, SHIBADAIMON MF BLDG., 2-1-16 SHIBADAIMON, MINATO-KU TOKYO 105 JAPAN. TEL NO. 03-5400-1971, FAX NO. 03-5400-1976.

    + PACKING LIST IN 5 COPIES

    + CERTIFICATE OF ORIGIN IN 5 COPIES

    + INSURANCE POLICY OR CERTIFICATE IN 2/2 AND ENDORSED IN BLANK FOR 110 PCT OF FULL TOTAL INVOICE VALUE COVERING ALL RISKS, WAR RISKS AS PER THE RELEVANT OCEAN MARINE CARGO CLAUSE OF P.I.C.C. DATED JAN. 1ST, 1981. WITH CLAIMS, IF ANY, PAYABLE AT DESTINATION

    + TELEX OR FAX COPY OF SHIPPING ADVICE DESPATCHED TO TIANJIN-DAIEI CO., LTD. (DIV: 1, DEPT: 3 FAX NO. 03-5400-1976) IMMEDIATELY AFTER SHIPMENT.

+ BENEFICIARY'S CERTIFICATE STATING THAT THREE SETS COPIES OF NON – NEGOTIABLE SHIPPING DOCUMENTS HAVE BEEN AIRMAILED DIRECTLY TO THE APPLICANT IMMEDIATELY AFTER SHIPMENT.

ADDITIONAL COND.   *47 B：

1) 5 PCT MORE OR LESS IN BOTH AMOUNT AND QUANTITY EACH ITEM WILL BE ACCEPTABLE.
2) BUYER'S IMPORT ORDER NO. 131283 MUST BE MENTIONED ON ANY SHIPPING DOCUMENTS.
3) ABOVE CARGO SHALL BE CONTAINERIZED.
4) SHIPPING MARK OF EACH CARTON SHOULD INCLUDE BUYER'S IMPORT ORDER NO. 131283.
5) T. T. REIMBURSEMENT IS NOT ACCEPTABLE.
6) ALL BANKING CHARGES OUTSIDE JAPAN ARE FOR ACCOUNT OF BENEFICIARY.
   ORDER IS ＜MAC：＞＜PAC：＞＜ENC：＞＜CHK：＞＜TNG：＞＜PDE：＞
   MAC：BF35294E
   CHK：6E452BBE2A45
   DLM：

制单相关信息（关于其中第一批货物的装船情况）：

ST／NO．353713

发票号 CPU04140A　　　　　发票日期 AUG. 10，2008

提单号 50100289BUS　　　　提单日期 AUG. 15，2008

保险单号 RGS354554　　　　产地证号 RQWT5525

船名 ULSAN V.501N　　　　H. S. 编码 5434.8764

商品数量 6 000 SETS　　　　包装 @30 SETS／CTN

集装箱号 MTU7045319/KB846421/40

毛重 @25 KGS／CTN　　　　净重 @24 KGS／CTN

尺码 @0.236 CBM／CTN

装箱单

ISSUER		PACKING LIST			
TO					
		NO.		DATE	
Marks and Numbers	Number and kind of package Description of goods	Quantity	G. W	N. W	Meas.
	Total：				
SAY TOTAL：					

第三章

托运和提单

第一节 托运操作

教学目标

最终目标：能进行出口托运。

促成目标：
1. 能填制托运单。
2. 能跟踪托运过程。

情景案例

机构：
外贸企业：宁波欧胜塑化有限公司（OCEAN PLASTIC & CHEMICAL PRODUCTS CO.，LTD）
货运代理：AFS – VISA INTERNATIONAL（HK）LTD

人物：
小余：宁波欧胜塑化有限公司单证员
张经理：宁波欧胜塑化有限公司业务经理
货代员陈小姐：AFS – VISA INTERNATIONAL（HK）LTD

背景资料：
（1）2016年11月6日宁波欧胜塑化有限公司外贸业务部张经理与阿拉伯联合酋长国的公司 ABC TRADING CO.，LLC 签订一份36 800支唇膏（LIP BALM）的出口合同，合同号为081106。
（2）小余打电话给货代员陈小姐，交流订舱事宜：陈小姐，您好！我需要一月份去迪拜的船期表、运费表，请用电子邮件发给我。
（3）12月20日，单证员小余制作托运单。当天下午，小余打电话给陈小姐：我刚传真过来一票托运单，查收下，我司货可在12月31日拉柜。
（4）12月23日，小余收到了货代员陈小姐的进仓单。

托运单（例）：

宁波欧胜塑化有限公司

地址：宁波沧海路1926号上东国际2号楼1101－1105室
电话：574/8766 3877 传真：574/8766 5377

出口货物配船单　　　08OS094　　　BY BOAT

SHIPPER：OCEAN PLASTIC & CHEMICAL PRODUCTS CO.，LTD
　　　　　Room1101－1105，Building#2，Shangdong Nationals，#1926 Canghai Rd.，
　　　　　Ningbo，315041，China
CONSIGNEE：To the order of ABC TRADING CO.，LLC P.O. BOX 13087 DUBAI, UAE
NOTIFY：ABC TRADING CO.，LLC P.O. BOX 13087 DUBAI, UAE
PORT OF LOADING：<u>NINGBO</u>
PORT OF DISCHARGE：<u>UAE</u>
FINAL DESTINATION：
OCEAN VESSEL：
VOY NO.：

MARKS	DESC. & QTY.	G.W./kg	CBM/m³
PRITTY FRUITFULLY YOURS LIP BALM	PO#080116 LIP BALM　　825CTNS The shipment contains no solid wooden packing material. FREIGHT PREPAID	3,300	27.62

PACKAGE：TTL EIGHT HUNDRED TWENTY FIVE CARTONS ONLY

TO：梁 R
　　您好！工厂货12/31完成拉柜，烦请配拼相应的船。
　　请与客人确认好，谢谢！

　　　　　　　　　　　　　　　　　　　　　　　　LANSING
　　　　　　　　　　　　　　　　　　　　　　　　12－26－2016

进仓单（例）：

DACHSER FAR EAST LTD.
SHANGHAI OFFICE

报关资料请注明进仓编号
谢谢配合

尊敬的客户，请提供完整的报关资料，我司不代为填写，谢谢合作

海运出口送货通知

ATTN: 关117 余小姐/Brand new days　　　FAX：
贵司所托货名：　　　　　　　　　　　　件数：10 CTNS
目的港：LE HAVRE　　　　　　　　　　VSL：
现预计开船日：2017 年 9 月 15 日
进仓编号：**D73200809004B**

1. 请于 2017 年 9 月 9 日 上午 9:00 时之前送正本报关单据至：
上海市南京西路1038号梅陇镇广场2305室上海德莎国际货运有限公司　邮政编码：200041
Tel 86-21-3217 4790 EXT 5116　　　Fax 86-21-62672748 / 6218 9612
联系人：赵小姐　（配载后提单、预录单联系人 5140 分机潘小姐）
（洋山三期），实行先报关，后进港，请务必按照我司要求时间进仓！
逾期请自行承担费用及责任，谢谢合作！
若退关，请于上周二告知我们。
***我司LOCAL CHARGE费用如下：
内装费：RMB95/CBM(MIN RMB95)　　报关费：RMB125/HB/L
文件费：RMB150/SHIPMENT　　　（如有商检，费用RMB100/SHIPMENT）***
安保费：RMB1/CBM(MIN RMB1)
以上费用如有任何异议，请在收到此通知后即与我司确认，否则视为默认。

2. 请于 2017 年 9 月 10 日 下午 16 时之前送货至：
上海市宝山区呼兰路455号华贸国际货运有限公司海运仓库
TEL:021-66203220/66212175/56994041　FAX:021-56994042/56749054
联系人：程剑峰,严晓明,任华,潘振宏
仓库24小时为客户服务,监督电话:13601877603(虞金篪)
****注意*** 通河路,爱辉路,虎林路 禁止8吨以上车辆通行船期、运费表（例）：

AFS-VISA INTERNATIONAL (HK) LTD

CROSS OCEAN

编号：YYJP08000801（上次编号：YYJP080705）生效日：7.28--8.3
航线客服：郑军 吉英 T:63935052 M:13918867053

生效日期：June.2008　　　　中东.红海.印巴运价　　　　编号：080801

国别	目的港	20'	40'	40'HQ	船东	开航日	航程	备注
U.A.E.	DUBAI (JEBEL ALI)	850	1450	1450	CSCL	SAT	15	ALL-IN DIR
	DUBAI (JEBEL ALI)	775	1375	1375	TSL	TUE	16	ALL-IN DIR
	DUBAI (JEBEL ALI)	750	1350	1350	TSL	SAT	17	ALL-IN DIR
	DUBAI (JEBEL ALI)	865	1575	1575	WHL	TUE/SAT	18	ALL-IN DIR
	DUBAI (JEBEL ALI)	775	1300	1300	CNC	TUE	16	ALL-IN DIR
	DUBAI (JEBEL ALI)	775	1330	1330	CMA	TUE	18	ALL-IN DIR
	DUBAI (PORT RASHID)	900	1530	1530	CMA	TUE	19	ALL-IN VIA:JEA
	DUBAI (JEBEL ALI)	825	1350	1350	EMI	MON	16	ALL-IN DIR
	DUBAI (JEBEL ALI)	1025	1775	1775	HEUNG-A	SUN	16	ALL-IN DIR
	DUBAI (JEBEL ALI)	800	1325	1325	KMTC	SUN	18	ALL-IN DIR
	DUBAI (JEBEL ALI)	850	1400	1400	NOR	WED	17	ALL-IN DIR
	ABU DHABI	1010	1665	1665	CSCL	SAT	22	ALL-IN VIA:DUB
	ABU DHABI	1050	1850	1850	TSL	TUE	22	ALL-IN VIA:DUB
	ABU DHABI	975	1685	1685	EMI	TUE	19	ALL-IN DIR
	ABU DHABI	1025	1700	1700	NOR	WED	28	ALL-IN VIA:JEA
IRAN	SHAHID RAJAEE SEZ (B)	1025	1850	1850	EMI	MON	21	ALL-IN VIA:JEA
	SHAHID RAJAEE SEZ (B)	1000	1900	1900	电询	TUE/SAT	20	ALL-IN DIR
	SHAHID RAJAEE SEZ (B)	1000	1600	1600	NOR	WED	28	ALL-IN VIA:JEA
	SHAHID RAJAEE SEZ (B)	925	1650	1650	CNC	MON	19	ALL-IN DIR
	B.ABBAS	875	1575	1575	KMTC	SUN	21	ALL-IN VIA:JEA
	SHAHID RAJAEE SEZ	900	1625	1625	CMA	TUE	21	ALL-IN DIR
	SHAHID RAJAEE SEZ	1100	1800	1800	TSL	TUE	22	ALL-IN VIA:PKL
	B.ABBAS	960	1565	1565	CSCL	TUE	19	ALL-IN DIR
	B.ABBAS	960	1665	1665	CSCL	SAT	22	ALL-IN VIA:DUB
	BAHRAIN	1175	1985	1985	EMI	MON	21	ALL-IN VIA:JEA
	BAHRAIN	1225	2200	2200	TSL	TUE	22	ALL-IN VIA:PKL

相关知识

一、托运单据概述

出口货物运输有海运、陆运和空运三种方式，其中海洋货物运输在国际贸易中使用最多。

国际货物运输的关系人承运人（Carrier）、发货人（Shipper）、收货人（Consignee）、货代（Freight Forwarder）。收货人与发货人是货主，货主一般都是通过货代向承运人办理货物的运输手续。

出口货物托运是指出口单位通过有权受理对外货物运输业务的单位，办理出口货物的海、陆、空等运输事宜，是国际货物运输的第一个步骤。不同的运输方式所对应的货物托运的流程及内容也不同。

二、托运单的流转

出口企业办理出口货物托运手续，使用出口货物托运单或出口货物明细单。托运单（Booking Note，B/N）俗称下货纸，是托运人根据贸易合同和信用证条款内容填制的，向承运人或其代理办理货物托运的单证。承运人根据托运单内容，并结合船舶的航线、挂靠港、船期和舱位等条件考虑，认为合适后，即接受托运。

分类：

（1）海运托运单。

（2）陆运托运单。
（3）空运托运单。
集装箱货物托运单各联：
第1联：货主留底
第2联：船代留底
第3联：运费通知（1）
第4联：运费通知（2）
第5联：装货单
第6联：收货单
第7联：场站收据
第8联：货代留底
第9、10联：配舱回单
第11、12联：货主机动联

其中，装货单（Shipping Order，S/O）、收货单（大副收据）、场站收据（Dock Receipt，D/R）为核心。

三、托运单制作注意事项

（1）目的港名称须明确具体，并与信用证描述一致，如有同名港，则须在港口名称后注明国家、地区或州、城市。如信用证规定目的港为选择港（Optional Ports），则应是同一航线上的、同一航次挂靠的基本港。

（2）运输编号，即委托书的编号。
每个具有进出口权的托运人都有一个托运代号（通常也是商业发票号），以便查核和财务结算。

（3）货物名称，应根据货物的实际名称，用中英文两种文字填写，更重要的是要与信用证所列货名相符。

（4）标记及号码，又称唛头（Shipping Mark），是为了便于识别货物，防止错发货，通常由型号、图形或收货单位简称、目的港、件数或批号等组成。

（5）货物的重量尺码，重量的单位为公斤[①]，尺码为立方米。

（6）托盘货要分别注明盘的重量、尺码和货物本身的重量、尺码，对超长、超重、超高货物，应提供每一件货物的详细的体积（长、宽、高）以及每一件的重量，以便货运公司计算货物积载因素，安排特殊的装货设备。

（7）运费付款方式。一般有运费预付（Freight Prepaid）和运费到付（Freight Collect）。有的转运货物，一程运输费预付，二程运费到付，要分别注明。

（8）可否转船、分批，以及装期、效期等均应按信用证或合同要求一一注明。

（9）通知人、收货人按需要决定是否填写。

（10）有关的运输条款、订舱、配载信用证或客户有特殊要求的也要一一列明。

---

① 1公斤＝1000克。

实训练习题

请根据前一章实训题给定业务信息，制作托运单

Shipper 托运人				
	SHIPPING ORDER 货物托运单			
Consignee 收货人				
	S/O No. 托运单号			
	CY Opening 开舱日期		CY Closing 截关日期	
	Vessel/Voyage 船名/航次			
	Size 柜型	Quantity 柜量	B/L Issued at：提单发放地点	
	20′		Shenzhen	
Notify Party 通知人	40′GP		HK	
	40′HQ		Taiwan	
	45′		Release B/L Way 放货方式	
	40′RD		Master B/L	
	40′RH		High Day B/L	
Place of Receipt	Place of Loading	其他	Telex Release	
Port of Discharge	Place of Delivery	Freight Confirm 费用确认		
Marks/Nos 唛头/号码	Quantity&Package 件数及包装	Description of Goods 货物品名及规格	Gross Weight （KG）毛重	Measurement （CBM）尺码
Prepaid 预付			Collect 到付	
如自拖自报，请注明： 拖车公司及联系方式、报关行及电话			Signature & Chop by Shipper 托运人签名及盖单	
拖柜地点、时间、联系人及电话：				

第二节　提单操作

教学目标

最终目标：能根据贸易信息审核确认提单。

促成目标：

1. 能审核确认提单。
2. 熟悉《UCP600》关于提单的规定。
3. 能阅读其他货运单据。

情景案例

机构：
外贸企业：宁波欧胜塑化有限公司（OCEAN PLASTIC & CHEMICAL PRODUCTS CO., LTD）
货运代理：AFS – VISA INTERNATIONAL（HK）LTD

人物：
小余：宁波欧胜塑化有限公司单证员
张经理：宁波欧胜塑化有限公司业务经理
货代员陈小姐：AFS – VISA INTERNATIONAL（HK）LTD

背景资料：
（1）2016年11月6日宁波欧胜塑化有限公司外贸业务部张经理与阿拉伯联合酋长国的公司 ABC TRADING CO., LLC 签订一份36 800支唇膏（LIP BALM）的出口合同，合同号为081106。
（2）12月7日，小余收到货代员提单传真件，要求确认提单。小余仔细阅读提单，觉得提单符合要求，就在提单上直接写确认 OK，并回传给货代员。
（3）12月13日，小余收到邮寄的提单正本。

提单确认件（例）：

提单（例）：

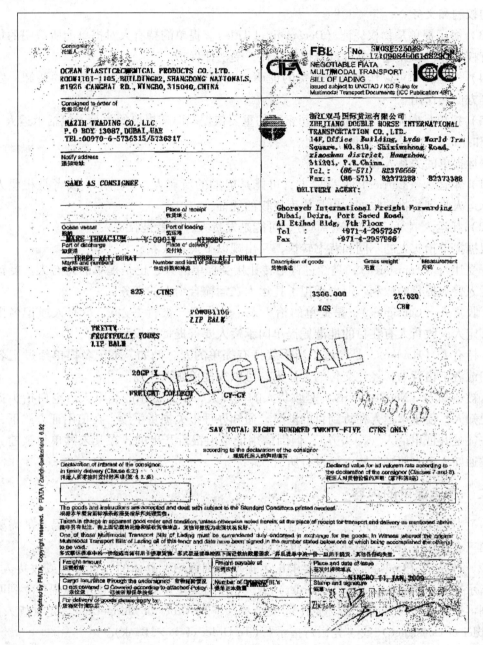

相关知识

一、海运提单的作用和关系人

海运提单的作用是：

（1）海运提单是承运人或其代理人签发的货物收据（Receipt for the Goods），确认承运人已经按海运提单所列内容收到货物。

(2) 海运提单是托运人和承运人之间的运输合约（Contract）。双方必须履行提单上所载明的权利和义务。

(3) 海运提单是物权凭证（Document of Title）。提单的持有人对提单上所载明的货物拥有所有权，并可以经过背书进行抵押、转让，受法律保护。

(4) 海运提单可以作为收取运费的证明，在运输过程中起到办理货物的装卸、发运和交付等方面的作用。

(5) 提单是向船公司或保险公司索赔的重要依据。海运提单的关系人包括承运人（Carrier）和托运人（Shipper）两个方面。

海运提单的关系人有：

(1) 承运人（Carrier）亦称船方，可能是船舶的所有人，即船东，或者是租船人。提单是承运人收到货物的收据，也是代表货权的凭证。

(2) 托运人（Shipper）亦称货方，可能是发货人，或者是收货人。

根据提单抬头人的不同和背书转让，又出现以下关系人：

①受让人（Transferee），是经过背书转让接受提单的人，也是提单的持有人。受让人有向承运人要求提货的权利，但也承担了托运人在运输合约上的义务。

②收货人（Consignee），是提单的抬头人、受让人（被背书人）、持有人或记名提单载明的特定人。收货人有在目的地港凭提单向承运人要求提货的权利。

③持有人（Holder），是经过正当手续持有提单的人。例如，不记名提单经过记名背书转让，或者空白背书，经过交付的受让人，可以凭提单领取货物。

④被通知人（Notified Party）是收货人的代理人，不是提单的当事人。空白抬头提单注明被通知人，便于承运人在货到目的港时，通知办理报关提货手续。在信用证方式下，被通知人往往是开证申请人（即买方），但因信用证是由银行开出的，在其未赎单付款前，只能作为被通知人负责照顾货物，而没有所有权。

二、海运提单的内容

(1) 托运人（Shipper），一般为信用证中的受益人。如果开证人为了贸易上的需要，要求做第三者提单（Thirdparty B/L），也可照办。

(2) 收货人（Consignee），如要求记名提单，则可填上具体的收货公司或收货人名称；如属指示提单，则填为"指示"（Order）或"凭指示"（To Order）；如需在提单上列明指示人，则可根据不同要求，作成"凭托运人指示"（To Order of Shipper）、"凭收货人指示"（To Order of Consignee）或"凭银行指示"（To Order of ×× Bank）。

(3) 被通知人（Notified Party），这是船公司在货物到达目的港时发送到货通知的收件人，有时即为进口人。在信用证项下的提单，如信用证上对提单被通知人有具体规定，则必须严格按信用证要求填写。如果是记名提单或收货人指示提单，且收货人又有详细地址，则此栏可以不填。如果是空白指示提单或托运人指示提单，则此栏必须填列被通知人名称及详细地址，否则船方就无法与收货人联系，收货人也不能及时报关提货，甚至会因超过海关规定申报时间被没收。

(4) 提单号码（B/L NO），一般列在提单右上角，以便于工作联系和查核。发货人向收货人发送装船通知（Shipment Advice）时，也要列明船名和提单号码。

（5）船名（Name of Vessel），应填列货物所装的船名及航次。

（6）装货港（Port of Loading），应填列实际装船港口的具体名称。

（7）卸货港（Port of Discharge），填列货物实际卸下的港口名称。如属转船，第一程提单上的卸货港填转船港，收货人填二程船公司；第二程提单装货港填上述转船港，卸货港填最后目的港，如由第一程船公司出联运提单（Through B/L），则卸货港即可填最后目的港，提单上列明第一程和第二程船名。如经某港转运，要显示"VIA ××"字样。在运用集装箱运输方式时，目前使用"联合运输提单"（Combined Transport B/L），提单上除列明装货港、卸货港外，还要列明"收货地"（Place of Rceipt）、"交货地"（Place of delivery）以及"第一程运输工具"（Pre-carriage by）、"海运船名和航次"（Ocean Vessel, Voy. No）。填写卸货港，还要注意同名港口问题，如属选择港提单，就要在这栏中注明。

（8）货名（Discription of Goods），在信用证项下货名必须与信用证上规定的一致。

（9）件数和包装种类（Number and Kind of Packages），要按箱子的实际包装情况填列。

（10）唛头（Shipping Marks），信用证有规定的，必须按规定填列，否则可按发票上的唛头填列。

（11）毛重、尺码（Gross Weight, Measurement），除信用证另有规定者外，一般以公斤为单位列出货物的毛重，以立方米列出货物体积。

（12）运费和费用（Freight and Charges），一般为预付（Freight Prepaid）或到付（Freight Collect）。如 CIF 或 CFR 出口，一般均填上运费预付字样，千万不可漏列，否则收货人会因运费问题提不到货，虽可查清情况，但拖延提货时间，也将造成损失。如系 FOB 出口，则运费处填写"运费到付"字样，除非收货人委托发货人垫付运费。

（13）提单的签发、日期和份数：提单必须由承运人或船长或他们的代理签发，并应明确表明签发人身份。一般表示方法有：Carrier, Captain, 或 "As Agent for the Carrier：×××"等。提单份数一般按信用证要求出具，如"Full set of"一般理解成三份正本、若干份副本。待凭借其中一份正本完成提货任务后，其余各份失效。提单还是结汇的必需单据，特别是在跟单信用证结汇时，银行要求所提供的单证必须一致，因此提单上所签的日期必须与信用证或合同上所要求的最后装船期一致或先于装期。如果卖方估计货物无法在信用证装船期前装上船，应尽早通知买方，要求修改信用证，而不应利用"倒签提单"、"预借提单"等欺诈行为取得货款。

三、提单制作注意事项

（1）整套正本提单注有张数、是否按信用证条款交呈。

（2）提单正面是否打明承运人（Carrier）的全名及"承运人（Carrier）"一词以表明其身份。

（3）如提单正面已作如上表示，在承运人自己签署提单时，签署处毋须再打明承运人一词及其全名。举例：如提单正面已打明（或印明）承运人全名为 XYZ LINE 及"CARRIER"一词以示明其身份，则在提单签署处（一般在提单的右下角）经由 XYZ LINE 及其负责人签章即可。如提单正面未作如（2）表示，且由运输行（Forwarder）签署提单，则必须在签署处打明签署人的身份。如：ABC FORWARDING CO. as agents for XYZ LINE, the carrier 或 ABC FORWARDING Co. on behalf of XYZ LINE the carrier。如提单正面已作如（2）表示，但由运输行（Fowarder）签署提单，则必须在签署处打明签署人的身份，如 ABC FORWARDING CO. as agents for the carrier 或 as agents for/on behalf of the carrier。

（4）提单上如果印有"已装船"（"Shipped in apparent good order and condition on board…"）字样，则毋须加"装船批注"（"On board notation"）；如果印有"收妥待运"（"Received in apparent good order and condition for shipment…"）字样，则必须加"装船批注"并且加上装船日期。

（5）提单上如果印有"intended vessel"、"intended port of loading"、"intended port of discharge"及/或其他"intended…"等不肯定的描述字样，则必须加注"装船批注"，其中须把实际装货的船名、装货港口、卸货港口等项目打明，即使和预期（Intended）的船名和装卸港口一样，也须重复打出。

（6）单式海运即港对港（装货港到卸货港）运输方式下，只需在装货港（Port of Loading）、海轮名（Ocean vessel），及卸货港（Port of Discharge）三栏内正确填写；如在中途转船（Transhipment），转船港（Port of transhipment）的港名，不能打在卸货港（Port of discharge）栏内。需要时，只可在提单的货物栏空白处打明"在××（转船港）转船""with transhipment at ××"。

（7）"港口"（Port）和"地点"（Place）是不同的概念。如果提单上印有"收货地点"（place of receipt/taking in charge）和"交货地点/最后目的地"（place of delivery/final destination）等栏目，则此提单可用作"多式联运"（multi-modal transport）或"联合运输"（combined transport）运输单据。单式海运时不能填注，否则会引起对运输方式究竟是单式海运还是多式联运的误解。

（8）提单上印有"前期运输由"（Precarriage by）栏也为"多式联运"方式所专用，不能作为转船提单时打明第一程海轮名称的栏目。只有作为多式联运运输单据时，方可在该栏内注明"铁路"、"卡车"、"空运"或"江河"（rail、truck、air、river）等运输方式。

（9）提单的"收货人"栏（Consigned to 或 Consignee）须按信用证要求注明。例如，信用证规定提单作成"made out to order"，则打"order"一词；"made out to order of the applicant（申请开证人）"，则打"order of ××××（applicant 全名）"；"made out to order of the inssuing bank"，则打"order of ×××× Bank（开证行全名）"。如信用证规定提单直接作成买主（即申请人）或开证行的抬头，则不可再加"order of"两词。

（10）提单不能有"不洁净"批注（Unclean Clause），即对所承载的该批货物及其包装情况有缺陷现象的批注。

（11）除非信用证许可，提单不能注有"Subject Charter Party"即租船契约提单。

（12）关于转船，这些是允许的：
①如信用证允许转船——指装货港和卸货港之间发生转船，同一份提单包括了整个航程；
②如信用证禁止转船，同一份提单包括整个航程，装货港和卸货港之间并不发生转船；
③如信用证禁止转船，货由集装箱、拖船、母子船载运，即使提单注明将有转船，也不作不符，但须由同一份提单包括整个航程。

（13）提单上关于货物的描述不得与商业发票上的货物描述有所不一致。如提单上货物用统称表示，则该统称须与信用证中货物描述一致，且与其他单据有共通连接（Link）特征，例如唛头等。

（14）提单上通知人（Notify Party）须注有符合信用证规定的名称和地址、通信号码等。

（15）提单上有关运费的批注须符合信用证的规定和《UCP600》相应的规定。

（16）提单上的任何涂改、更正须加具提单签发者的签章。

（17）提单必须由受益人及装货人（Shipper）背书。

四、信用证中有关提单条款举例

（1）Full set clean on board ocean bill of lading issued to order, blank endorsed marked freight payable at destination notify party as ABC company and showing invoice value, unit price, trade terms, contract number and L/C number unacceptable.

（2）Full set of clean on board B/L issued to our order, marked notifying applicant and freight prepaid and showing full name and address of the relative shipping agent in Egypt.

（3）Full set clean on board port to port bill of lading, made to the order and blank endorsed to our order, marked freight prepaid dated not later than the latest date of shipment not prior to the date of this credit, plus three non-negotiable copies.

实训练习题

请根据交易信息制作提单

```
MT700 --------------------- ISSUE OF A DOCUMENTARY CREDIT ---------------------

SEQUENCE OF TOTAL                    27: 1/1
FORM OF DOCUMENTARY CREDIT           40A: IRREVOCABLE
DOCUMENTARY CREDIT NUMBER            20: 00IM01413
DATE OF ISSUE                        31C: 160731
DATE AND PLACE OF EXPIRY             31D: 160915 CHINA
APPLICANT                            50: NEW WORLD INTERNATIONAL INC.
                                         NWI C AND A CO.
                                         129 HAYWARD WAY
                                         SO. EL MONTE, CA 91733
BENEFICIARY                          59: QINGDAO YUANDA INDUSTRY
                                         AND COMMERCE CO. LTD.
                                         PINGDU BRANCH
                                         QINGDAO, CHINA
CURRENCY CODE, AMOUNT                32B: USD30,940.00
AVAILABLE WITH...BY...               41D: ANY BANK
                                         BY NEGOTIATION
DRAFTS AT...                         42C: AT SIGHT FOR 100 PCT OF INVOICE VALUE
DRAWEE                               42D: CATHAY BANK
                                         LOSANGELES, CA.
```

PARTIAL SHIPMENT	43P:	NOT ALLOWED
TRANSHIPMENT	43T:	NOT ALLOWED
LOADING/DISPATCH/TAKING IN CHARGE/FM	44A:	QINGDAO PORT, CHINA
FOR TRANSPORTATION TO…	44B:	LOSANGELES PORT, CA, USA
LATEST DATE OF SHIPMENT	44C:	160831
DESCRIPTION OF GOODS/SERVICES	45A:	LANDIES SLIPPERS

FOB QINGDAO, CHINA

DOCUMENTS REQUIRED: 46A:

+ SIGNED COMMERCIAL INVOICE IN 1 ORIGINAL AND 3 COPIES
+ PACKING LIST IN 1 ORIGINAL AND 3 COPIES
+ FULL SET OF CLEAN ON BOARD OCEAN BILLS OF LANDING CONSIGNED TO ORDER OF NEW WORLD INTERNATIONAL INC., MARKED FREIGHT COLLECT

NOTIFY: NEW WORLD INTERNATIONAL INC. NWI C AND A CO.

   129 HAYWARD WAY   SO. EL MONTE, CA 91733

ADDITIONAL CONDITIONS   47A:

+ INSURANCE TO BE COVERED BY BUYER.
+ A DISCREPANCY FEE OF USD50.00 WILL BE DEDUCTED FROM PROCEEDS ON EACH SET OF DISCREPANT DOCUMENTS PRESENTED.
+ THE REQUIRED DOCUMENTS MUST BE SENT TO CATHAY BANK, 777 NORTH BROADWAY, LOS-ANGELES, CALIFORNIA 90012, USA ATTN. INTERNATIONAL DEPT. IN ONE LOT BY EX-PRESS AIRMAIL.

CHARGES   71B: ALL BANKING CHARGES OUTSIDE OF OUR COUNTER ARE FOR ACCOUNT OF THE BENEFICIARY.

PERIOD FOR PRESENTATIONS   48: DOCUMENTS MUST BE PRESENTED FOR NEGOTIATION WITHIN 15 DAYS AFTER BILL OF LADING DATE, BUT WITHIN THE VALIDITY OF THIS CREDIT.

CONFIRMATION INSTRUCTION   49: WITHOUT

ADVISE THROUGH BANK   57A: YOUR PINGDU SUB-BRANCH

                                             98 ZHENGYANG ROAD

                                             PINGDU DISTRICT

                                             QINGDAO, CHINA

SENDER TO RECEIVER INFO   72: THIS CREDIT IS SUBJECT TO UCP 2007 ICC PUB. NO. 600. THIS IS OPERATIVE INSTRUMENT AND NO MAIL CONFIRMATION WILL FOLLOW.

TRAILER

        MAC: A75A8689 CHK: 39D0ADB5BC9A

NNNN

参考资料:

(1) Commodity: Ladies slippers。

(2) Quantity: 2,000 pairs。

(3) Size: Each carton containing 37/10 38/10 39/10 40/10。

(4) Unit Price: USD15.47 per pair FOB Qingdao, China。

(5) Total Amount: USD30,940。
(6) S/C No. 00628; invoice No. LS628。
(7) Packing: in cartons of 40 pairs each。
(8) Measurement: 0.356m^3。
(9) Shipping mark: N/M, shipped by S.S Caihong V125 on 28th Aug., 2016。

提　　单

托运人 Shipper				B/L No. 中 国 对 外 贸 易 运 输 总 公 司 联 运 提 单 COMBINED TRANSPORT BILL OF LADING
收货人或指示 Consignee or order				RECEIVED the foods in apparent good order and condition as specified below unless otherwise stated herein. THE carrier, in accordance with the provisions contained in this document,
通知地址 Notify address				1) undertakes to perform or to procure the performance of the entire transport from the place at which the goods are taken in charge to the place designated for delivery in this document, and 2) assumes liability as prescribed in this document for such transport. One of the Bills of Lading must be surrendered duty indorsed in exchange for the goods or delivery order
前段运输 Pre-carriage by	收货地点 Place of Receipt			
海运船只 Ocean vessel	装货港 Port of loading			
卸货港 Port of discharge	交货地点 Place of delivery	运费支付地 Freight payable at	正本提单份数 Number of original Bs/L	
标志和号码 Marks and Nos.	件数和包装种类 Number and kind of packages	货　名 Description of goods	毛重（公斤） Gross weight（kg）	尺码（立方米） Measurement（m³）
以上细目由托运人提供 ABOVE PARTICULARS FURNISHED BY SHIPPER				
运费和费用 Freight and charges	REVENUE TONS	RATE	IN WITNESS whereof the numbers of original Bills of Lading stated above have been signed, one of which being accomplished, the other (s) to be void.	
PREPAID AT	PAYABLE AT		签单地点和日期 Place and date of issue	
TOTAL PREPAID	NUMBER OF ORIGINAL B/L (S)		代表承运人签字 Signed for or on behalf of the carrier 代　理 as agents	

报检

第一节 报检操作

教学目标

最终目标：能提交报检单据取得通关单。

促成目标：

1. 能进行报检单据的制作（除发票、装箱单）。
2. 熟悉报检通关程序、报检资格、时间、地点。
3. 熟悉报检单据种类、出单人、出单时间。
4. 了解通关单的来源、作用、内容。

情景案例

机构：

外贸企业：宁波欧胜塑化有限公司（OCEAN PLASTIC & CHEMICAL PRODUCTS CO., LTD）

工厂：金华市佳隆日化有限公司

商检局（CIQ）

人物：

小余：宁波欧胜塑化有限公司单证员

张经理：宁波欧胜塑化有限公司业务经理

小朱：金华市佳隆日化有限公司跟单员

背景资料：

（1）2016年11月6日，宁波欧胜塑化有限公司外贸业务部张经理与阿拉伯联合酋长国的公司 ABC TRADING CO., LLC 签订一份36 800支唇膏（LIP BALM）的出口合同，合同号为081106。

（2）单证员小余备齐发票、装箱单、合同、报检委托书等单据和海文的报检号：3800601740，给金华佳隆日化有限公司跟单员小朱发邮件，将以上附件随发。

（3）小余打电话给工厂跟单员小朱，电话协商产品的法定检验，小余与工厂跟单员小朱对话：小朱您好，商检资料看附件，请安排商检，烦请12月30日前，将电子传单发给我。谢谢！

（4）12月29日，小余收到了工厂传真来的电子传单（商检换单）。

报检委托书：

NBQS 务 T-R09

报 检 委 托 书

_____出入境检验检疫局：

　　本委托人郑重声明，保证遵守出入境检验检疫法律、法规的规定。如有违法行为，自愿接受检验检疫机构的处罚并负法律责任。

　　本委托人委托受委托人向检验检疫机构提交"报检申请单"和各种随附单据。具体委托情况如下：

本单位将于_____年____月间进口/出口如下货物：

品　　名		HS 编码	
数（重）量		合 同 号	
信用证号		审批文号	
其他特殊要求			

特委托_____（单位/注册登记号），代表本公司办理下列出入境检验检疫事宜：
- □ 1.办理代理报检手续；
- □ 2.代缴检验检疫费；
- □ 3.负责与检验检疫机构联系和验货；
- □ 4.领取检验检疫证单；
- □ 5.其他与报检有关的相关事宜。

请贵局按有关法律法规予以办理。

委托人（公章）　　　　　　　　受委托人（公章）

　　年　月　日　　　　　　　　　年　月　日

本委托书有效期至____年____月____日。

报检单样本（例）：

中华人民共和国出入境检验检疫
出境货物报检单

报检单位（加盖公章）：						*编 号 _____	
报检单位登记号：		联系人：		电话：		报检日期： 年 月 日	

发货人	（中文）
	（外文）

收货人	（中文）
	（外文）

货物名称（中/外文）	H.S.编码	产地	数/重量	货物总值	包装种类及数量

运输工具名称号码		贸易方式		货物存放地点	
合同号		信用证号		用途	
发货日期		输往国家（地区）		许可证/审批号	
启运地		到达口岸		生产单位注册号	
集装箱规格、数量及号码					

合同、信用证订立的检验检疫条款或特殊要求	标记及号码	随附单据（画"√"或补填）	
		□合同	□厂检单
		□信用证	□包装性能结果单
		□发票	□许可/审批文件
		□换证凭单	□
		□装箱单	□

需要的证单名称（画"√"或补填）			*检验检疫费	
□品质证书 __正__副	□植物检疫证书 __正__副	总金额（人民币元）	
□重量证书 __正__副	□熏蒸/消毒证书 __正__副		
□数量证书 __正__副	□出境货物换证凭单	计费人	
□兽医卫生证书 __正__副	□出境货物通关单		
□健康证书 __正__副		收费人	
□卫生证书 __正__副			
□动物卫生证书 __正__副			

报检人郑重声明：	领取证单
1. 本人被授权报检。	日期
2. 上列填写内容正确属实，货物无伪造或冒用他人的厂名、标志、认证标志，并承担货物质量责任。 签名：_____	签名

注：有"*"号栏由出入境检验检疫机关填写　　◆国家出入境检验检疫局制

通关单样本（例）：

中华人民共和国出入境检验检疫
出境货物通关单

编号：3103002082871630000

1. 发货人		5. 标记及号码
2. 收货人		
3. 合同/信用证号	4. 输往国家或地区	
6. 运输工具名称及号码	7. 发货日期	8. 集装箱规格及数量
9. 货物名称及规格	10. H.S. 编码	11. 申报总值	12. 数/重量、包装数量及种类

13. 证明

上述货物业经检验检疫，请海关予以放行。
本通关单有效期至 二〇〇九 年 一 月 四 日

签字： 日期： 2008

14. 备注

I 7078669　　① 货物通关　印刷流水号：17078669　　[2-2(2000.1.1)]

电子传单样本（例）：

贵单位报检的该批货物，经我局检验检疫，已合格。请执此单到宁波局本部办理出境验证业务。本单有效期截止于 2017 年 03 月 01 日。

text
330200208087784T   6609   330200208091302

金华市佳隆日化有限公司

唇膏

081106   3304100000

36 800 个   825 纸箱   11040 美元

相关知识

一、报检单据概述

报检是指办理商品出入境检验检疫业务的行为。报检单位一般是专门的报检公司或者货运代理。

报检所需资料一般有：

（1）报检单（原件，出口企业若自己报检则盖出口企业公章；若委托代理企业报检，则盖代理报检企业章）。

（2）工厂检验报告（原件，盖工厂检验章）。

（3）该批货物外包装生产厂提供的出口包装证（由商检局签发，复印件即可；若出口包装为纸箱，则还需纸箱厂向商检局申请办理《出境货物运输包装性能检验结果单》，2～3 个工作日办好，办好后需将原件交商检局，以便由其根据此批货物所用纸箱数进行相应的核销）。

（4）出口合同（复印件或传真件）。

（5）出口形式发票（复印件或传真件）。

（6）出口 Packing List 装箱单（复印件或传真件）。

将上述全套报检资料交商检局相关负责商检抽样的部门，请他们安排商检。

第一次商检，商检局一般会要求到工厂实地抽样商检（熟悉后可以有所变通，可以将货物拉到某个就近的地点进行商检），出口企业需严格遵守跟商检局抽样人士约定的时间，绝对不能晚到。如果商检局人士提出产品在某些方面不符合商检程序要求或规定，出口企业则应当积极配合，做好记录，以便整改。

检后一般两个工作日内出单，如果急于发货，应当提前 3～5 天去商检。

二、出境报检单具体填写要求

（1）发货人：填合同中的卖方。

（2）收货人：一般填合同中的买方，证书中不要求写上收货人的可留空。

（3）货物名称：按实际填写货物的中英文名称。

（4）H.S编码：根据海关公布的H.S编码填写，每份申请单一般可填5个不同的编码。

（5）产地：填报检货物生产所在地县（市）。

（6）数/重量：填货物具体数量，如衣服的件数，重量填净重，饮料填容积（如升）；有多个H.S编码的，要根据每个H.S编码对应填写数/重量。

（7）货物总值：根据合同或发票的金额填写并注明币种，有多个H.S编码的，要根据每个H.S编码对应填写金额、币种。

（8）包装种类及数量：填写货物的外包装种类（如纸箱、木箱等）及包装种类代码和具体的件数；有多个H.S编码的，要根据每个H.S编码对应填写包装种类及数量。

（9）运输工具名称号码：填写运输工具的类别（如海运、空运等）及运输工具名称（如船名等）。

（10）贸易方式：按实际的贸易方式填写（如一般贸易、进料加工等）。

（11）货物存放地点：填写货物存放具体地点。

（12）合同号：填外贸合同号（或内贸合同号）。

（13）信用证号：用信用证结汇的要填写信用证号码，没有的可留空。

（14）用途：填写入境货物用途。

（15）发货日期：按货物实际发货日期填写。

（16）输往国家（地区）：填货物到达国家或地区的相应代码。

（17）许可证/审批号：对需质量许可证或卫生注册证或出口审批的货物填写许可证号或卫生许可证号或审批单号，不需质量许可证或卫生注册证或出口审批的货物可留空。

（18）启运地：填货物出运的港口。

（19）到达口岸：填货物到达的港口。

（20）生产单位注册号：填报检单位注册登记编号。

（21）集装箱规格、数量及号码：按实际填写，不用集装箱运输的可留空。

（22）合同、信用证订立的检验检疫条款或特殊要求：合同、信用证上有条款或有其他要求（如在检验检疫证书上要注明信用证号码等）的应写明，没有要求的可留空。

（23）标记及号码：根据所附单据上的唛头填写。

（24）随附单据：根据所附单据在相应的"□"内打勾，申请单上未列明的，可自己添加。

（25）需要证单名称：根据所列证书名称在相应的"□"内打勾，申请单上未列明的，可自己添加；如需电子转单的，也需注明。

三、入境报检单具体填写要求

（1）收货人：填外贸合同中的买方。

（2）企业性质：如果收货人是"三资企业"，就在对应的"□"内打勾，其他企业可留空。

（3）发货人：填外贸合同中的卖方。
（4）货物名称：按实际填写货物的中英文名称。
（5）H.S编码：根据海关公布的H.S编码填写，每份申请单一般可填5个不同的编码。
（6）原产国（地区）：填入境货物的原生产国或地区。
（7）数/重量：填货物具体数量，如衣服的件数，重量填净重；有多个H.S编码的，要根据每个H.S编码对应填写数/重量。
（8）货物总值：根据合同或发票的金额填写并注明币种，有多个H.S编码的，要根据每个H.S编码对应填写金额、币种。
（9）包装种类及数量：填写货物的外包装种类（如纸箱、木箱等）及包装种类代码和具体的件数；有多个H.S编码的，要根据每个H.S编码对应填写包装种类及数量。
（10）运输工具名称号码：填写运输工具的类别（如海运、空运等）及运输工具名称（如船名等）。
（11）合同号：填外贸合同号。
（12）贸易方式：按实际的贸易方式填写（如一般贸易、进料加工等）。
（13）贸易国别（地区）：按买卖合同中卖方所在的国家或地区填写。
（14）提单/运单号：填提单或运单的编号。
（15）到货日期：按货物实际到达港口的日期填写。
（16）启运国家（地区）：填写货物启运国家或地区。
（17）许可证/审批号：对需入境安全质量许可证或进口审批的货物填写许可证号或审批单号，不需入境安全质量许可证或进口审批的货物可留空。
（18）卸毕日期：填货物在港口的卸毕日期。
（19）启运口岸：填货物出运的港口。
（20）入境口岸：填货物到达我国的港口。
（21）索赔有效期：根据合同约定的索赔有效期填写。
（22）经停口岸：填货物运输过程中停靠过的口岸，未停靠过任何口岸的可留空。
（23）目的地：填货物最终到达地。
（24）集装箱规格、数量及号码：按实际填写，不用集装箱运输的可留空。
（25）合同订立的特殊条款以及其他要求：合同上有条款或有其他要求（如在检验检疫证书上要注明信用证号码等）的应写明，没有要求的可留空。
（26）货物存放地点：填写入境货物存放的具体地点。
（27）用途：填写入境货物用途。
（28）随附单据：根据所附单据在相应的"□"内打勾，申请单上未列明的，可自己添加。
（29）标记及号码：根据所附单据上的唛头填写。

四、商检证书的种类

商检证书，是各种进出口商品检验证书、鉴定证书和其他证明书的统称。其是对外贸易有关各方履行契约义务、处理索赔争议、仲裁或诉讼举证的具有法律依据的有效证件，也是海关验放、征收关税、优惠减免关税的必要证明。商检证书的种类及用途主要有：

（1）品质检验证书，是出口商品交货结汇和进口商品结算索赔的有效凭证，法定检验商品的证书是进出口商品报关、输出输入的合法凭证。商检机构签发的放行单和在报关单上加盖的放行章具有与商检证书同等通关效力。签发的检验情况通知单也具有商检证书性质。

（2）重量或数量检验证书，是出口商品交货结汇、签发提单和进口商品结算索赔的有效凭证；出口商品的重量证书，也是国外报关征税和计算运费、装卸费用的证件。

（3）兽医检验证书，是证明出口动物产品或食品经过检疫合格的证件；适用于冻畜肉、冻禽、禽畜罐头、冻兔、皮张、毛类、绒类、猪鬃、肠衣等出口商品；是对外交货、银行结汇和进口国通关输入的重要证件。

（4）卫生/健康证书，是证明可供人类食用的出口动物产品、食品等经过卫生检验或检疫合格的证件；适用于肠衣、罐头、冻鱼、冻虾、食品、蛋品、乳制品、蜂蜜等；是对外交货、银行结汇和通关验放的有效证件。

（5）消毒检验证书，是证明出口动物产品经过消毒处理，保证安全卫生的证件；适用于猪鬃、马尾、皮张、山羊毛、羽毛、人发等商品；是对外交货、银行结汇和国外通关验放的有效凭证。

（6）熏蒸证书，是用于证明出口粮谷、油籽、豆类、皮张等商品，以及包装用木材与植物性填充物等已经过熏蒸灭虫的证书。

（7）残损检验证书，是证明进口商品残损情况的证件；适用于进口商品发生残、短、渍、毁等情况；可作为受货人向发货人或承运人或保险人等有关责任方索赔的有效证件。

（8）积载鉴定证书，是证明船方和集装箱装货部门正确配载积载货物，作为证明履行运输契约义务的证件；可供货物交接或发生货损时处理争议之用。

（9）财产价值鉴定证书，是作为对外贸易关系人和司法、仲裁、验资等有关部门索赔、理赔、评估或裁判的重要依据。

（10）船舱检验证书，证明承运出口商品的船舱清洁、密固、冷藏效能及其他技术条件是否符合保护承载商品的质量和数量完整与安全的要求；可作为承运人履行租船契约适载义务，对外贸易关系方进行货物交接和处理货损事故的依据。

（11）生丝品级及公量检验证书，是出口生丝的专用证书；其作用相当于品质检验证书和重量/数量检验证书。

（12）产地证明书，是出口商品在进口国通关输入和享受减免关税优惠待遇和证明商品产地的凭证。

（13）舱口检视证书、监视装/卸载证书、舱口封识证书、油温空距证书、集装箱监装/拆证书，作为证明承运人履行契约义务，明确责任界限，便于处理货损货差责任事故的证明。

（14）价值证明书，作为进口国管理外汇和征收关税的凭证。在发票上签盖商检机构的价值证明章与价值证明书具有同等效力。

（15）货载衡量检验证书，是证明进出口商品的重量、体积吨位的证件；可作为计算运费和制订配载计划的依据。

（16）集装箱租箱交货检验证书、租船交船剩水/油重量鉴定证书，可作为契约双方明确履约责任和处理费用清算的凭证。

五、检验机构

国际上的检验机构，有官方的，也有民间私人或社团经营的。

官方的检验机构只对特定商品（粮食、药物等）进行检验，如美国食品药物管理局（FDA）。

国际贸易中的商品检验主要由民间机构承担，民间商检机构具有公证机构的法律地位。比较著名的有：瑞士日内瓦通用鉴定公司（SGS）、日本海外货物检验株式会社（OMIC）、美国保险人实验室（UL）、英国劳合氏公证行（Lloyd's Surveyor）、法国船级社（B.V）等。

我国进出口商品检验主要由官方的"中华人民共和国国家出入境检验检疫局"及其分支机构承担。此外还有各种专门从事动植物、食品、药品、船舶、计量器具等检验的官方检验机构。

1980 年成立的中国进出口商品检验总公司（CCIC）及其分公司，是接受国家委托从事进出口商品检验的具有法人资格的公司。我国商检机构和一些国外检验机构建立了委托代理关系（如 SGS）或合资检验机构（如 OMIC）。外国检验机构经批准也可在我国设立分支机构，在指定范围内接受进出口商品检验和鉴定业务。

实训练习题

根据交易信息填制报检单

```
------------------------------- Message Header -------------------------------
              Swift Output：FIN 700 Issue of a Documentary Credit
                        Sender：BNPAFRPPAGS
                       Receiver：ICBCCNSHXXX

-------------------------------- Message Text --------------------------------
    27      Sequence of Total
                Number              1
                Total               1
    40A     Form of Documentary Credit
            IRREVOCABLE
    20      Documentary Credit Number
            30004LCC09XXXXXX
    31C     Date of Issue
            091009
    40E     Applicable Rules
            Applicable Rules UCP LATEST VERSION
    31D     Date and Place of Expiry
                Date                091224
                Place               IN CHINA
    50      Applicant
                        AA ECLAIRAGE SA
                        PARIS, FRANCE
    59      Beneficiary-Name & Address
                Name and Address    ZHEJIANG LIGHT INDUSTRY CO LTD
                                    ZHEJIANG, CHINA
```

32B   Currency Code, Amount
      Currency   USD
      Amount   45,791.60
39A   Percentage Credit Amt Tolerance
      Tolerance 1   10
      Tolerance 2   10
41D   Available with…by…   Name & Addr.
      Name and Address ANY BANK IN CHINA
      Code   BY NEGOTIATION
42C   Drafts at…
      60 DAYS AFTER SHIPMENT DATE
42A   Drawee   BIC
      BIC   BNPAFRPP×××
43P   Partial Shipments
      NOT ALLOWED
43T   Transhipment
      ALLOWED
44E   Port of Loading/Airport of Dep.
      SHANGHAI PORT IN CHINA
44F   Port of Discharge/Airport of Dest.
      LE HAVRE PORT IN FRANCE
44C   Latest Date of Shipment
      091209
45A   Description of Goods &/or Services
      + INCO TERM：
      FOB SHANGHAI PORT IN CHINA
      + GOODS：
      73620 PIECES OF HALOGEN LAMPS AS PER PROFORMA INVOICES
      ×××××× DATED 07/10/2009
46A   Documents Required
      1/COMMERCIAL INVOICE IN QUINTUPLICATE.
      2/FULL SET ORIGINAL OF CLEAN ON BOARD FIATA BILLS OF LADING
      ISSUED BY BLD INTERNATIONAL LOGISTICS CO LTD 6 MINOR FLOOR
      SHANGHAI HONGKOU DISTRICT NO 358 HAINING ROAD SHANGHAI
      200080 PHONE：86 21 630 399 33 FAX：86 21 635 709 00 MADE
      OUT TO THE ORDER OF AA ECLAIRAGE SA WITH FULL ADDRESS, NOTIFY
           AA ECLAIRAGE SA WITH FULL ADDRESS AND MARKED FREIGHT COLLECT.
      3/CERTIFICATE OF ORIGIN GSP FORM A ISSUED BY CHINESE AUTHORITIES
      MENTIONING THE MANUFACTURER ZHEJIANG LIGHT INDUSTRY CO LTD
      4/PACKING LIST IN QUINTUPLICATE.
      5/CERTIFICATE CERTIFYING GOODS IN CONFORMITY WITH EEC STANDARDS
      ESPECIALLY EN60432 AND EN60357.

	6/CERTIFICATE CERTIFYING GOODS IN CONFORMITY WITH ROHS STANDARDS
	7/ASIA OR SGS INSPECTION REPORT CERTIFYING GOODS ARE IN CONFORMITY WITH APPLICANT'S ORDER AND ECC AND ROHS STANDARDS
	8/PRODUCT QUALITY COMMITMENT SIGNED AND STAMPED BY ZHEJIANG LIGHT INDUSTRY CO LTD
47A	Additional Conditions
	+ ALL THE DOCUMENTS MUST BE ISSUED IN ENGLISH LANGUAGE
	+ THE AMOUNT OF THE DRAWING MUST BE ENDORSED ON THE REVERSE OF ORIGINAL CREDIT INSTRUMENT BY NEGOTIATING BANK.
	+ MORE OR LESS 10 PER CENT FOR QUANTITY AND AMOUNT ACCEPTABLE
	+ A COPY OF SHIPPING DOCUMENTS IS REQUIRED FOR ISSUING BANK FILES AN EUR 10.00 WILL BE DEDUCTED FROM REMITT PROCEEDS.
	+ ANY CLAUSE ON BILLS OF LADING AUTHORIZING A CARRIER OR SHIPPING CPY TO DELIVER GOODS WITHOUT PRESENTATION OF AN ORIGINAL BILL OF LADING IS PROHIBITED.
71B	Charges
	+ BANK CHARGES OUTSIDE OF FRANCE ARE FOR BENEFICIARIES ACCOUNT
	+ IF DISCREPANT DOCUMENTS ARE PRESENTED TO US, WE SHALL DEDUCT EUR 95.00 PLUS SWIFT CHARGES FROM PROCEEDS REMITTED.
48	Period for Presentation
	15 DAYS AFTER SHIPMENT DATE BUT WITHIN THE VALIDITY OF THE CREDIT.
49	Confirmation Instructions
	WITHOUT
78	Instr to Payg/Accptg/Negotg Bank
	+ DOCUMENTS TO BE COURIERED TO BNP PARIBAS – APAC COMMERCE INTERNATIONAL, IMMEUBLE AXA, 35 RUE DU CHATEAU D'ORGEMONT 49003 ANGERS FRANCE IN TWO SEPARATE EXPRESS COURIER.
	+ UPON RECEIPT OF DOCUMENTS IN STRICT COMPLIANCE WITH L/C TERMS WE SHALL CABLE COVER THE NEGOTIATING BANK AS PER ITS INSTRUCTIONS AT MATURITY DATE
72	Sender to Receiver Information
	/TELEBEN/

有关资料：

发票号码：ZJGIE201076587　　　提单号码：PWT668798
发票日期：2009 年 11 月 21 日　　提单日期：2009 年 12 月 4 日
船名：MOONLIGHT V. 877658　　商品编码：5476.4396
包装：180PCS/CTN　　　　　　　出口口岸：宁波海关
集装箱：1×40′CY/CY　　　　　　运费：USD1 600/CONTAINER（40′）
　　　　HJGJ76576 SEAL675876　保费：USD320
净重：15.00KG/CTN　　　　　　 外汇核销单号：545767968
毛重：18.00KG/CTN　　　　　　 原材料情况：完全中国产
尺码：（50×40×30）CM/CTN　　唛头：（请根据交易信息自行设计）

原产地证号：89768765　　　　　　FORM A 号：GZ9/76578/876

中华人民共和国出入境检验检疫
出境货物报检单

报检单位（加盖公章）：　　　　　　　　　　　　　　*编　号 _____

报检单位登记号：　　　联系人：　　　电话：　　　报检日期：　年　月　日

发货人	（中文）
	（外文）

收货人	（中文）
	（外文）

货物名称（中/外文）	H.S. 编码	产地	数/重量	货物总值	包装种类及数量

运输工具名称号码		贸易方式		货物存放地点	
合同号		信用证号		用途	
发货日期		输往国家（地区）		许可证/审批号	
启运地		到达口岸		生产单位注册号	

集装箱规格、数量及号码	

合同、信用证订立的检验检疫条款或特殊要求	标记及号码	随附单据（画"√"或补填）	
		□合同	□厂检单
		□信用证	□包装性能结果单
		□发票	□许可/审批文件
		□换证凭单	□
		□装箱单	□

需要的证单名称（画"√"或补填）		*检验检疫费
□品质证书　　__正__副	□植物检疫证书　　__正__副	总金额
□重量证书　　__正__副	□熏蒸/消毒证书　　__正__副	（人民币元）
□数量证书　　__正__副	□出境货物换证凭单	
□兽医卫生证书　　__正__副	□出境货物通关单	计费人
□健康证书　　__正__副		
□卫生证书　　__正__副		收费人
□动物卫生证书　　__正__副		

报检人郑重声明： 1. 本人被授权报检。 2. 上列填写内容正确属实，货物无伪造或冒用他人的厂名、标志、认证标志，并承担货物质量责任。 　　　　　　　　　　　签名：_____	领取证单
	日期
	签名

注：有"*"号栏由出入境检验检疫机关填写　　◆国家出入境检验检疫局制

第五章

报关

第一节 出口报关操作

教学目标

最终目标：能进行出口报关操作。

促成目标：

1. 能填写出口报关单。
2. 熟悉报关程序。
3. 能跟踪出口报关过程。

情景案例

机构：
外贸企业：宁波欧胜塑化有限公司（OCEAN PLASTIC & CHEMICAL PRODUCTS CO.，LTD）。
货运代理：AFS – VISA INTERNATIONAL（HK）LTD。
人物：
小余：宁波欧胜塑化有限公司单证员。
张经理：宁波欧胜塑化有限公司业务经理。
货代员陈小姐：AFS – VISA INTERNATIONAL（HK）LTD。
背景资料：
(1) 2016年11月6日，宁波欧胜塑化有限公司外贸业务部张经理与阿拉伯联合酋长国的公司 ABC TRADING CO.，LLC 签订一份36 800支唇膏（LIP BALM）的出口合同，合同号为081106。
(2) 12月4日，小余准备和制作报关单据寄给货代员陈小姐。单据有：发票、装箱单、合同、报关单、核销单、报关委托书、商检换单。下班前申通公司投递员来到小余办公室，小余填写面函，快递公司取走全套的报关单据。
(3) 12月5日小余与货代员陈小姐电话确认报关单据收到事宜："陈小姐，您好！我昨天有寄一票报关资料过来，抬头是×××公司，825箱，是否有收到？"陈小姐："收到了。"

报关委托书（例）：

代理报关委托书

编号：00108813813

我单位现　　（A 逐票、B 长期）委托贵公司代理　　等通关事宜。（A、填单申报 B、辅助查验 C、垫缴税款 D、办理海关证明联 E、审批手册 F、核销手册 G、申办减免税手续 H、其他）详见《委托报关协议》。

我单位保证遵守《海关法》和国家有关法规，保证所提供的情况真实、完整、单货相符。否则，愿承担相关法律责任。

本委托书有效期自签字之日起至　　年　月　日止。

委托方（盖章）：

法定代表人或其授权签署《代理报关委托书》的人（签字）：　　年　月　日

委托报关协议

为明确委托报关具体事项和各自责任，双方经平等协商签定协议如下：

委托方		被委托方	
主要货物名称		*报关单编码	No.
HS 编码	□□□□□□□□	收到单证日期	年 月 日
货物总价		收到单证情况	合同 □　发票 □ 装箱清单 □　提(运)单 □ 加工贸易手册 □　许可证件 □ 其他
进出口日期	年 月 日		
提单号			
贸易方式		报关收费	人民币　　元
原产地/货源地			
其他要求：		承诺说明：	

背面所列通用条款是本协议不可分割的一部分，对本协议的签署构成了对背面通用条款的同意。

委托方业务签章：

被委托方业务签章：

经办人签章：

经办报关员签章：

联系电话：　　年 月 日

联系电话：　　年 月 日

CCBA

（白联：海关留存、黄联：被委托方留存、红联：委托方留存）　　中国报关协会监制出口报关单（例）：

JG02	**中华人民共和国海关出口货物报关单**

预录入编号：		海关编号：		
出口口岸 NINGBO	备案号		出口日期	申报日期
经营单位 NINGBO HAIWEN IMP&EXP.CORP.,LTD. 3302967493	运输方式 BY BOAT	运输工具名称	提运单号	
发货单位 NINGBO HAIWEN IMP&EXP.CORP.,LTD. 3302967493	贸易方式 G.T.	征免性质		结汇方式 T/T
许可证号	运抵国（地区）	指运港 FOB NINGBO		境内货源地
批准文号	成交方式 825	运费 CTNS	保费 3300.00	杂费 2475.00
合同协议号	件数	包装种类	毛重(公斤)	净重(公斤)
集装箱号	随附单据		生产厂家	
标记唛码及备注 AS PER INV 0905002				

项号	商品编号	商品名称、规格型号	数量及单位	最终目的国(地区)	单价	总价 FOB NINGBO	币制	征免
1	3304100000	LIP BALM 唇膏	2475.00KGS			USD11040.00		

税费征收情况

录入员	录入单位	兹声明以上申报无讹并承担法律责任	海关审单批注及放行日期(签章)	
报关员			审单	审价
单位地址		申报单位(签章) 报关专用章 宁波	征税	统计
邮编	电话	填制日期	查验	放行

相关知识

一、报关货物和报关流程

（一）报关货物分类

（1）一般进出口货物是指在进出境环节缴纳了应征的进出口税费并办结了所有必要的

海关手续，海关放行后不再进行监管的进出口货物。

（2）保税货物是指经海关批准未办理纳税手续进境，在境内储存加工装配后复运出境的货物。

（3）特定减免税货物是指海关根据国家的政策规定准予减免税进境使用于特定地区特定企业特定用途的货物。

（4）暂准进出口货物是指为了特定的目的经海关批准暂时进境并在规定的期限内复运进境或复运出境的货物。

（二）出口报关过程中的单据流程

报关流程是：接受申报→审核单证→查验货物→办理征税→结关放行。

第一步，要做的就是订舱，首先得到货物的相关信息，包括品名、数量、毛重、立方、要求出运时间。

这个时候做的是准备工作，品名是为了找到相对应的 HS 编码、确定退税和海关监管条件，毛重、立方和出运时间是为了去货代员那里订舱，做一份定舱单给货代员，货代员会给你订舱编号和进舱单（把这个交给工厂让他们按时送货即可）。

第二步，根据品名找到 HS 编码的海关监管条件，准备相应的报检文件（有监管条件的话），以做商检为例，需要准备报关单、发票、装箱单、合同、厂检单、报检单。这些单证都是由报检员送进海关审批的。

第三步，等到商检证拿到后，再做一份报关文件给货代报关（一般会委托货代报关，这样比较方便）。报关文件应该包括报关单、发票、装箱单、合同、商检单（或者其他能够证明报检通过的文件）、核销单。如出口需缴纳税费的，应及时缴纳税费。

第四步，海关现场审单结束、货物单证放行后，货主应在海关规定的时间内将货物运至海关监管区内进行验放。如需查验，报关行应及时与海关联系，进行货物查验，验完后需封指定铅封。不需查验的应及时进行实货放行，将装货单按截关时间送到港区装船。

接着待货物出口，船公司就将出口舱单数据传送海关，海关接收到数据后报关行待海关数据结关后，及时到海关打印退税核销联。接下来需要做的工作就是跟货代员联系，在开船后尽快拿到提单。再之后要做的就是收汇动作了。

（三）出口报关所需单据

装箱单、发票、报关委托、报检委托（需商检货）、非木质包装证明（非木质包装货）、核销单、药品证明（出口货为药品）、场站收据。

出口货物报关一定遵循货到后方可报关的原则，其中需要注意的地方有：

（1）报关单据准备齐全并都需要正本，HS 编码一定要确认准确，以便判断有没有特殊的监管条件（如电子产品更新换代比较快，没有注册商品编码，可在出口时向海关询问，找一个相似货物的商品编码）。

（2）报关之前确认船公司是否已输入 EDI，否则会影响报关速度。

（3）报关的数据要和装箱单、发票相符，否则会影响输入目的港舱单、影响提货。

填制报关单：出口报关单一般为六联，即海关留存联、海关作业联、报关企业留存联（海关三天之内有审核权，所以报关企业要留存）、海关核销联、出口收汇证明联、出口退税证明联。

二、进出口报关单概述

进出口货物报关单是指进出口货物收发货人或其代理人,按照海关规定的格式对进出口货物的实际情况做出书面申明,以此要求海关对其货物按适用的海关制度办理通关手续的法律文书。它在对外经济贸易活动中具有十分重要的法律地位。它既是海关监管、征税、统计以及开展稽查和调查的重要依据,又是加工贸易进出口货物核销,以及出口退税和外汇管理的重要凭证,也是海关处理走私、违规案件,及税务、外汇管理部门查处骗税和套汇犯罪活动的重要证书。

按货物的流转状态、贸易性质和海关监管方式的不同,进出口货物报关单可以分为以下几种类型:

1. 按进出口状态分
(1)进口货物报关单。
(2)出口货物报关单。

2. 按表现形式分
(1)纸质报关单。
(2)电子数据报关单。

3. 按使用性质分
(1)进料加工进出口货物报关单(粉红色)。
(2)来料加工及补偿贸易进出口货物报关单(浅绿色)。
(3)外商投资企业进出口货物报关单(浅蓝色)。
(4)一般贸易及其他贸易进出口货物报关单(白色)。
(5)需国内退税的出口贸易报关单(浅黄色)。

4. 按用途分
(1)报关单录入凭单。
(2)预录入报关单。
(3)电子数据报关单。
(4)报关单证明联。

三、中华人民共和国海关进出口货物报关单填制规范(节选)

1. 预录入编号
本栏目填报预录入报关单的编号,预录入编号规则由接受申报的海关决定。

2. 海关编号
本栏目填报海关接受申报时给予报关单的编号,一份报关单对应一个海关编号。

3. 进口口岸/出口口岸
本栏目应根据货物实际进出境的口岸海关填报海关规定的《关区代码表》中相应口岸海关的名称及代码。

4. 备案号
本栏目填报进出口货物收发货人在海关办理加工贸易合同备案或征、减、免税备案审批等手续时,海关核发的《中华人民共和国海关加工贸易手册》、电子账册及其分册(以下统称《加工贸易手册》)、《进出口货物征免税证明》(以下简称《征免税证明》)或其他备案审批文件的编号。

5. 合同协议号

本栏目填报进出口货物合同（包括协议或订单）编号。

6. 进口日期/出口日期

进口日期填报运载进口货物的运输工具申报进境的日期。

出口日期指运载出口货物的运输工具办结出境手续的日期，本栏目供海关签发打印报关单证明联用，在申报时免予填报。

本栏目为8位数字，顺序为年（4位）、月（2位）、日（2位）。

7. 申报日期

申报日期指海关接受进出口货物收发货人、受委托的报关企业申报数据的日期。以电子数据报关单方式申报的，申报日期为海关计算机系统接受申报数据时记录的日期。以纸质报关单方式申报的，申报日期为海关接受纸质报关单并对报关单进行登记处理的日期。

8. 经营单位

本栏目填报在海关注册登记的对外签订并执行进出口贸易合同的中国境内法人、其他组织或个人的名称及海关注册编码。

9. 收货单位/发货单位

收货单位填报已知的进口货物在境内的最终消费、使用单位的名称。发货单位填报出口货物在境内的生产或销售单位的名称。

10. 申报单位

自理报关的，本栏目填报进出口企业的名称及海关注册编码；委托代理报关的，本栏目填报经海关批准的报关企业名称及海关注册编码。

本栏目还包括报关单左下方用于填报申报单位有关情况的相关栏目，包括报关员、报关单位地址、邮政编码和电话号码等栏目。

11. 运输方式

运输方式包括实际运输方式和海关规定的特殊运输方式，前者指货物实际进出境的运输方式，按进出境所使用的运输工具分类；后者指货物无实际进出境的运输方式，按货物在境内的流向分类。

12. 运输工具名称

本栏目填报载运货物进出境的运输工具名称或编号。填报内容应与运输部门向海关申报的舱单（载货清单）所列相应内容一致。

13. 航次号

本栏目填报载运货物进出境的运输工具的航次编号。

14. 提运单号

本栏目填报进出口货物提单或运单的编号。一份报关单只允许填报一个提单或运单号，一票货物对应多个提单或运单时，应分单填报。

15. 贸易方式（监管方式）

本栏目应根据实际对外贸易情况按海关规定的《监管方式代码表》选择填报相应的监管方式简称及代码。一份报关单只允许填报一种监管方式。

16. 征免性质

本栏目应根据实际情况按海关规定的《征免性质代码表》选择填报相应的征免性质简称及代码，持有海关核发的《征免税证明》的，应按照《征免税证明》中批注的征免性质填报。一份报关单只允许填报一种征免性质。

17. 征税比例/结汇方式

进口报关单本栏目免予填报。

出口报关单填报结汇方式，按海关规定的《结汇方式代码表》选择填报相应的结汇方式名称或代码。

18. 许可证号

本栏目填报以下许可证的编号：进（出）口许可证、两用物项和技术进（出）口许可证、两用物项和技术出口许可证（定向）、纺织品临时出口许可证、出口许可证（加工贸易）、出口许可证（边境小额贸易）。

19. 启运国（地区）/运抵国（地区）

启运国（地区）填报进口货物启始发出直接运抵我国或者在运输中转国（地）未发生任何商业性交易的情况下运抵我国的国家（地区）。

运抵国（地区）填报出口货物离开我国关境直接运抵或者在运输中转国（地区）未发生任何商业性交易的情况下最后运抵的国家（地区）。

不经过第三国（地区）转运的直接运输进出口货物，以进口货物的装货港所在国（地区）为启运国（地区），以出口货物的指运港所在国（地区）为运抵国（地区）。

经过第三国（地区）转运的进出口货物，如在中转国（地区）发生商业性交易，则以中转国（地区）作为启运/运抵国（地区）。

20. 装货港/指运港

装货港填报进口货物在运抵我国关境前的最后一个境外装运港。

指运港填报出口货物运往境外的最终目的港；最终目的港不可预知的，按尽可能预知的目的港填报。

21. 境内目的地/境内货源地

境内目的地填报已知的进口货物在国内的消费、使用地或最终运抵地，其中最终运抵地为最终使用单位所在的地区。最终使用单位难以确定的，填报货物进口时预知的最终收货单位所在地。

境内货源地填报出口货物在国内的产地或原始发货地。出口货物产地难以确定的，填报最早发运该出口货物的单位所在地。

22. 批准文号

进口报关单中本栏目免予填报。

出口报关单中本栏目填报出口收汇核销单编号。

23. 成交方式

本栏目应根据进出口货物实际成交价格条款，按海关规定的《成交方式代码表》选择填报相应的成交方式代码。

24. 运费

本栏目填报进口货物运抵我国境内输入地点起卸前的运输费用，出口货物运至我国境内输出地点装载后的运输费用。进口货物成交价格包含前述运输费用或者出口货物成交价格不包含前述运输费用的，本栏目免于填报。

运费可按运费单价、总价或运费率三种方式之一填报，注明运费标记（运费标记"1"表示运费率，"2"表示每吨货物的运费单价，"3"表示运费总价），并按海关规定的《货币代码表》选择填报相应的币种代码。

25. 保费

本栏目填报进口货物运抵我国境内输入地点起卸前的保险费用，出口货物运至我国境内输出地点装载后的保险费用。进口货物成交价格包含前述保险费用或者出口货物成交价格不包含前述保险费用的，本栏目免于填报。

保费可按保险费总价或保险费率两种方式之一填报，注明保险费标记（保险费标记"1"表示保险费率，"3"表示保险费总价），并按海关规定的《货币代码表》选择填报相应的币种代码。

26. 杂费

本栏目填报成交价格以外的、按照《中华人民共和国进出口关税条例》相关规定应计入完税价格或应从完税价格中扣除的费用。可按杂费总价或杂费率两种方式之一填报，注明杂费标记（杂费标记"1"表示杂费率，"3"表示杂费总价），并按海关规定的《货币代码表》选择填报相应的币种代码。

27. 件数

本栏目填报有外包装的进出口货物的实际件数。

本栏目不得填报为"0"，裸装货物填报为"1"。

28. 包装种类

本栏目应根据进出口货物的实际外包装种类，按海关规定的《包装种类代码表》选择填报相应的包装种类代码。

29. 毛重（千克）

本栏目填报进出口货物及其包装材料的重量之和，计量单位为千克，不足一千克的填报为"1"。

30. 净重（千克）

本栏目填报进出口货物的毛重减去外包装材料后的重量，即货物本身的实际重量，计量单位为千克，不足一千克的填报为"1"。

31. 集装箱号

本栏目填报装载进出口货物（包括拼箱货物）集装箱的箱体信息。一个集装箱填一条记录，分别填报集装箱号（在集装箱箱体上标示的全球唯一编号）、集装箱的规格和集装箱的自重。非集装箱货物填报为"0"。

32. 随附单证

本栏目根据海关规定的《监管证件代码表》选择填报除本规范第十八条规定的许可证件以外的其他进出口许可证件或监管证件代码及编号。

优惠贸易协定项下出口货物，本栏目填报原产地证书代码和编号。

33. 用途/生产厂家

进口货物本栏目填报用途，应根据进口货物的实际用途按海关规定的《用途代码表》

选择填报相应的用途代码。

出口货物本栏目填报其境内生产企业。

34. 标记唛码及备注

本栏目填报要求如下：

（1）标记唛码中除图形以外的文字、数字。

（2）受外商投资企业委托代理其进口投资设备、物品的进出口企业名称。

35. 项号

本栏目分两行填报及打印。第一行填报报关单中的商品顺序编号；第二行专用于加工贸易、减免税等已备案、审批的货物，填报和打印该项货物在《加工贸易手册》或《征免税证明》等备案、审批单证中的顺序编号。

优惠贸易协定项下实行原产地证书联网管理的报关单，第一行填报报关单中的商品顺序编号，第二行填报该项商品对应的原产地证书上的商品项号。

加工贸易项下进出口货物的报关单，第一行填报报关单中的商品顺序编号，第二行填报该项商品在《加工贸易手册》中的商品项号，用于核销对应项号下的料件或成品数量。

36. 商品编号

本栏目应填报由《中华人民共和国进出口税则》确定的进出口货物的税则号列和《中华人民共和国海关统计商品目录》确定的商品编码，以及符合海关监管要求的附加编号组成的10位商品编号。

37. 商品名称、规格型号

本栏目分两行填报及打印。第一行填报进出口货物规范的中文商品名称，第二行填报规格型号。

38. 数量及单位

本栏目分三行填报及打印。

（1）第一行应按进出口货物的法定第一计量单位填报数量及单位，法定计量单位以《中华人民共和国海关统计商品目录》中的计量单位为准。

（2）凡列明有法定第二计量单位的，应在第二行按照法定第二计量单位填报数量及单位。无法定第二计量单位的，本栏目第二行为空。

（3）成交计量单位及数量应填报并打印在第三行。

39. 原产国（地区）/最终目的国（地区）

原产国（地区）应依据《中华人民共和国进出口货物原产地条例》、《中华人民共和国海关关于执行〈非优惠原产地规则中实质性改变标准〉的规定》以及海关总署关于各项优惠贸易协定原产地管理规章规定的原产地确定标准填报。同一批进口货物的原产地不同的，应分别填报原产国（地区）。进口货物原产国（地区）无法确定的，填报"国别不详"（代码701）。

最终目的国（地区）填报已知的出口货物的最终实际消费、使用或进一步加工制造国家（地区）。不经过第三国（地区）转运的直接运输货物，以运抵国（地区）为最终目的国（地区）；经过第三国（地区）转运的货物，以最后运往国（地区）为最终目的国（地区）。同一批出口货物的最终目的国（地区）不同的，应分别填报最终目的国（地区）。出口货物不能确定最终目的国（地区）时，以尽可能预知的最后运往国（地区）为最终目的国（地区）。

40. 单价

本栏目填报同一项号下进出口货物实际成交的商品单位价格。无实际成交价格的，本栏目填报单位货值。

41. 总价

本栏目填报同一项号下进出口货物实际成交的商品总价格。无实际成交价格的，本栏目填报货值。

42. 币制

本栏目应按海关规定的《货币代码表》选择相应的货币名称及代码填报，如《货币代码表》中无实际成交币种，需将实际成交货币按申报日外汇折算率折算成《货币代码表》列明的货币填报。

43. 征免

本栏目应按照海关核发的《征免税证明》或有关政策规定，对报关单所列每项商品选择海关规定的《征减免税方式代码表》中相应的征减免税方式填报。

44. 税费征收情况

本栏目供海关批注进（出）口货物税费征收及减免情况。

45. 录入员

本栏目用于记录预录入操作人员的姓名。

46. 录入单位

本栏目用于记录预录入单位名称。

47. 填制日期

本栏目填报申报单位填制报关单的日期。本栏目为 8 位数字，顺序为年（4 位）、月（2 位）、日（2 位）。

48. 海关审单批注及放行日期（签章）

本栏目供海关作业时签注。

实训练习题

根据给定信息填制一份一般贸易出口报关单

中国江苏省张家港市对外贸易公司
ZHANGJIAGANG FOREIGN TRADE CORP. DEPT
ZHANGJIAGANG CITY, JIANGSU, CHINA
INVOICE

NO. ZY07032173
Sales Contract No. MUY5895
Date NOV. 27th, 2016

装运口岸
From SHANGHAI, CHINA

目的地
To ZURICH

信用证号数
Letter Credit No. UYT145638

开证银行
Issued by BANK OF CHINA

Marks & Nos.	Quantities and Descriptions		Amount
HAMBURG IN TRANSIT TO ZURICH SWITZERLAND NO1－1533 MADE IN CHINA 预录入编号：757171029 2003.12.4 装"VD TAURUS V. A23W"轮从上海出口 由上海××报关有限责任公司代理申报	MEN'S 100 PCT COTTON WOVEN CH UNDER PANTS 10220DOZS USD22.08／DOZ AS PER CONTRACT NO. 410／496 GROSS WT：13，797kg NET WT：10，424kg L／C NO：35487 外汇核销单号：29／1900780 全棉男式内裤 HSCODE：62071100 法定计量单位：件／kg 经营单位海关注册编号：3215910101，发货人同经营单位 由张家港服装厂生产		USD225，657.60 CIF F 5％ I 0.25％ 提单号： CMA2584HAM
SHIPPER BLUE ANCHOR LINE C/O KUEHNE & NAGEL（HONKONG）LTD. SHANGHAI REPRESENTATIVE OFFICE		BILL OF LADING SEA WAY BILL　　　VGE： 　　　　　　　　B/L NO. 　　　　　　　　CMA29584HAM FW0103700064	
CONSIGNEE BLUE ANCHOR LINE C/O KUEHNE & NAGEL（AG & CO） PINKERTWEG 20（HH－BILLBROOK）D－22113 HAMBURG （HBG ISW）		CMA COMPAGNIE MARITIME D'AFFRETEMENT Societe Anonyme au Capital de 30.000.000 de France 4 quai d'Arend. 13002 Marseille phone 91.39.30.00. telex 401667 F. telefax 91.39.30.95 r. c. marseille b 340 353 911	
NOTIFY PARTY CARRIER NOT TO BE RESPONSIBLE FOR FAILURE TO NOTIFY SAME AS COSIGNEE			
PRE CARRIAGE BY	PLACE OF RECEIPT	FREIGHT TO BE PAID AT	NUMBER OF ORIGINAL B/L
OCEAN VESSEL VE TAURUS V A23W	PORT OF LOADING SHANGHAI	PORT OF DISCHARGE HAMBURG	FINAL PLACE OF DELIVERY

MARKS AND NOS SEALS	NO ANY KIND OF PACKAGES	DESCRIPTION OF PACKAGES AND GOODS	GROSS WEIGHT	TARE	MEASUREMENT
HAMBURG IN TRANSIT TO ZURICH SWITZERL AND NO. 1－1533 MADE IN CHINA	MEN'S 100PCT COTTON WOV- EN UNDER WEAR 1533 CA RTONS CY TO CY	AS STATED BY SHIPPER SHIPPERS LOAD COUNT AND SEAL			87.920CBM

1×20′FCL + 1×40′HQ GSTU246243/ CMA1322819 DFDU7967385/1806785	SAY ONE THOUSAND FIVE HUN-DRED THIRTY THREE CARTONS ONLY ABOVE PARTICULARS DE-CLARED BY SHIPPER CARRIER NOT RE-SPONSIBLE		

中华人民共和国海关出口货物报关单

预录入编号：　　　　　　　　海关编号：

出口口岸	备案号	出口日期	申报日期
经营单位	运输方式	运输工具名称	提运单号
发货单位	贸易方式	征免性质	结汇方式
许可证号	运抵国（地区）	指运港	境内货源地
批准文号	成交方式	运费	保费	杂费
合同协议号	件数	包装种类	毛重（公斤）	净重（公斤）
集装箱号	随附单据		生产厂家
标记唛码及备注			

项号	商品编号	商品名称	规格型号	数量及单位	最终目的国（地区）	单价	总价	币制征免

税费征收情况

录入员　录入单位	兹声明以上申报无讹并承担法律责任	海关审单批注及放行日期（签章）	
报关员		审单	审价
单位地址	申报单位（签章）	证税	统计
邮编	电话	填制日期	查验	放行

第二节 进口报关操作

教学目标

最终目标：能进行进口报关操作。

促成目标：

1. 能填写进口报关单。
2. 能跟踪进口报关过程。

情景案例

机构：

外贸企业：宁波对外贸易发展有限公司（NINGBO FOREIGN TRADE DEVELOPMENT CO., LTD.）。

货运代理：AFS – VISA INTERNATIONAL（HK）LTD。

人物：

小徐：宁波对外贸易发展有限公司单证员。

蔡经理：宁波对外贸易发展有限公司业务经理。

货代员陈小姐：AFS – VISA INTERNATIONAL（HK）LTD。

背景资料：

（1）2017年3月23日，宁波对外贸易发展有限公司蔡经理与新加坡公司DU PONT SINGAPORE签订了一份外贸合同，进口10 332公斤氨纶弹力丝。

（2）2017年4月6日，货物到达宁波口岸，小徐联系AFS – VISA INTERNATIONAL（HK）LTD的陈小姐："我们公司一批进口货物到宁波港了，合同、发票、装箱单、提单现在传真给你，你赶紧帮我们报关。"

发票、装箱单、合同、提单信息：

1 MARITIME SQUARE # 07 – 01
WORLD TRADE CENTRE
SINGAPORE 09925
PHONE：2732244（12 LINES）
CABLES：FORELPONT
TELEX：DUFE RS 21963

DU PONT SINGAPORE FIBRES PTE LTD

SOLD TO

INVOICE

NINGBO FOREIGN TRADE DEVELOPMENT
CO., LTD.
RM 723 7/F NO.14 HEYI ROAD NINGBO
CHINA 315010

INVOICE NUMBER 1G20303463	PAGE1
27 MAR, 2017	
ACCOUNT NUMBER 00352125	

宁波对外贸易发展有限公司 CONTACT PERSON: MR. QIAN WEIFENG TEL 0086-574-63033442	CUSTOMER NO CUSTOMER PURCHASE ORDER NO 10152345 04L-025SH
	DU PONT ORDER NO PAYMENT TERMS XCBS07258A00 N 90
	SHIPPING TERMS CIF NINGBO VIA: OCEAN FREIGHT PREPAID SHIP FROM: SINGAPORE SG

PRODUCT AND DESCRIPTION	QUANTITY	UNIT	UNIT PRICE	AMOUNT
* * * * * * * * * * * * * * * * * * "LYCRA" ELASTANE 氨纶弹力丝 40 DENIER TYPE 149B MERGE 17 124.5 kg TUBE COUNTRY OF ORIGIN: SINGAPORE KENNETH CHOY, LYCRA 企业海关注册编号: 3122210376 预录入编号: 108007846 H.S 10152345	10,332.00 TOTAL	kg PAYABLE IN US DOLLAR	19.000,0	196,308.00 196,308.00

DU PONT SINGAPORE
PACKING LIST

27 MAR, 2017

CUSTOMER REF   : \
VESSEL/VOYAGE: HYUNDAI BARON VOY. 3068
DEPARTURE DATE ON/ABOUT   : 2703/2017
PORT OF DISCHARGE   : NINGBO

MARKING DESCRIPTION	GROSS WEIGHT (kg)	NET WEIGHT (kg)	MEASUREMENT (m^3)

NINGBO
04L-025SH   1×40'CIBTAUBER
C/NO. 1-420 420 CARTONS OF
    10,332 kg "LYCRA" ELASTANE 40.5kg TUBE
        COUNTRY OF ORIGIN: SINGAPORE
        (CONTRACT NO: 04L-025SH)
	13,285.10	10,332.00	50,400

CONTAINER NO   SEAL NO
NOSU4371790   NOLZ00349

DU PONT SINGAPORE

DATE: 23/03/2017

SALES AGREEMENT

Whereby DU PONT SINGAPORE PTE LTD. The sellers have this day sold to the buyer No. 04L025SH NINGBO FOREIGN TRADE DEVELOPMENT CO. , LTD.
RM 723 7/F NO. 14 HEYI ROAD NINGBO CHINA 315010

All the goods stated in the Schedule hereto subject to the terms and conditions below and on the reverse of this form

Place of Delivery	NINGBO
Time of Delivery	March – APRIL
Price	40 DENIER TYPE 149B 17124 – USD19/kg
Terms of Payment	CIF NINGBO – NET 90 DAYS

SCHEDULE

Item No	Quantity	Details of Goods	Amount
04L – 025SH	10,332kg	"LYCRA" ELASTANE 40 DENIER TYPE 149B MERGE 17, 124.5 kg TUBE	196,308
TOTAL AMOUNT		US $ 196,308.00	

APL   CAL #1（Q00001/）

BILL OF LADING

03/27/2017   STB

SHIPPER（Principal or seller licensee and full address） DU PONT SINGAPORE FIBRES PTE LTD 1 MARITIME SQUARE NO. 07 – 01 WORLD TRADE CENTRE SINGAPORE 099253	BOOKING NUMBER B/L NUMBER 007137686 APLU 7137686
CONSIGNEE（Name and full address） （Unless provided otherwise a consignment "To Order" means "To Order of Shipper".） NINGBO FOREIGN TRADE DEVELOPMENT CO. , LTD. RM 723 7/F NO. 14 HEYI ROAD NINGBO CHINA 315010	EXPORT REFERENCES FORWARDING AGENT
NOTIFY PARTY（Name and full address） NINGBO FOREIGN TRADE DEVELOPMENT CO. , LTD. RM 723 7/F NO. 14 HEYI ROAD NINGBO CHINA 315010	POINT AND COUNTRY OF ORIGIN OF GOODS
INITIAL CARRIAGE（MODE） PLACE OF RECEIPT SINGAPORT	

EXPORT CARRIER (Vessel, voyage, & flag) PORT OF LOADING			ALSO NOTIFY (Name and Full Address) /DOMESTIC ROUTING EXPORT INSTRUCTIONS/PIER TERMINAL/ONWARD ROUTING	
Hyundai Baron 3068 SINGAPORE				
PORT OF DISCHARGE NINGBO	PLACE OF DELIVERY NINGBO			
Excess Valuation Please refer to Clause 7 iii on Reverse Side			＊ MR. QIAN WEIFENG FAX：0086－21－62033441 ＊＊ MR QIAN WEIFENG FAX：0086－21－62033442	
MKS A NOS/COS/ CONTAINER NOS	NO OF	PKGS DESCRIPTION OF PACKAGES AND GOODS	GROSS WEIGHT	MEASUREMENT
NINGBO 04L－025SH C/NO. 1－420	420	CTNS AA FA07－0550 SLAC CY/CY 1×40′CIBTAUBER 420 CARTONS OF 10,332KG "LYCRA" ELAS-TANE 40 DENIER TYPE 149B MERGE 17 124.5 kg TUBE COUNTRY OF ORIGIN： ORDER NO：04L－025SH	13,285kg	50,400
＊＊＊CTR NRB＊ ＊＊＊SEAL NOSU437179－0 NOL Z00349 ON BOARD HYU NDA 1 BARON	CIF 306B	NBR＊＊＊ T/X MODE 4.06 QUANT/TYPE D40 CY/CY 420 CTBS 新加坡 HYUNDAI BARON 420 ON MAR 27, 2008 AT SINGA-PORE	APLU007137686 FREIGHT	PREPAID
/E TO BE RELEASED AT SINGAPORE OCEAN FREIGHT PAYABLE AT SINGAPORE				

中华人民共和国海关出口货物报关单

预录入编号：　　　　　　　　　海关编号：

出口口岸	备案号	出口日期	申报日期
经营单位	运输方式	运输工具名称	提运单号
发货单位	贸易方式	征免性质	征税比例
许可证号	起运国（地区）	装运港	境内目的地

批准文号		成交方式		运费		保费		杂费	
合同协议号		件数		包装种类		毛重（公斤）		净重（公斤）	
集装箱号		随附单据						用途	
标记唛码及备注									
项号	商品编号	商品名称	规格型号	数量及单位		原产国（地区）	单价	总价	币制征免
税费征收情况									
录入员　　录入单位　　兹声明以上申报无讹并承担法律责任 报关员						海关审单批注及放行日期（签章） 审单　　　　　　审价			
单位地址　　　　　　　申报单位（签章）						证税　　　　　　统计			
邮编　　　　　电话　　　　填制日期						查验　　　　　　放行			

相关知识

一、进口报关流程

报关流程是：接受申报→审核单证→查验货物→办理征税→结关放行。

1. 用换来的提货单（1、3）联并附上报关单据前去报关

报关单据：提货单（1、3）联海关放行后，在白联上加盖放行章，发还给进口方作为提货的凭证。正本装箱单、正本发票、合同、进口报关单一式两份、正本报关委托协议书、海关监管条件所涉及的各类证件。

注意事项：

（1）接到客户全套单据后，应确认货物的商品编码，然后查阅海关税则。确认进口税率，确认货物需要什么监管条件，如需做各种检验，则应在报关前向有关机构报验。报验所需单据：报验申请单、正本装箱单发票，合同、进口报关单两份。

（2）换单时应催促船舶代理部门及时给海关传舱单，如有问题应与海关舱单室取得联系，确认舱单是否转到海关。

（3）当海关要求开箱查验货物时，应提前与场站取得联系，调配机力将所查箱子调至海关指定的场站（事先应现场确认好调箱费、掏箱费）。

2. 若是法检商品应办理验货手续

如需商检，则要在报关前，拿进口商检申请单（带公章）和两份报单办理登记手续，并在报关单上盖商检登记在案章以便通关。验货手续在最终目的地办理。

如需动植检，也要在报关前拿装箱单发票合同报关单去代报验机构申请报验，在报关单上盖放行章以便通关，验货手续可在通关后堆场进行。

3. 海关通关放行后

应去三检大厅办理三检，向大厅内的代理报验机构提供装箱单、发票、合同报关单，由他们代理报验。报验后，可在大厅内统一窗口交费，并在白色提货单上盖三检放行章。

4. 三检手续办理后

去港池大厅交港杂费。

港杂费用结清后，港方将提货联退给提货人供提货用。

5. 所有提货手续办妥后

可通知事先联系好的堆场提货。

注意事项：

（1）首先应与港池调度室取得联系，安排计划。

（2）根据提箱的多少与堆场联系足够的车辆，尽可能按港方要求时间内提清，以免产生转栈堆存费用。

（3）提箱过程中应与堆场有关人员共同检查箱体是否有重大残破，如有，要求港方在设备交接单上签残。

6. 重箱由堆场提到场地后，应在免费期内及时掏箱以免产生滞箱

7. 货物提清后，从场站取回设备交接单证明箱体无残损，去船公司或船舶代理部门取回押箱费

二、进口报关所需单据

（1）Consignee 若有进出口经营权：代理进口报关委托书；进口报关单证；提货证明（D/O；少部分地方用 B/L 或 B/L Copy）；运单 Copy（空运下）；销售合同（一般贸易下）；装箱单（Packing List）；发票（Invoice）。

（2）Consignee 若无进出口经营权：除以上全部单证外还需"代理进口委托书"。

实训练习题

请根据下列单据（发票、提单），在报关单填写的选项中选出最合适的答案

<table>
<tr><td colspan="5" align="center">**INVOICE**</td></tr>
<tr><td colspan="2">CONSIGNEE：
DALIAN CHEMICALS I/E CORP
大连化工进出口公司（2102911013）
No. 61 RENMINLU ROAD DALIAN CHINA</td><td colspan="3">NO.：　　　　　　DATE：
CDFG5618　　　　NOV. 14, 2016</td></tr>
<tr><td colspan="2">NOTIFY PARTY：
BEIJING YUDU COMMERCIAL & TRADE CO., LTD
北京宇都商贸有限公司
NO. 365 DONGSIBEIDAJIE, BEIJING, CHINA</td><td colspan="3">L/C NO.：　　　　DATE：
LC810A00228　　MAY 25, 2016
BANK OF CHINA
LIAONING BRANCH
DALIAN CN</td></tr>
<tr><td>PORT OF LOADING：
ROTTERDAM</td><td>VESSEL：
EAST EXPRESS</td><td colspan="3"></td></tr>
<tr><td>VOYAGE No.
151E</td><td>PORT DISCHARGE：
DALIAN PORT, CHINA
via HONGKONG</td><td colspan="3">CONTRACT No.
OOXFFFG – 78017KR</td></tr>
<tr><td>MARKS &
NO. OF PKGS</td><td>DESCRIPTION OF
GOODS</td><td>QUANTITY/
UNIT</td><td>UNIT PRICE</td><td>AMOUNT</td></tr>
<tr><td colspan="5">　　　　　　　　　　　　　　　　　　　　　　　　　　　DM（币制代码304）DM</td></tr>
<tr><td colspan="5">OOXFFFG – 78017KR
DALIAN CHINA
DELIVERY OF CIF DALIAN CHINA OF 3 UNITS & 6 PKGS OF
B30S FORKLIFT TRUCK INCLUDING FFT4730MM S/S BATTERY & CHARGER
H. S. CODE：84271090
DETAILS AS PER THE ATTACHED SHEET

　　　　B30S – 2　　　　17951.00　　　535 853.00
　　　　FREIGHT CHARGES（F）　　　2 050.00
　　　　INSURANCE（I）　　　　　　1 346.00
　　　　TOTAL　　　　　　　　　　57 249.00

DADAI CORPORATION
P. O. BOX：7955 SEOUL, KOREA　　　**DADAI CORPORATION**
TELEPHONE：　　　　　　　　　　SIGNED BY</td></tr>
</table>

BILL OF LADING

CONSIGNOR: DADAI CORPORATION 7955 SEOUL, KOREA		OUR BOOK NO.:	B/L NO.: EEW7865435
CONSIGNEE: DALIAN CHEMICAL I/E CORP 大连化工进出口公司 2102911013 NO. 61 RENMINLU ROAD, DALIAN, CHINA		REMARKS: 注：北京宇都商贸有限公司委托大连化工进出口公司与韩国签约，为长春特钢厂进口 B30S 型电动叉车，委托大连外轮代理公司向大连海关申报。	
NOTIFY PARTY: BEIJING YUDU COMMERCIAL & TRADE CO., LTD 北京宇都商贸有限公司 1101250756 NO. 365 DONGSIBEIDAJIE, BEIJING, CHINA			
PORT OF LOADING: ROTTERDAM［鹿特丹］	VESSEL: EAST EXPRESS	VOYAGE NO.: 151E	FLAG: DENMARK
PORT OF DISCHARGE: DALIAN CHINA via HONGKONG		PLACE OF DELIVERY:	

MARK	NO. OF PKGS	DESCRIPTION OF GOODS	GROSS WEIGHT	NET WEIGHT	MEASUREMENT
	1×20" SCZU7854343 (3 PACKAGES) 1×40" SCZU7855243 (2 PACKAGES)		15,025KG		18,900CBM
OOXFFFG-78017KR DALIAN CHINA		SAID TO CONTAIN: 3 UNITS OF B30S FORKLIFT TRUCK ——————— 6 PKGS OF FFT4730MM S/S BATTERY & CHARGER PACKING: TOB BUSTABLE FOR LONG DISTANCE OCEAN TRANSPORTATION QUANTITY: 3 UNITS MANUFACTURER: GEERLOFS TRUCK B.V, GERMANY CONTRACT NO: OOXFFFG-78017KR			

TOTAL NUMBER OF CONTAINERS
OF PACKAGES (IN WORDS)

LADEN ON BOARD THE VESSEL BATE: Nov. 16, 2000 BY _____	FLYSEA FERRY CO., LTD BY _____

单项选择题

1. 备案号栏应填：
   A. EEW7865435　　B. CDFG5618　　C. LC810A000228　　D. 不填
2. 经营单位栏应填：
   A. 大连化工进出口公司 2102911013　　B. 北京宇都商贸有限公司 1101250756
   C. 长春特钢厂　　D. 大连外轮代理公司
3. 运输工具名称栏应填：
   A. 江海
   B. EAST EXPRESS
   C. EAST EXPRESS2000.11.16
   D. EAST EXPRESS 151E
4. 提运单号栏应填：
   A. EEW7865435　　B. CDFG5618
   C. LC810A000228　　D. 00XFFFG-78017KR
5. 收货单位栏应填：
   A. 大连化工进出口公司 2102911013　　B. 北京宇都商贸有限公司
   C. 长春特钢厂　　D. 大连外轮代理公司
6. 贸易方式栏应填：
   A. 一般贸易　　B. 加工贸易设备　　C. 中外合资　　D. 合资合作设备
7. 征免性质栏应填：
   A. 照章　　B. 一般征税　　C. 中外合资　　D. 全免
8. 装运港栏应填：
   A. 丹麦港口　　B. 荷兰港口　　C. 香港　　D. 鹿特丹
9. 境内目的地栏应填：
   A. 北京其他　　B. 大连其他　　C. 长春其他　　D. 长春特钢厂
10. 成交方式栏应填：
    A. CIF　　B. FOB　　C. L/C　　D. 一般贸易
11. 保费栏应填：
    A. 304/0250/3　　B. 304/1346/1　　C. 1346/3　　D. 不填
12. 合同协议号栏应填：
    A. CDFG5618　　B. LC810A000228　　C. 00XFFFG-78017KR　　D. EEW7865435
13. 件数栏应填：
    A. 9　　B. 12　　C. 3　　D. 2
14. 净重栏应填：
    A. 18.90　　B. 15，025　　C. 17，951　　D. 不填
15. 集装箱号栏应填：
    A. SCZU7854343/SCZU7855234　　B. SCZU7854343*2（3）
    C. SCZU7854343*1（3）　　D. SCZU7854343*2（2）
16. 标记唛码及备注栏应填：
    A. 00XFFFG-78017KR DALIAN CHINA SCZU7855234 委托化工进出口公司签约
    B. 00XFFFG-78017KR DALIAN CHINA SCZU7855234 受长春钢厂委托

C. 00XFFFG-78017KR DALIAN CHINA SCZU7855243（备注）

D. 00XFFFG-78017KR DALIAN CHINA SCZU7855234/SCZU7854343

17. 商品名称、规格型号栏应填：

A. FORKLIFT TRUCK/BATTERY & CHARGE

B. 电动叉车 FFT4730MM

C. 电动叉车 B30S

D. 电动叉车 84271090

18. 原产国（地区）栏应填：

A. 丹麦　　　　　　B. 德国　　　　　　C. 荷兰　　　　　　D. 韩国

19. 总价栏应填：

A. 53,853　　　　　B. 55,903　　　　　C. 55,199　　　　　D. 57,249

20. 征免栏应填：

A. 一般征税　　　　B. 全免　　　　　　C. 照章　　　　　　D. 征免

第六章

申请产地证

第一节 一般原产地证

教学目标

最终目标：能根据贸易信息办理一般原产地证。

促成目标：

1. 理解一般原产地证的作用。
2. 能办理（制作）一般原产地证。
3. 能跟踪一般原产地证的办理过程。

情景案例

机构：
外贸企业：宁波欧胜塑化有限公司（OCEAN PLASTIC & CHEMICAL PRODUCTS CO., LTD）。
外贸代理：宁波海文进出口有限公司（NINGBO HAIWEN IMP&EXP. CORP., LTD）。
贸促会（CCPIT）

人物：
小余：宁波欧胜塑化有限公司单证员。
张经理：宁波欧胜塑化有限公司业务经理。
外贸代理公司单证员小刘：宁波海文进出口有限公司。

背景资料：
(1) 2016年11月6日宁波欧胜塑化有限公司外贸业务部张经理以宁波海文进出口有限公司业务员的身份与阿拉伯联合酋长国的公司ABC TRADING CO., LLC签订一份36 800支唇膏（LIP BALM）的出口合同，合同号为081106。
(2) 海文单证员小刘先网上申请做原产地证（http：//www.zform.net/select.htm），1~2天后，贸促会确认无误，凭自动生成的打印后的发票到贸促会领正本产地证。

申请页面1、2（例）：

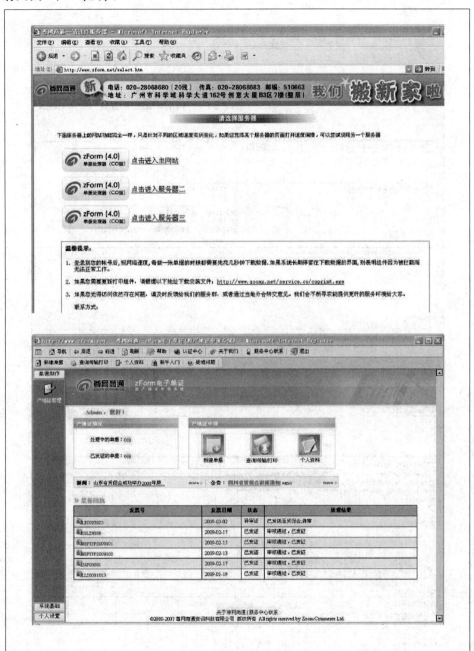

申请页面3（例）：

*红色标题字段为必填项

1.Exporter [选择受益人]	Certificate No.
	CERTIFICATE OF ORIGIN OF THE PEOPLE'S REPUBLIC OF CHINA
2.Consignee [选择客户]	
3.Means of transport and route [疑难问题]	5.For certifying authority use only
4.Country / region of destination	10.Number and date of invoices 发票号码 发票日期 2009-03-05 进口成份标志(全部国产填P，含进口成份填W): 毛净重标识:

6.Marks and numbers	7.Number and kind of packages; description of goods	8.H.S. code	9.Quantity

[↑] [↓] [汇总] [拷贝] [粘贴] [增加商品] [编辑] [插入] [删除] [疑难问题]

特殊条款（货物前描述）

特殊条款（货物后描述）

11.Declaration by the exporter The undersigned hereby declares that the above details and statements are correct, that all the goods were produced in China and that they comply with the Rules of Origin of the People's Republic of China.	12.Certification It is hereby certified that the declaration by the export is correct.
申请地点： 申请日期： 2009-03-05	签署地点： 签署日期： 2009-03-05
Place and date, signature and stamp of authorized signatory	Place and date, signature and stamp of certifying authority

EDI补充内容
发票打印份数：2
录入备注：

一般原产地证（例）：

ORIGINAL	
NINGBO HAIWEN IMP.&EXP. CORP., LTD. 9FL, NO. 428, ZHONGSHAN EAST ROAD, NINGBO CHINA	Certificate No. **CCPIT 083235134** 09C3302A1756/00002 **CERTIFICATE OF ORIGIN** **OF** **THE PEOPLE'S REPUBLIC OF CHINA**
MAZEN TRADING CO., LLC P. O. BOX 13087, DUBAI, UAE TEL:00971-6-6739392, FAX:00971-6-5736315/5736317	
PORT OF DISPATCH/DESTINATION: JEBEL ALI, UAE BY SEA	5. For certifying authority use only
UNITED ARAB EMIRATES	

6. Marks and numbers	7. Number and kind of packages; description of goods	8. H.S.Code	9. Quantity	10. Number and date of invoices
PRITTY FRUITFULLY YOURS LIP BALM	REMARKS: PO#081106 EIGHT HUNDRED AND TWENTY FIVE (825) CTNS OF LIP BALM ************************	3304	36800PCS	09OS005 JAN. 4, 2009

| 11. Declaration by the exporter
The undersigned hereby declares that the above details and statements are correct, that all the goods were produced in China and that they comply with the Rules of Origin of the People's Republic of China.

宁波海文进出口有限公司
NINGBO HAIWEN IMP.&EXP. CORP LTD
9FL, NO. 428, ZHONGSHAN EAST ROAD, NINGBO CHINA

任蒋超
NINGBO CHINA   JAN. 6, 2009
Place and date, signature and stamp of authorized signatory | 12. Certification
It is hereby certified that the declaration by the exporter is correct.

(CHINA COUNCIL FOR THE PROMOTION OF INTERNATIONAL TRADE 宁波 90)

NINGBO CHINA   JAN. 6, 2009
Place and date, signature and stamp of certifying authority |

打印页面（例）：

```
请核对单据信息是否有误                                   打印原产地证 ▾   🖨 打印输出
                                                      打印原产地证
         商业/退税发票              产地证                打印发票

1.Exporter                               Certificate No. 09C3302A1756/00016
NINGBO HAIWEN IMP.& EXP.CORP., LTD.
9FL,NO.428, ZHONGSHAN EAST ROAD, NINGBO CHINA
                                              CERTIFICATE OF ORIGIN
2.Consignee                                              OF
MR. ING. JUAN PABLO VARELA                   THE PEOPLE'S REPUBLIC OF CHINA
RG GROUP S.R.L
PINO 1166 HAEDO NORTE - CP.1684 - BUENOS
AIRES-ARGENTINA

3.Means of transport and route           5.For certifying authority use only
FROM NINGBO TO BUENOSAIRES BY SEA

4.Country / region of destination
ARGENTINA

6.Marks and   7.Number and kind of packages;description of goods  8.H.S.code  9.Quantity  10.Number
  numbers                                                                                 and date
                                                                                          of
                                                                                          invoices

RG GROUP S.R.L   ONE HUNDRED AND TWELVE (112) CTNS OF ALUMINUM WIR  7615      9600PCS    09LZH006
MADE IN CHINA    E KNITTED HOSE                                                          FEB
                                                                                         17,2009
                 ONE HUNDRED AND TWO (102) CTNS OF STAINLESS STEEL  7411      11200PCS
                 RIPPLE HOSE
```

相关知识

一、原产地证书作用和种类

产地证书（Certificate of Origin），是出口商应进口商的要求而提供的、由公证机构或政府或出口商出具的证明货物原产地和制造地的一种证明文件。

原产地证书作用：

（1）供进口国海关掌握进出口货物的原产地国别，从而采取不同的国别政策，决定进口税率和确定税别待遇。

（2）是对某些国家或某种商品采取控制进口额度和进口数量的依据。

（3）也是进口国进行贸易统计的依据。

原产地证书的种类：

（1）普通产地证：出口商签发的厂商产地证书；中国国际贸易促进委员会与商检机构签发的一般原产地证书。

（2）特殊产地证：普遍优惠制产地证书表格A（GSP FORM A）；纺织品产地证。

二、一般原产地证书的申请

出口单位最迟于每批货物报关出运前3天向签证机构（商检机构或商会）申请，并按要求提交以下材料。

（1）《出口货物原产地/加工装配证明书申请书》。

(2)《出口货物原产地证明书》。
(3) 商业发票。
(4) 合同、装箱单等其他证明文件。

三、产地证书的填写

一般原产地证书 C/O 是蓝色的，一式三份，一正两副。

办理地点：

(1) 如果信用证上没有要求要盖商会章的话，就在商检局或者贸促会办理。
(2) 如果要盖商会章的话，就只能在贸促会办理。

第一栏（Exporter）：出口商品名称、地址、国别。

此栏出口商名称必须是经检验检疫局登记注册，其名称、地址必须与注册档案一致。必须填明在中国境内的出口商详细地址、国名（CHINA）。如果出口单位是其他国家或地区某公司的分公司，申请人要求填境外公司名称时可填写；但必须在中国境内的出口商名称后加上 ON BEHALF OF（O/B）或 CARE OF（C/O）再加上境外公司名称。

第二栏（Consignee）：收货人的名称、地址和国别。

一般应填写最终收货人名称，即提单通知人或信用证上特别声明的受货人，如最终收货人不明确或为中间商时可填"TO ORDER"字样。

第三栏（Means of Transport and Route）：运输方式和路线。

填明装货港、目的港名称及运输方式（海运、空运或陆运）。经转运的，应注明转运地。

第四栏（Country/Region of Destination）目的地。

指货物最终运抵港，或国家、地区，一般应与最终收货人（第二栏）一致。

第五栏（For Certifying Authority Use Only）：签证机构专用栏。

此栏留空。签证机构在签发后发证书、补发证书或加注其他声明的使用。

第六栏（Marks and Numbers）：唛头及包装号。

此栏应照实填具完整的图案、文字标记及包装号。如唛头多，本栏填不下，可填在第七、八、九栏的空白处，如还不够，可以附页填写。如图案文字无法缮制，可附复印件，但须加盖签证机构印章。如无唛头，应填 N/M 字样。此样不得出现"香港、台湾或其他国家和地区制造"等的字样。

第七栏（Number and Kind of Packages；Description of Goods）：商品名称，包装数量及种类。

此栏应填明商品总称和具体名称。在商品名称后须加上大写的英文数字并用括号加上阿拉伯数字及包装种类或度量单位。

如同批货物有不同品种，则要有总包装箱数。最后应加上截止线，以防止填伪造内容。国外信用证有时要求填具合同、信用证号码等，可加在截止线下方空白处。

第八栏（H. S Code）：商品编码。

此栏要求填写四位数的 H. S. 税目号，若同一证书含有多种商品，应将相应的税目号全部填写。

第九栏（Quantity）：数量和重量。

此栏应填写商品的计量单位。

第十栏（Number）：发票号与日期。

此栏不得留空。月份一律用英文缩写。该栏日期应早于或同于第十一栏和第十二栏的申报和签发日期。

第十一栏（Declaration by the Exporter）：出口商声明。

该栏由申领单位已在签证机构注册的人员签字并加盖企业中英文印章，同时填定申领地点和日期，该栏日期不得早于发票日期（第十栏）。

第十二栏（Certification）：签证机构注明。

申请单位在此栏填写签证日期和地点，然后，由签证机构已授权的签证人签名、盖章。

签发日期不得早于发票日期（第十栏）和申请日期（第十一栏）。如有信用证要求填写签证机关名称、地址、电话、传真以及签证人员姓名，则仔细核对，确保准确无误。

实训练习题

根据下列信息填写一般原产地证书

```
MT700 ---------------- ISSUE OF A DOCUMENTARY CREDIT ----------------
SEQUENCE OF TOTAL               27：1/1
FORM OF DOCUMENTARY CREDIT      40A：IRREVOCABLE
DOCUMENTARY CREDIT NUMBER       20：31173
DATE OF ISSUE                   31C：050401
DATE AND PLACE OF EXPIRY        31D：DATE 050531 PLACE CHINA
APPLICANT                       50：MAMUT ENTERPRISESAV
                                    TARRAGONA, SPAIN
ISSUING BANK                    52A：CREDIT ANDORRA
                                    ANDORRA LA VELLA, ANDORRA
BENEFICIARY                     59：SHANGHAI TOOL IMPORT&
                                    EXPORT CO., LTD
                                    31, GANXIANG ROAD
                                    SHANGHAI, CHINA
CURRENCY CODE, AMOUNT           32B：CURRENCY USD AMOUNT 21,892.00
AVAILABLE WITH...BY...          41D：ANY BANK IN CHINA
                                    BY NEGOTIATION
DRAFTS AT...                    42C：30 DAYS AFTER SIGHT
DRAWEE                          42D：CREDIT ANDORRA
                                    ANDORRA LA VELLA, ANDORRA
                                    LOADING/DISPATCH/TAKING
IN CHARGE/FM                    44A：SHANGHAI
FOR TRANSPORTATION TO...        44B：BARCELONA (SPAIN)
LATEST DATE OF SHIPMENT         44C：050510
DESCRIPTION OF GOODS/SERVICES   45A：
    HAND TOOLS AS PER PROFORMA INVOICE No. 2005032 DATED MARCH. 10, 2005
```

FOB SHANGHAI
DOCUMENTS REQUIRED：　　　　　46A：
　　+ SIGNED COMMERCIAL INVOICE，2 ORIGINAL AND 4 COPIES.
　　+ PACKING LIST，1 ORIGINAL AND 4 COPIES
　　+ CERTIFICATE OF ORIGIN THE PEOPLE'S REPUBLIC OF CHINA，ISSUED BY THE CHAMBER OF COMMERCE OR OTHER AUTHORITY DULY ENTITLED FOR THIS PURPOSE.
CHARGES　　　　　　　　　　　71B：
　　ALL BANKING CHARGES OUTSIDE SPAIN ARE FOR BENEFICIARY'S ACCOUNT
PERIOD FOR PRESENTATIONS　　48：
　　DOCUMENTS MUST BE PRESENTED FOR NEGOTIATION WITHIN 15 DAYS AFTER BILL OF LADING DATE, BUT WITHIN THE VALIDITY OF THIS CREDIT.
CONFIRMATION INSTRUCTION　　49：WITHOUT
SENDER TO RECEIVER INFO　　　72：
　　THIS LC IS SUBJECT TO UCP 1993 ICC PUB. NO. 500. THIS IS OPERATIVE INSTRUMENT AND NO MAIL CONFIRMATION WILL FOLLOW.
　　补充资料：
　　（1）INVOICE NO.：TY034
　　（2）PACKING

	G. W/kg	N. W/kg	MEAS/（m³）	
9 pc Extra Long Hex Key Set				
Packing：10 SETS / Plastic carton	20/CTN	18/CTN	0.2/CTN	20CTNS
8 pc Double Offset Ring Spanner				
Packing：16 SETS / Plastic carton	20/CTN	18/CTN	0.2/CTN	20CTNS
12 pc Double Offset Ring Spanner				
Packing：8 SETS / Plastic carton	19/CTN	17/CTN	0.2/CTN	20CTNS
12 pc Combination Spanner				
Packing：10 SETS / Plastic carton	19/CTN	17/CTN	0.2/CTN	20CTNS
10 pc Combination Spanner				
Packing：10 SETS / Plastic carton	18/CTN	16/CTN	0.2/CTN	20CTNS

　　（3）H. S. CODE：8204.1100
　　（4）证书号：1283890096
　　（5）注册号：66778W
　　（6）B/L NO.：COSU57687546
　　（7）B/L DATE：MAY. 10，2005
　　（8）VESSEL：GOLDEN GATE BRIDGE V. 10W

ORIGINAL

1. Exporter（full name and address）	CERTIFICATE NO
2. Consignee（full name, address, country）	**CERTIFICATE OF ORIGIN OF THE PEOPLE'S REPUBLIC OF CHINA**

3. Means of transport and route	5. For certifying authority use only			
4. Country / region of destination				
6. Marks and numbers	7. Number and kind of packages description of goods	8. H. S. Code	9. Quantity	10. Number and date of invoices
11. Declaration by the exporter The undersigned hereby declares that the above details and statement are correct; that all the goods were produced in China and that they comply with the Rules of Origin of the People's Republic of China. -------- Place and date, signature and stamp of authorized signatory	12. Certification It is hereby certified that the declaration by the exporter is correct. -------- Place and date, signature and stamp of certifying authority			

第二节 普惠制产地证

教学目标

最终目标：能根据贸易信息办理普惠制产地证。
促成目标
1. 理解普惠制产地证的作用。
2. 能办理（制作）普惠制产地证。
3. 能跟踪普惠制产地证的办理过程。

情景案例

机构：
外贸企业：宁波保税区益友国际贸易有限公司。
中华人民共和国出入境检验检疫局。
人物：
小李：宁波保税区益友国际贸易有限公司。
郑经理：宁波保税区益友国际贸易有限公司业务经理。

背景资料：

（1）2016年6月14日，宁波保税区益友国际贸易有限公司外贸业务部郑经理与波兰某公司签订一份9 600个起钉器（STAPLES REMOVER）的出口合同。合同要求我方提供普惠制产地证。

（2）单证员小李先向出入境检验检疫局提出申请，2天后，出入境检验检疫局确认无误，小李凭自动生成的打印后的发票到出入境检验检疫局领正本普惠制产地证。

产地证凭条（例）：

产地证领证凭条

申请单位注名称：宁波保税区益友国际贸易有限公司		领证人签收：	
证书号码	G083800037500008	种类	GSP
		份数	1

以下由签证机构填写：

申请受理日期：2008-07-01

申请单位缴纳签证费后，凭此领证

》》》》》》》产地证制证凭条《《《《《《《

申请单位注名称：宁波保税区益友国际贸易有限公司			
证书号码	G083800037500008	种类	GSP
		份数	1

备注：

申请受理日期：2008-07-01

如需打印唛头附页的请提交专用的空白唛头附页纸。

FORM A（例）：

相关知识

一、普惠制产地证书表格 A（G.S.P. FORM A）的申请

出口企业在货物出运前 5 天向签证机构申请，并提交申请书及商业发票，商检机构审核无误即予签发。

实施普惠制必须遵循的三个原则：非歧视性原则、惠遍原则、非互惠原则。

实施普惠制必须符合三个要求：产地原则、直接运输、普惠制原产地证明书。

二、普惠制产地证书的填写

第一栏，注册企业的英文名称、地址、国家（强制性添加，不得以任何理由删改）。

中文地名采用汉语拼音。国家名称不可以有"ROC"字样。

第二栏，收货人名称、地址、国家。

必须填写给惠国最终收货人名称，但不可填写中间转口商名称。

到日本、加拿大的货物必须填写最终收货人名称地址。除此之外，如有特殊要求，可填"to order"，不得留空。

第三栏，运输方式及路线。

填写货物最终离境口岸和到货口岸。如有转运，可分段填写。转口国须在申请书信息内显示。

第四栏，正常情况下此栏空白。

第五栏，商品顺序号。

按照商品品名顺序："1""2""3""4""5"等，以此类推。切记不能只写最大的号。对于单项商品，此栏填"1"，也可以留空。

第六栏，唛头及包装号。

如无唛头，应填"N/M"或"NO MARK"。此栏应与货物外包装和发票唛头一致。不得出现他国制造字样，不得出现香港、澳门、台湾原产字样。

第七栏，包装数量及种类、商品的名称。

包装数量必须用英文和阿拉伯数字同时表示，品名必须具体填明，不能笼统填"MA-CHINE"，"GARMENTS"等模糊的名称，具体到可以判断出其前四位税目号。化工产品等必须填具体品名，不能只填如"B-11"这样的代号。商品名称等列完后，应紧接着加上截止符，防止加添伪造内容。

第八栏，原产地标准。

（1）完全原产的填"P"。

（2）加拿大：在两个或以上受惠国内加工的填"G"，利用给惠国成分的填"F"，原产地标准：非原产成分的价值未超过产品出厂价的 40%。

（3）日、挪、瑞士、欧盟、土、波："W"和产品的四位 HS 品目号。

（4）俄、白、乌、哈、捷、斯：在我国增值的填"Y"和非原产成分占产品 FOB 的百分比，对在其他受惠国和我国生产的并在我国完成最后工序的填"PK"，原产地标准：非原

产成分的价值未超过产品离岸价的50%。

（5）澳、新：此栏留空。原产地标准：非原产成分的价值未超过工厂成本价的50%。

第九栏，以商品正常计量单位填写。

如"只""件""打"等。以重量计算的，则填毛重；只有净重的，填净重，但要标上"N.W."或"NET WEIGHT"字样。

第十栏，发票号码及日期。

月份用英文显示，此栏的日期必须与商业发票一致，发票日期不得迟于出货日期。发票号码之间不得留空格。

第十一栏，签证当局的证明。

此栏填写签证当局的签证地点、日期。如有企业异地签证，则必须填写签证所在地的签证地点。

第十二栏，出口商声明。

此栏填写最终进口国名称，进口国必须与第三栏目的港国别保持一致。申请单位手签人员在此栏右下角签字，此栏盖单位中英文对照印章，不得出现除单位名外任何字样。申请日期必须早于签证日期、晚于发票日期，极特殊情况下此三日期可以是同一天。

实训练习题

请根据下列信息填写普惠制产地证书

```
BASIC HEADER F 01 BKCHCNBJA5XX 9109 069905
APPL。HEADER O 700 1332990223 SMITJPJSAXXX 4956 850438 9902231232 N
                        + SUMITOMO BANK LTD OSAKA JAPAN
（BANK NO：2632001）      + OSAKA, JAPAN
USER HEADER             BANK. PRIORITY 113：
                        MSG USER REF. 108：G/FO - 7752807
MT700 ---------------- ISSUE OF A DOCUMENTARY CREDIT ----------------

SEQUENCE OF TOTAL                  27：1/1
FORM OF DOCUMENTARY CREDIT         40A：IRRVOCABLE
DOCUMENTARY CREDIT NUMBER          20：G/FO7752807
DATE OF ISSUE                      31C：160223
DATE AND PLACE OF EXPIRY           31D：160610 QINGDAO CHINA
APPLICANT                          50：TOSHU CORPORATION OSALM
                                       12 - 36, KYUTARO - MACHI 4 - CHOME
                                       CHUO - KU, OSAKA 561 - 8177 JAPAN
BENEFICIARY                        59：DONGYUE KNITWEARS AND HOMETEXTILES
                                       IMPORT AND EXPORT CORPORATION
                                       197 ZHONGHUA ROAD, QINGDAO, CHINA
CURRENCY CODE, AMOUNT              32B：USD201, 780, 00
AVAILABLE WITH...BY...             41D：ANY BANK
                                       BY NEGOTIATION
```

DRAFTS AT…	42C: AT SIGHT
DRAWEE	42D: THE SUMITOMO BANK, LTD. OSAKA
PARTIAL SHIPMENT	43P: ALLOWED
TRANSHIPMENT	43T: PROHIBITED
LOADING/DISPATCH/TAKING IN CHARGE/FM	44A: QINGDAO
FOR TRANSPORTATION TO…	44B: YOKOHAMA
LATEST DATE OF SHIPMENT	44C: 160531
DESCRIPTION OF GOODS/SERVICES	45A:

CIF YOKOHAMA

    MAN SHIRT (CONTRACT NO. 99JA7031KL)

    ST/NO.   Q'TY   UNIT PRICE

    71 – 800   67,200PCS   USD1.43/PC

    71 – 801   48,000PCS   USD1.46/PC

    71 – 802   27,600PCS   USD1.29/PC

DOCUMENTS REQUIRED: 46A:

    + COMMERCIAL INVOICE IN QUINTUPLICATE

    + FULL SET LESS ONE ORIGINAL CLEAN ON BOARD OCEAN BILL OF LADING MARKED FREIGHT PREPAID MADE OUT TO ORDER OF THE SHIPPER BLANK ENDORSED NOTIFY APPLICANT

    + PACKING LIST IN 3 COPIES

    + G.S.P CERTIFICATE OF ORIGIN FORM A IN 3 COPIES

    + INSURANCE POLICY OR CERTIFICATE IN DUPLICATE ENDORSED IN BLANK WITH CLAIM PAYABLE IN JAPAN IN THE CURRENCY OF THE DRAFT COVERING 110 PERCENT OF INVOICE VALUE INCLUDING INSTITUTE WAR CLAUSES INSTITUTE CARGO CLAUSES (ALL RISKS) INSTITUTE S.R.C.C. CLAUSES

    + BENEFICIARY'S CERTIFICATE STATING THAT ONE SET OF ORIGINAL SHIPPING DOCUMENTS INCLUDING CERTIFICATE OF ORIGINAL FORM A HAS BEEN SENT DIRECTLY TO THE APPLICANT (ATTN. OSALM SECTION) WITHIN 2 DAYS AFTER SHIPMENT BY AIR COURIER.

ADDITIONAL CONDITIONS   47A:

    THIS CREDIT IS SUBJECT TO UNIFORM CUSTOMS AND PRACTICE FOR DOCUMENTARY CREDITS (1993 REVISION) ICC. PUBLICATION NO. 500

    T.T REIMBURSEMENT: UNACCEPTABLE

    X) THE GOODS SHOULD BE CONTAINERIZED.

    X) A COPY OF CABLE ADVISING SHIPPING DETAILS FAX TO THE ACCOUNTEE WITHIN 2 DAYS AFTER SHIPMENT.

    X) CLEAN ON BOARD COMBINED TRANSPORT B/L OF ITOCHU EXPRESS CO., LTD IS ACCEPTABLE.

CHARGES	71B: ALL BANKING CHARGES AND COMMISSIONS INCLUDING REIMBURSEMENT COMM. OUTSIDE JAPAN ARE FOR ACCOUNT OF BENEFICIARY.
PERIOD FOR PRESENTATIONS	48: DOCUMENTS MUST BE PRESENTED FOR NEGOTIATION WITHIN 10 DAYS AFTER BILL OF LADING DATE, BUT WITHIN THE VALIDITY OF THIS CREDIT.

CONFIRMATION INSTRUCTION	49：WITHOUT
INSTR. TO PAY/ACPT/NGG BANK	78：

TO NEGOTIATING BANK：

　　ALL SHIPPING DOCUMENTS TO BE SENT DIRECTLY TO THE OPENING OFFICE BY REGISTERED AIRMAIL IN ONE LOT.

　　UPON RECEIPT OF THE DRAFTS AND DOCUMENTS IN ORDER, WE WILL REMIT THE PROCEEDS TO YOUR ACCOUNT WITH THE BANK DESIGNATED BY YOU.

TRAILER

　　MAC：51EF556F CHK：D3A3A848E00C

NNNN

参考资料：

（1）CIF YOKOHAMA。

（2）SHIPPED BY S.S. HONG V26 ON MAY 28TH, 2016。

（3）B/L NO. 9905358。

（4）INVOICE NO. JYS698。

（5）20PCS/CTN。

colspan="4"	ORIGINAL		
colspan="4"	1. Goods consigned from (Exporter's business name, address, country)		Reference No. GENERALIZED SYSTEM OF PREFERENCES CERTIFICATE OF ORIGIN (Combined declaration and certificate) FORM A Issued in *THE PEOPLE'S REPUBLIC OF CHINA* (country) See Notes overleaf
	2. Goods consigned to (Consignee's name, address, country)		
colspan="4"	3. Means of transport and route (as far as known)		4. For official use
5. Item number	6. Marks and numbers of packages	7. Number and kind of packages; description of goods	8. Origin criterion (see Notes overleaf)	9. Gross weight or other quantity	10. Number and date of invoices

11. Certification It is hereby certified, on the basis of control carried out, that the declaration by the exporter is correct. -- Place and date, signature and stamp of certifying authority	12. Declaration by the exporter The undersigned hereby declares that the above details and statements are correct, that all the goods were produced in <u>CHINA</u> ------------------------------------ (country) and that they comply with the origin requirements specified for those goods in the Generalized System of Preferences for goods exported to -- -- Place and date, signature and stamp of authorized signatory

第七章

投保

第一节　投保单和保险单

教学目标

最终目标：能根据贸易信息办理保险。

促成目标：

1. 能理解合同或信用证关于保险的条款。
2. 能填制投保单并审核保险单。

情景案例

机构：

外贸企业：宁波欧胜塑化有限公司（OCEAN PLASTIC & CHEMICAL PRODUCTS CO., LTD）。

保险公司：中国人民财产保险股份有限公司（PICC）。

人物：

小余：宁波欧胜塑化有限公司单证员。

张经理：宁波欧胜塑化有限公司业务经理。

背景资料：

(1) 2016年11月6日，宁波欧胜塑化有限公司外贸业务部张经理与阿拉伯联合酋长国的公司 ABC TRADING CO., LLC 签订一份 36 800 支唇膏（LIP BALM）的出口合同，合同号为 081106。

(2) 12月7日小余制作投保单并传真给保险公司。保险公司回传确认件，小余审核无误，在确认件上写 "OK"，再传回 PICC。

(3) 单证员小余 12 月 8 日到 PICC 拿正本保险单。

投保单（例）：

PICC 中国人民财产保险股份有限公司 宁波市分公司
PICC Property and Casualty Company Limited Ningbo Branch

地址：中国宁波大来街 50 号　邮编(POST CODE)：315000
ADD: NO.50 DA LAI STREET NINGBO CHINA
电话(TEL): 0574-87196111　传真(FAX): 0574-87199058

货物运输保险投保单
APPLICATION FORM FOR CARGO TRANSPORTATION INSURANCE

被保险人：
Insured:
发票号(INVOICE NO.)
合同号(CONTRACT NO.)
信用证号(L/C NO.)
发票金额(INVOICE AMOUNT) ＿＿＿＿＿＿　投保加成(PLUS) ＿＿＿＿＿＿ %

兹有下列物品向中国人民财产保险股份有限公司宁波市分公司投保。(INSURANCE REQUIRED ON THE FOLLOWING COMMODITIES:)

标记 MARKS & NOS.	包装及数量 QUANTITY	保险货物项目 DESCRIPTION OF GOODS	保险金额 AMOUNT INSURED

起运日期：　　　　　　　　　装载运输工具：
DATE OF COMMENCEMENT＿＿＿　PER CONVEYANCE:＿＿＿
自　　　　　　　　经　　　　　　　　　至
FROM ＿＿＿＿＿　VIA ＿＿＿＿＿　TO ＿＿＿＿＿
提单号：　　　　　　　　　　赔款偿付地点：
B/L NO.:＿＿＿＿＿　　CLAIM PAYABLE AT:＿＿＿＿＿
投保险别：(PLEASE INDICATE THE CONDITIONS &/OR SPECIAL COVERAGES:)

请如实告知下列情况:(如"是"在[ ]中打"√") IF ANY, PLEASE MARK "√":
1. 货物种类：　袋装[ ]　散装[ ]　冷藏[ ]　液体[ ]　活动物[ ]　机器/汽车[ ]　危险品等级[ ]
   GOODS:　BAG/JUMBO　BULK　REEFER　LIQUID　LIVE ANIMAL　MACHINE/AUTO　DANGEROUS CLASS
2. 集装箱种类：普通[ ]　开顶[ ]　框架[ ]　平板[ ]　冷藏[ ]
   CONTAINER:　ORDINARY　OPEN　FRAME　FLAT　RAFRIGERATOR
3. 转运工具：　海轮[ ]　飞机[ ]　驳船[ ]　火车[ ]　汽车[ ]
   BY TRANSIT:　SHIP　PLANE　BARGE　TRAIN　TRUCK
4. 船舶资料：　船籍[ ]　　　　　　　　船龄[　　　　　　]
   PARTICULAR OF SHIP　REGISTRY　　　　　　　AGE

备注：被保险人确认本保险合同条款和内容已经完全了解。　　　投保人（签名盖章）APPLICANT'S SIGNATURE
　　　THE ASSURED CONFIRMS HEREWITH THE TERMS AND
　　　CONDITIONS OF THESE INSURANCE CONTRACT FULLY
　　　UNDERSTOOD.

　　　　　　　　　　　　　　　　　　　　　　　　电话：(TEL)
投保日期：(DATE) ＿＿＿＿＿　　　　　　　　　　地址：(ADD)

本公司自用（FOR OFFICE USE ONLY）

费率：　　　　　　　保费：　　　　　　　备注：
RATE:　　　　　　　PREMIUM
经办人：　　　核保人：　　　负责人：
BY

No PICC

保单确认件（例）：

```
05/01 2009 15:08 FAX 057487315600    PICC NINGBO UNDERWRITING                    @001

                                                              PYIE200933020810000042
         08CS095
         OCEAN PLASTIC & CHEMICAL PRODUCTS CO.,LTD




         DER WERBEKONTAKT    13 CTNS         LIP BALM                  USD2,860.00
         QUANTITY PER BOX:
         N.W.:
         G.W.:
         SIZE OF CARTON:


                        USD TWO THOUSAND EIGHT HUNDRED AND SIXTY ONLY
                                                                          Dec.30, 2008
              AS ARRANGED      CSCL ZEEBRUGGE V.0023W
         NINGBO                                              HAMBURG
              COVERING ALL RISKS AS PER OCEAN MARINE CARGO CLAUSES OF THE PICC
                    PROPERTY AND CASUALTY COMPANY LIMITED DATED 1/1/81.




         THE CLAIM IS UNDER USD300, IT IS NOT NECESSARY TO APPLY FOR SURVEY.CLAIM IF ANY,PAYABLE ON SURRENDER
         RECTLY TO THIS COMPANY OF THIS POLICY,INVOICE,BILL OF LADING,STATEMENT OF CLAIM AND THE PHOTOGRAPHS
         THE DAMAGED GOODS. IF THE CLAIM AMOUNT IS OVER USD300, THE BELOW AGENT MUST BE APPLIED FOR SURVEY.
         RECK & CO GMBH
         PHONE: +49 40 2780 6375
         AFTER HOURS: +49 40 2780 6375 (24 HOURS)
         FAX: +49 40 2780 141
         EMAIL: CLAIMS@RECK.DE
         HAMBURG@RECK.DE

              HAMBURG IN USD
              Dec.29, 2008
```

保险单（例）：

相关知识

一、货物运输保险险别和投保手续

（一）保险条款与险别

1. 中国保险条款（China Insurance Clause，CIC）

由中国人民保险公司（PICC）制定。货物运输保险分为基本险和附加险两大类，基本险为平安险、水渍险和一切险，可以单独投保其中一种，附加险不能单独投保。目前我国出口业务中，一般多选用一切险。

2. 协会货物险条款（Institute Cargo Clause，ICC）

由伦敦保险协会制定。包括：ICC（A）险、ICC（B）险、ICC（C）险、协会战争险条款—货物（Institute War Clause—Cargo）、协会罢工险条款—货物（Institute Strikes Clause—Cargo）、恶意损坏险条款（Malicious Damage Clause）等。

（二）保险业务的一般手续

出口商备妥货，并确定了装运日期和运输工具后（收到经船公司签署的配舱回单后），即填制投保单向保险公司投保。保险公司接受投保后即签发保险单。

出口货物明细单，加注了运输方式、承保险别等的出口发票也可作为投保单使用。

二、出口货物运输保险投保单的填写

凡按 CIF 和 CIP 条件成交的出口货物，由出口企业向当地保险公司逐笔办理投保手续。在办理时注意：应根据出口合同或信用证规定，在备妥货物并已确定装运日期和运输工具后，按约定的保险险别和保险金额，向保险公司投保。投保时应填制投保单并支付保险费（保险费＝保险金额×保险费率），保险公司凭以出具保险单或保险凭证。

投保的日期应不迟于货物装船的日期。投保金额若合同没有明示规定，应按 CIF 或 CIP 价格加成 10%，如买方要求提高加成比率，一般情况下可以接受，但增加的保险费应由买方负担。

具体投保单的填写如下：

1. 投保人

填投保人公司名称（如为出口商投保请填公司中文名称）。

2. 投保日期

填投保单的日期。

3. 发票号码

填写此批货物的发票号码。

4. 被保险人

被保险人即投保人，或称"抬头"，这一栏填投保人公司的名称。实务上，有些公司会填写"见发票"字样。货物出运后，风险转由进口商负担。因此，如属出口商投保，可将自己公司的中文名称填在"客户抬头"栏，而将进口商公司名称填在"过户"栏，这样填写便于货物发生意外后进口商向保险公司索赔；如属进口商投保，则直接将自己公司名称填

在"抬头"栏,而"过户"栏留空。

5. 保险货物项目

填写货物名称。

6. 标记

填写运输标志。

7. 数量及包装

按实际情况填写。

8. 保险金额

保险金额 = CIF 货价 × (1 + 保险加成率)。

在进出口贸易中,根据有关的国际贸易惯例,保险加成率通常为 10%。当然,出口人也可以根据进口人的要求与保险公司约定不同的保险加成率。

由于保险金额的计算是以 CIF(或 CIP)货价为基础的,因此,对外报价时如果需要将 CFR(或 CPT)价格变为 CIF(CIP)价格,或是在 CFR(或 CPT)合同项下买方要求卖方代为投保时,均不应以 CFR 价格为基础直接加保险费来计算,而应先将 CFR(或 CPT)价格换算为 CIF(或 CIP)价格后再求出相应的保险金额和保险费。

(1)按 CIF 进口时:保险金额 = CIF 货价 × 1.1。

(2)按 CFR 进口时:保险金额 = CFR 货价 × 1.1/(1 - 1.1 × r),其中 r 为保险费率。

(3)按 FOB 进口时:保险金额 =(FOB 货价 + 海运费)× 1.1/(1 - 1.1 × r),其中海运费请在装船通知中查找,由出口商根据配舱通知填写。

注意:因为一切险(或 A 险)已包括了所有一般附加险的责任范围,所以在投保一切险(或 A 险)时,保险公司对一般附加险的各险别不会再另收费。投保人在计算保险金额时,一般附加险的保险费率可不计入。

9. 启运港

按提单填写。

10. 目的港

按提单填写。

11. 转内陆

按实际情况填写。

12. 开航日期

可只填"As Per B/L",也可根据提单签发日期具体填写。如为备运提单,则应填装船日。

13. 船名航次

海运方式下填写船名加航次。例如:FENG NING V. 9103;如整个运输由两次运输完成,则应分别填写一程船名及二程船名,中间用"/"隔开。此处可参考提单内容填写。例如:如果提单中一程船名为"Mayer",二程船名为"Sinyai",则填"Mayer/Sinyai"。

铁路运输加填运输方式"by railway"加车号;航空运输为"By air";邮包运输为"By parcel post"。

14. 赔款地点

严格按照信用证规定打制;如来证未规定,则应打目的地或目的港。如信用证规定不止一个目的港或赔付地，则应全部照打。

15. **赔付币别**

按出口合同规定的赔付币别填写。

16. **保单份数**

中国人民保险公司出具的保险单 1 套 5 份，由 1 份正本（Original）、1 份副本（Duplicate）和 3 份副本（Copy）构成。具体如下：

（1）如果来证要求提供保单为"In duplicate"、"In two folds"或"in 2 copies"，则应提供 1 份正本（Original）、1 份副本（Duplicate）构成全套保单。

（2）根据跟单信用证《UCP600》规定，如保险单据表明所出具正本为 1 份以上，则必须提交全部正本保单。

17. **投保条款和险别**

投保条款包括：中国人民保险公司保险条款（PICC CLAUSE），伦敦协会货物险条款（ICC CLAUSE），两种任选其一。

投保险别包括：一切险（ALL RISKS）；水渍险（W. P. A./W. A.）；平安险（F. P. A.）；战争险（WAR RISKS）；罢工、暴动、民变险（S. R. C. C.）；罢工险（STRIKE）；协会货物（A）险条款（ICC CLAUSE A）；协会货物（B）险条款（ICC CLAUSE B）；协会货物（C）险条款（ICC CLAUSE C）；航空运输综合险（AIR TPT ALL RISKS）；航空运输险（AIR TPT RISKS）；陆运综合险（O/L TPT ALL RISKS）；陆运险（O/L TPT RISKS）；转运险（TRANSHIPMENT RISKS）；仓至仓条款（W TO W）；偷窃、提货不着险（T. P. N. D.）；存仓火险责任扩展条款（货物出口到香港，包括九龙或澳门）（F. R. E. C.）；淡水雨淋险（R. F. W. D.）；包装破裂险（RISKS OF BREAKAGE）；不计免赔率（I. O. P.）。

其中，中国保险条款的基本险险别为一切险、水渍险、平安险，一切险承保范围最大，水渍险次之，平安险最小。伦敦协会货物险条款包括协会货物（A）险条款、协会货物（B）险条款、协会货物（C）险条款，A 险条款承保范围最大，B 险条款次之，C 险条款最小。

注意：由于一切险（或 A 险）条款承保范围最大，包括了一般附加险，所以在填写投保单时，一般附加险的条款可不勾选。但若对方要求在保险单上列明一般附加险中的若干险别，投保人则需在投保单中勾选这些险别，这样保险公司在出具保险单时，才会把这些险别一一列出。

18. **其他特别条款**

有其他特殊投保条款可在此说明，以分号隔开。

三、保险单分类

保险单是保险公司在接受投保人投保后签发的，证明保险人（即保险公司）与被保险人（即投保人）之间订有保险合同的文件。当货物出险后，它是投保人索赔和保险公司理赔的主要依据。

保险单据的分类：

（1）保险单（Insurance Policy），即大保单。

（2）保险凭证（Insurance Certificate），即小保单。

（3）预约保险单/总保险单（Open Cover/Open Policy）。
（4）保险声明书/通知书（Insurance Declaration）。
（5）联合保险凭证（Combined Insurance Certificate），不能转让，很少使用。
（6）暂保单。
（7）批单。
（8）其他保险证明和单据有保险公司保费收据（Premium Receipt）和保险公司证明书（Certificate of Insurance Company）。

四、保单的内容

出口货物保险单主要内容如下：
（1）保险人及保险公司。
（2）保险单编号。
（3）被保险人，即投保人。在 CIF 或 CIP 条件下，出口货物由出口商申请投保，在信用证没有特别规定的前提下，信用证受益人为被保险人，并加空白背书，以转让保险权益。在信用证要求下，也可以做成"出口公司名称 + Held to order of ×××bank"，或者"To whom it may concern"。
（4）标记。指运输标志应和提单、发票及其他单据上的标记一致。通常在标记栏内注明"按××号发票"（as per Invoice No. ×××）。
（5）包装及数量。应与发票内容相一致。
（6）保险货物名称。可参照商业发票中描述的商品名称填制。也可填货物的统称。信用证有时要求所有单据都要显示出信用证号码，那么可在本栏空白处表示。
（7）保险金额。按信用证规定金额投保，若信用证未规定，则按 CIF 或 CIP 价格的 110% 投保。
（8）保费及费率。保费及费率一般没有必要在保险单上表示。该栏仅填"AS ARRANGED"。但来证如果要求标明保费及费率时，则应打上具体数字及费率。
（9）装载运输工具。海运货物应填写船名和航次。如果需在中途转船，而且投保时已确定二程船名，则把二程船名也填上。如二程船名未能预知，则在第一程船名后加注"and/or steamers"。
（10）开航日期、起运地和目的地。开航日期可填写"as per B/L"（见提单），地点参照提单填写。
（11）承保险别。本栏是保险单的核心内容。它主要规定了保险公司对该批货物承保的责任范围，也是被保险人在货物遭受损失后，确定是否属保险公司责任的根据。本栏应按投保资料缮制，并要严格符合信用证条款的要求。如果信用证规定"Irrespective of percentage"（不计免赔率），则不可以加注免赔率条款。
（12）赔付地点和赔付代理人。一般为保险公司在目的地或就近地区的代理人。
（13）保险单签发日期和地点。保险单的出单日期不迟于提单或其他货运单据签发日期，以表示货物在装运前已办理保险。
（14）保险公司签章。
（15）背书。常见的是空白背书（Blank Endorsed），也有信用证要求做记名背书"En-

dorsed in the name of ×××", 或者记名指示背书 "Endorsed to the order of ×××"。

五、L/C 中有关保险条款举例

(1) INSURANCE POLICY OR CERTIFICATE IN THREE COPIES MADE OUT TO APPLICANT, COVERING INSTITUTE CARGO CLAUSES (A), AND INSTITUTE WAR CLAUSES (CARGO) AS PER ICC CLAUSE, INCLUDING WAREHOUSE TO WAREHOUSE UP TO FINAL DESTINATION AT OSAKA FOR AT LEAST 110% OF CIF VALUE, MARKED PREMIUM PREPAID AND SHOWING CLAIMS IF ANY PAYABLE IN JAPAN.

(2) 2/2 SETS OF ORIGINAL INSURANCE POLICY OR CERTIFICATE, BLANK ENDORSED, COVERING ALL RISKS AND WAR RISKS FOR 110% INVOICE VALUE, SHOWING CLAIMS PAYABLE IN INDIA.

实训练习题

根据下列信息填写保险单

```
THE HONGKONG AND SHANGHAI BANKING CORPORATION
INCORPORATED IN HONGKONG WITH LIMITED LIABILITY
SHANGHAI OFFICE: 185 YUAN MING YUANG ROAD,
P. R. CHINA SHANGHAI 20002
OUR REF. EXP DC 007545
SHANDONG HOPE NATIVE PRODUCE I/E CORP.,
62, GUANGXI ROAD, QINGDAO.
DATE 23 MAY, 2000
WE ADVISE HAVING RECEIVED THE FOLLOWING TELETRANSMISSION DATED 22 MAY, 2000 FROM:
    THE HONGKONG AND SHANGHAI BANKING CORP LTD., DOWNING
        STREET, PENANG
```

ISSUE OF A DOCUMENTARY CREDIT	
SEQUENCE OF TOTAL	27: 1/1
FORM OF DOCUMENTARY CREDIT	40A: IRREVOCABLE
DOCUMENTARY CREDIT NUMBER	20: PGH000348DC
DATE OF ISSUE	31C: 21 MAY, 2000
DATE AND PLACE OF EXPIRY	31D: 21 JULY, 2000—CHINA
APPLICANT	50: SOO HUP SENG TRADING CO. SDN BHD. 165 1ST FLOOR, VICTORIA STREET, 10300 PENANG MALAYSIA
BENEFICIARY	59: SHANGDONG HOPE NATIVE PRODUCE I/E CORP., 62, GUANGXI ROAD, QINGDAO, CHINA

CURRENCY CODE, AMOUNT	32B: HKD46,150.00
AVAILABLE WITH…BY…	41D: ANY BANK
	BY NEGOTIATION
DRAFTS AT…	42C: AT SIGHT FOR FULL INVOICE VALUE
DRAWEE	42D: OURSELVES
PARTIAL SHIPMENT	43P: FORBIDDEN
TRANSHIPMENT	43T: PERMITTED
LOADING/DISPATCH/TAKING IN CHARGE/FM	44A: ANY PORT IN CHINA
FOR TRANSPORTATION TO…	44B: PENANG
LATEST DATE OF SHIPMENT	44C: 06 JULY, 2000
DESCRIPTION OF GOODS/SERVICES	45A:

5M/TONS SHANDONG BLACK DATES HIGH QUALITY AT HKD9,230 PER M/TON CIF PENANG AS PER BUYER'S ORDER NO. SOO—6378

DOCUMENTS REQUIRED: 46A:

+ INVOICE IN TRIPLICATE
+ FULL SET ORIGINAL CLEAN ON BOARD BILL (S) OF LADING MADE "FREIGHT PREPAID" AND NOTIFY APPLICANT AND ISSUING BANK.
+ MARKING INSURANCE POLICY OR CERTIFICATE CLAUSES ALL RISKS (INCLUDING WAREHOUSE TO WAREHOUSE CLAUSES) AND WAR RISKS CLAUSES (1/1/1981) OF THE PEOPLE'S INSURANCE COMPANY OF CHINA

ADDITIONAL CONDITIONS   47A:

1) WEIGHT LIST IN TRIPLICATE TO BE ISSUED BY THE SHANDONG/QINGDAO IMP AND EXP COMMODITY INSPECTION BUREAU OF THE PEOPLE'S REPUBLIC OF CHINA TO STATE THAT GOODS ARE PACKED IN 25KG NET OR 26.2KG PER CARTON REQUIRED.

2) CERTIFICATE OF CHINESE ORIGIN IN TRIPLICATE ISSUED BY CHINA COUNCIL FOR THE PROMOTION OF INTERNATIONAL TRADE TO STATE THAT GOODS ARE OF SHANDONG/QINGDAO ORIGIN REQUIRED.

3) DOCUMENTS TO EVIDENCE THAT ALL PACKINGS BEAR SHIPPING MARKS: SHA/PENANG/1 - UP.

4) DOCUMENTS TO EVIDENCE THAT PACKING IS DONE AS FOLLOWS: IN CARDBOARD CARTONS OF 25KG NET OR 26.2KG GROSS PER CARTON.

5) BENEFICIARY TO ADVISE OPENER BY TELEX/FAX ALL DETAILS OF SHIPPMENT AND SUCH TELEX/FAX COPY TO ACCOMPANY DOCUMENTS.

6) BENEFICIARY TO AIRMAIL DIRECT OPENER ONE SET OF NON - NEGOTIABLE DOCUMENTS IMMEDIATELY AFTER SHIPPMENT AND A CERTIFICATE OF COMPLIANCE TO THIS EFFECT IS REQUIRED.

7) PLUS MINUS 05 PERCENT ON BOTH QUANTITY AND AMOUNT ACCEPTABLE.

8) A USD30.00 (OR EQUIVALENT) FEE SHOULD BE DEDUCTED FROM THE REIMBURSEMENT CLAIM FOR EACH PRESENTATION OF DISCREPANT DOCUMENTS UNDER THIS DOCUMENTARY CREDIT NOTWITHSTANDING ANY INSTRUCTIONS TO THE CONTRARY, THIS CHARGE SHALL BE FOR THE ACCOUNT OF THE BENEFICIARY.

CHARGES	71B: ALL BANKING CHARGES OUTSIDE MALAYSIA INCLUDING ADVISING, NEGOTIATING COMMISSION AND REIMBURSING BANK'S FEES ARE FOR APPLICANT'S ACCOUNT
PERIOD FOR PRESENTATIONS	48: DOCUMENTS MUST BE PRESENTED FOR NEGOTIATION WITHIN 15 DAYS AFTER BILL OF LADING DATE, BUT WITHIN THE VALIDITY OF THIS CREDIT.
CONFIRMATION INSTRUCTION	49: WITHOUT
INSTR. TO PAY/ACPT/NGG BANK	78:

WE HEREBY ENGAGE WITH DRAWERS AND/OR BONA FIDE HOLDERS THAT DRAFTS DRAWN AND NEGOTIATED ON PRESENTATION, SO LONG AS THERE HAS BEEN STRICT COMPLIANCE WITH ALL TERMS AND CONDITIONS (INCLUDING SPECIAL CONDITIONS) OF THIS CREDIT, SAVE TO THE EXTENT THAT THE SAME HAVE BEEN AMENDED IN WRITING AND SIGNED ON OUR BEHALF.

DIRECTIONS TO ADVISING BANK:
+ YOUR CHARGES ARE FOR APPLICANT'S ACCOUNT
DIRECTIONS TO NEGOTIATING BANK:
+ THE AMOUNT OF EACH NEGOTIATION MUST BE ENDORSED BELOW.
+ DOCUMENTS MUST BE DESPATCHED Y REGISTERED AIRMAIL IN ONE COVER.
REIMBURESEMENT INSTRUCTION:
ON RECEIPT OF DOCUMENTS CONFIRMING TO THE TERMS OF THIS DOCUMENTARY CREDIT, WE UNDERTAKE TO REIMBURSE YOU IN THE CURRENCY OF THIS DOCUMENTARY CREDIT IN ACCORDANCE WITH YOUR INSTRUCTIONS. NEGOTIATING BANK'S DISCOUNT AND/OR INTEREST, IF ANY, PRIOR TO REIMBURSEMENT BY US ARE FOR ACCOUNT OF BENEFICIARY.

SENDER TO RECEIVER INFO	72: THIS LC IS SUBJECT TO UCP 1993 ICC PUB. NO. 500. THIS IS OPERATIVE INSTRUMENT AND NO MAIL CONFIRMATION WILL FOLLOW.

COL HKD46, 150-00

参考资料:

(1) Commodity: Shandong Black Dates。

(2) Quantity: 5 m/t。

(3) Packed in cardboard cartons of 25kg each and then shipped in one container of 200 cartons。

(4) Container No. EISU2628205。

(5) GR. WT: 5,240kg。

(6) Measurement: 13.427CBM。

(7) Shipping Mark: SHS/PENANG/1-up。

(8) Shipped per m/v "Victoria" on July 5, 2000。

(9) B/L No. 19。

中国人民保险公司
THE PEOPLE'S INSURANCE COMPANY OF CHINA

总公司设于北京　　　　　一九四九年创立
Head Office: BEIJING　　　Established in 1949

保　险　单　　　　号次
INSURANCE POLICY　　No.

中国人民保险公司（以下简称本公司）
This Policy of Insurance witnesses that The People's Insurance Company of China (hereinafter called "the Company"), at the request of _____
根据（以下简称被保险人）的要求，由被保险人向本公司缴付约定
(hereinafter called "the Insured") and in consideration of the agreed premium paid to the Company by the
的保险费，按照本保险单承保险别和背面所载条款与下列
Insured, undertakes to insure the undermentioned goods in transportation subject to the conditions of this Policy
条款承保下述货物运输保险，特立本保险单。
as per the Clause printed overleaf and other special clauses attached hereon.

标　记 Marks & Nos.	包装及数量 Quantity	保险货物项目 Description of Goods	保险金额 Amount Insured

总保险金额：
Total Amount Insured: _____

保　费　　　　　　　　费　率　　　　　　　　装载运输工具
Premium: as arranged　　Rate: as arranged　　Per conveyance S. S. _____

开行日期　　　　　　　自　　　　　　　　　至
Slg. on or abt. _____ From _____ to _____

承保险别
Conditions

　　所保货物，如遇出险，本公司凭本保险单及其他有关证件给付赔款。
Claims, if any, payable on surrender of this Policy together with other relevant documents.
　　所保货物，如发生本保险单项下负责赔偿的损失或事故，
In the event of accident whereby loss or damage may result in a claim under this Policy immediate notice applying
应立即通知本公司下述代理人查勘。
for survey must be given to the Company's Agent as mentioned hereunder:

赔款偿付地点
Claim payable at _____

日期　　　　　　　上海　　　　　　　中国人民保险公司上海分公司
Date _____ Shanghai　　　　THE PEOPLE'S INSURANCE CO. OF CHINA
　　　　　　　　　　　　　　　　　　　　　　　SHANGHAI BRANCH
地址：中国上海中山东一路23号。
Address: 23 Zhongshan Dongyilu, Shanghai, China.
Cables: 42001 Shanghai.　　　　　　　_____
Telex: 33128 PICCS CN　　　　　　　　　　　General Manager

第八章

制作其他单据

第一节 装船通知和受益人证明

教学目标

最终目标：能根据贸易信息制作装船通知和受益人证明。
促成目标：
1. 理解装船通知和受益人证明的作用、内容。
2. 能够制作装船通知和受益人证明。

情景案例 1

机构：
外贸企业：宁波欧胜塑化有限公司（OCEAN PLASTIC & CHEMICAL PRODUCTS CO.，LTD）。
人物：
小余：宁波欧胜塑化有限公司单证员。
张经理：宁波欧胜塑化有限公司业务经理。
背景资料：
（1）2016 年 11 月 6 日，宁波欧胜塑化有限公司外贸业务部张经理与阿拉伯联合酋长国的公司 ABC TRADING CO.，LLC 签订一份 36 800 支唇膏（LIP BALM）的出口合同，合同号为 081106。
（2）小余在办公室制作、补齐、整理客户清关用单据。
制作：客户用的发票、装箱单及其他单据。
整理：产地证、保险单、提单。
背书：保险单、提单。
（3）小余在取得提单后马上给客人传真装船通知。

装运通知（例）：

OCEAN PLASTIC & CHEMICAL PRODUCTS CO., LTD
Rm 1105, Building#2, Shangdong Nationals, #1926 Canghai Rd.,
315040, Ningbo, China

SHIPPING ADVICE

Messrs.: ABC TRADING CO., LLC, P. O. BOX 13087 DUBAI, UAE
Dear Sirs:
　　　　　　　　Re: PO# 081106　　L/C NO. HSBC657708467464
In accordance with the stipulations of the above credit, we hereby declare that the goods have been shipped. The details of the shipment are stated below.

COMMODITY:	36800 PCS LIP BALM
AMOUNT:	US $11,040.00
PACKAGE:	825 CTN, MEAS. 27.62CBM, G.W. 3300KGS, N.W. 2475KG
MEANS OF CONVEYANCE:	MARE THRACIUM V. 0901W
DATE OF SAILING:	2009-1-11
PORT OF LOADING:	Ningbo
DESTINATION:	JEBEL ALI, UAE
SHIPPING MARK:	PRITTY
	FRUITFULLY YOURS
	LIP BALM

OCEAN PLASTIC & CHEMICAL
PRODUCTS CO., LTD

情景案例 2

机构：
工贸企业：宁波机械有限公司（NINGBO MACHINERY CO., LTD）。
人物：
小白：宁波机械有限公司单证员。
贾经理：宁波机械有限公司业务经理。
背景资料：
(1) 2016 年 5 月 12 日，宁波机械有限公司外贸业务部贾经理与叙利亚某公司签订了一份注塑机的出口合同，FOB NINGBO PORT。8 月 29 日收到信用证。
(2) 由于工期延误，我方后来要求修改信用证，将船期和效期都延后一个月。
(3) 10 月 21 日—11 月 4 日，小白在办公室制作、补齐、整理客户清关用单据。
制作：商业发票、装箱单、重量单、受益人证明、声明等。
整理：产地证、提单、熏蒸证明、各种证明等。

信用证（例）：

```
                                                    TERMINAL  KT7:
                                                    PAGE  00001
                          DOCUMENTARY CREDIT         FUNC  ZJNBBPRQ
                                                    UMR   37264976

{S:S7651 AUTH OK, KEY DIGEST, BKCHCNBJ GBTFSYDA RECORD
{1:BASIC HEADER          F  01 BKCHCNBJA92A 1659 983233
{2:APPLICATION HEADER    O 700 1815 030828 GBTFSYDAAXXX 5297 062997 030828 2315 N
                        *INTERNATIONAL BANK FOR TRADE AND
                        *FINANCE, THE
                        *DAMASCUS
USER HEADER              SERVICE CODE  :103:
                         BANK PRIORITY :113:
                         MSG USER REF. :108:
                         INFO. FROM CI :115:
SEQUENCE OF TOTAL        *27 :       1/1
FORM OF DOC. CREDIT      *40 A :     IRREVOCABLE
DOC. CREDIT NUMBER       *20   :     OCE 6C1/21/08/03
DATE OF ISSUE            *31 C :     030828
APPLICABLE RULES         *40 E :     UCPURR LATEST VERSION
EXPIRY                   *31 D :     DATE 081028 PLACE CHINA
APPLICANT BANK           *51 A :     GBTFSYDA
                        *INTERNATIONAL BANK FOR TRADE AND
                        *FINANCE, THE
                        *DAMASCUS
APPLICANT                *50   :     RATEB KHADEM AL JAMB SONS COMPANY.
                                     DAMASCUS, SYRIA.
                                     TEL: 963118335835
                                     FAX: 963118825559
BENEFICIARY              *59   :     8830320809304
                                     LTD EXPORT PROCESSING ZONE NINGBO
                                     CHINA. ZIP CODE: 315800 TEL:86574861
                                     77242 FAX:865748622186417725
AMOUNT                   *32 B :     CURRENCY USD AMOUNT 27,500,
MAX. CREDIT AMOUNT        39 B :     NOT EXCEEDING
AVAILABLE WITH/BY        *41 A :     BKCHCNBJ92A
                                    *BANK OF CHINA
                                    *NINGBO
                                    *(NINGBO BRANCH)
                                     BY DEF PAYMENT
DEFERRED PAYM. DET.       42 P :     AT 360 FROM B/L DATE
PARTIAL SHIPMENTS         43 P :     NOT ALLOWED
TRANSHIPMENT              43 T :     NOT ALLOWED
PORT OF LOADING           44 E :
                                     NINGBO PORT CHINA
PORT OF DISCHARGE         44 F :
                                     LATTAKIA PORT SYRIA BY VESSEL
LATEST DATE OF SHIP.      44 C :     081018
DESCRIPT. OF GOODS        45 A :
                                     ONE SET PVC PLASTIC INJECTION MOLDING MACHINES INCLUDING AUTO
                                     LOADER AND HOPPER DRYER FOR PCV POWDER MATERIAL
                                     DETAILS AS PER PROFORMA INVOICE DATED 12/05/2003
                                     FOB NINGBO PORT - SYRIA BY VESSEL
DOCUMENTS REQUIRED        46 A :
                                     1 - SIGNED BENEFICIARY'S COMMERCIAL INVOICES IN ONE ORIGINAL AND
                                     3 COPIES CERTIFIED BY CCPIT IN CHINA AND BEARING THE FOLLOWING
                                     DECLARATIONS:
                                     A- WE CERTIFY THAT THIS INVOICE IS AUTHENTIC, AND IS THE ONLY
                                     INVOICE ISSUED BY US FOR THE GOODS, HEREIN DESCRIBED, MENTIONING
                                     EXACT VALUE OF THE SAID GOODS, WITHOUT ANY DEDUCTION OF PAYMENTS
                                     IN ADVANCE, AND THAT THE ORIGIN OF THE GOODS IS CHINA AND THE
                                     COMMERCIAL INVOICE MUST BE MADE OUT IN THE NAME OF L/C APPLICANT.
                                     B- WE CERTIFY THAT RAW MATERIALS WHICH HAVE BEEN USED FOR THE
```

PRODUCTION OR PREPARATION OF THE GOODS MENTIONED IN THIS INVOICE ARE PURE OF CHINESE ORIGIN..
C - WE HEREBY CERTIFY THAT THE GOODS SHIPPED ACCORDING TO THIS INVOICE ARE IN CONFORMITY WITH PROFORMA INVOICE DATED 22/05/2008
2 - CERTIFICATE OF ORIGIN IN ONE ORIGINAL AND THREE COPIES ISSUED OR CERTIFIED BY CCPIT IN CHINA TO THE EFFECT THAT THE GOODS UNDER EXPORT ARE OF CHINESE ORIGIN AND THAT SAID CERTIFICATE SHOULD SHOW THE NAME OF FACTORY OR PRODUCER OF SUCH GOODS.
3 - FULL SET OF CLEAN ON BOARD MARINE BILLS OF LADING MADE OUT OR ENDORSED TO THE ORDER OF THE INTERNATIONAL BANK FOR TRADE AND FINANCE SHOWING FREIGHT PAYABLE AT DISTENATION AND MARKED NOTIFY BUYERS AND INDICATING NAME AND ADDRESS OF THE SHIPPING COMPANY'S AGENT IN SYRIA.
4 - PACKING LIST IN ONE ORIGINAL AND 3 COPIES
5 - CERTIFICATE OF WEIGHT IN ONE ORIGINAL AND 3 COPIES.
6 - CERTIFICATE ISSUED BY THE OWNER AGENT OR MASTER OF THE VESSEL CARRYING THE GOODS, ATTESTING THAT THIS VESSEL IS NOT BANNED ENTRY TO SYRIAN PORTS FOR ANY REASON WHATSOEVER ACCORDING TO SYRIAN LAWS AND REGULATIONS.
7 - CERTIFICATE ISSUED, SIGNED AND STAMPED BY THE OWNER CARRIERS, MASTER, CHARTERER OR AGENT OF THE VESSEL CERTIFYING THAT THE CARRYING VESSEL IS SUBJECT TO INTERNATIONAL SAFETY MANAGEMENT CODE (ISM) CARRIES VALID SAFETY MANAGEMENT CERTIFICATE (SMC) AND DOCUMENT OF COMPLIANCE (DOC) FOR THE PURPOSE OF PRESENTING THEM TO THE PORT AUTHORITIES.
8 - CERTIFICATE ISSUED BY THE MASTER OR THE CARRIER OWNER OR THE AGENT CERTIFYING THAT THE CARRYING VESSEL INDICATED IN THE B/L IS CLASSIFIED AND NOT OVER AGE.
9 - CERTIFICATE ISSUED BY THE BENEFICIARIES INDICATING THAT THE GOODS ARE BRAND NEW AND IN CONFORMITY WITH THE CREDIT.
10 - A DECLARATION ISSUED BY BENEFICIARY STATING THAT
WE DECLARE UNDER OUR OWN RESPONSIBILITY THAT WE ARE NOT REPRESENTED FOR SYRIA AND THAT SYRIA IS NOT INCLUDED IN THE TERRITORY OF ANY OTHER AGENT WHO WOULD BENEFIT FROM ANY COMMISSION WHATEVER IN OUR PRODUCTS IMPORTED INTO SYRIA.

ADDITIONAL COND.   47 A :
1 - ALL DOCUMENTS SHOULD BE DATED AND INDICATE THIS L/C NUMBER AND THE INTERNATIONAL BANK FOR TRADE AND FINANCE NAME AND ISSUANCE DATE.
2 - NEGOTIATION OF DOCUMENTS UNDER RESERVE/GUARANTEE IS NOT ACCEPTABLE.
3 - DOCUMENTS BEARING DATE OF ISSUANCE PRIOR TO THAT OF THIS CREDIT ARE NOT ACCEPTABLE.
4 - ALL DOCUMENTS SHOULD BE ISSUED IN ENGLISH LANGUAGE.
5 - THIRD PARTY DOCUMENTS ARE NOT ACCEPTABLE.
6 - SHORT FORM B/L IS NOT ACCEPTABLE.
7 - FREIGHT FORWARDER TRANSPORT DOCUMENT IS NOT ACCEPTABLE.
8 - A FLAT FEE FOR USD 70.- OR EQUIVALENT WILL BE DEDUCTED FROM EACH SET OF DISCREPANT DOCUMENTS AS DISCREPANCY FEES.
9 - L/C AMOUNT TO READ: NOT EXCEEDING USD TWENTY SEVEN THOUSAND FIVE HUNDRED.
10 - REIMBURSEMENT IS SUBJECT TO URR 525.
11 - THIS CREDIT IS SUBJECT TO THE UNIFORM CUSTOMS AND PRACTICE FOR COMMERCIAL DOCUMENTARY CREDITS FIXED BY THE INTERNATIONAL CHAMBER OF COMMERCE - PUBLICATION NO. 600.
12 - NVOCC (NON VESSEL OPERATING COMMON CARRIER) B/L IS NOT ACCEPTABLE.
13 - B/L SHOWING 'ON BEHALF OF THE CARRIER' OR 'AS CARRIER' INSTEAD OF 'CARRIER' OR 'THE CARRIER' ARE NOT ACCEPTABLE.
14 - B/L MUST BE ISSUED ON THE HEADING PAPER OF THE CARRIER

```
  TELEX                                              LOGICAL TERMINAL  SI71
 0370027 08:03:15          ISSUE OF A DOCUMENTARY CREDIT    PAGE 00003
S700                                                        FUNC ZJNBBFRQ
                                                            UMR  37264976
        HIMSELF.
        14 - BENEFICIARY TO BE INDICATED AS SHIPPER IN ALL DOCUMENTS.
        15 - SENDING DOCUMENTS IN TRUST, APPROVAL OR COLLECTION BASIS
        WITHOUT INDICATING THE DISCREPANCIES IS STRICTLY PROHIBITED.
DETAILS OF CHARGES   71 B : ALL BANKS CHARGES AND COMMISSIONS
                            OUTSIDE SYRIA INCLUDING REIMB. AND
                            PMT. TRANSFER CHARGES ARE ON
                            BENEFICIARY'S A/C.
CONFIRMATION          *49 : WITHOUT
INSTRUCTIONS          78
        A- PLS FORWARD TO THE INTERNATIONAL BANK FOR TRADE AND FINANCE,
        HEAD OFFICE BLDG, PAKISTAN STREET P. O. BOX 11058 DAMASCUS - SYRIA
        THE NEGOTIATED SET OF DOCUMENTS BY FAST COURIER AND THE DUPLICATE
        SET BY REGISTERED AIRMAIL IN STRICT CONFORMITY WITH L/C TERMS AND
        CONDITIONS.
        B- UPON RECEIVING THE COMPLYING DOCS AT YOUR COUNTER AND AT
        MATURITY DATE, WE WILL REIMBURSE YOU FOR THE INVOICE VALUE AS PER
        YOUR INSTRUCTIONS MENTIONED IN YOUR COVERING SCHEDULE PROVIDED
        THAT WE MUST RECEIVE YOUR SWIFT MSG ADVISE 5 WORKING DAYS BEFORE
        MATURITY.
TRAILER         ORDER IS (MAC: 2 (REF: 2 (ENC) (CHK) (TNG) (PDE: 5
                MAC: F3922B4F
                CHK: DE4ED1640961
```

发票（例）：

COMMERCIAL INVOICE

Buyers:	Shipping Marks & Numbers:
RATEB KHADEM AL JAME SONS COMPANY. DAMASCUS, SYRIA TEL: +963118835835 FAX: +963118825510	N/M

Invoice Number:	2008-1259	Date:	OCT.21.2008
From:	NINGBO PORT-CHINA	L/C No.:	OLC 601/21/08/93
To:	LATTAKIA PORT SYRIA	Payment:	

Descriptions	Q'ty	Unit Price	Amount
ONE SET PVC PLASTIC INJECTION MOLDING MACHINES INCLUDING AUTO LOADER AND HOPPER DRYER FOR PCV POWDER MATERIAL SA1600/600 DETAILS AS PER PROFORMA INVOICE DATED 12/05/2008 A- WE CERTIFY THAT THIS INVOICE IS AUTHENTIC, AND IS THE ONLY INVOICE ISSUED BY US FOR THE GOODS, HEREIN DESCRIBED, MENTIONING EXACT VALUE OF THE SAID GOODS, WITHOUT ANY DEDUCTION OF PAYMENTS IN ADVANCE, AND THAT THE ORIGIN OF THE GOODS IS CHINA AND THE COMMERCIAL INVOICE IS MADE OUT IN THE NAME OF L/C APPLICANT. B- WE CERTIFY THAT RAW MATERIALS WHICH HAVE BEEN USED FOR THE PRODUCTION OR PREPARATION OF THE GOODS MENTIONED IN THIS INVOICE ARE PURE OF CHINESE ORIGIN. C-WE HEREBY CERTIFY THAT THE GOODS SHIPPED ACCORDING TO THIS INVOICE ARE IN CONFORMITY WITH PROFORMA INVOICE DATED 12/05/2008 L/C NUMBER: OLC 601/21/08/93 INTERNATIONAL BANK FOR TRADE AND FINANCE ISSUANCE DATE: 080828 SHIPPER: PROCESSING ZONE NINGBO CHINA, ZIP CODE:315800 TEL: FAX:	1 SET	FOB NINGBO PORT-SYRIA BY VESSEL	

Authorized Signature

装箱单（例）：

PACKING LIST					
Buyers: RATEB KHADEM AL JAME SONS COMPANY. DAMASCUS, SYRIA TEL: +963118835835 FAX: +963118825510			Shipping Marks &Numbers: N/M		
Invoice Number: 2008-1259			Date: OCT.21,2008		
From: NINGBO PORT-CHINA			L/C No.: OLC 601/21/08/93		
To: LATTAKIA PORT SYRIA			Payment:		
Descriptions	Q'ty	PACKING	G.W.	N.W.	DIMENSION
ONE SET PVC PLASTIC INJECTION MOLDING MACHINES INCLUDING AUTO LOADER AND HOPPER DRYER FOR PCV POWDER MATERIAL SA1600/600 DETAILS AS PER PROFORMA INVOICE DATED 12/05/2008 L/C NUMBER: OLC 601/21/08/93 INTERNATIONAL BANK FOR TRADE AND FINANCE ISSUANCE DATE: 080828 SHIPPER: /28307208093014 NINGBO CHINA, ZIP CODE:315800 TEL:	1 SET	3 PALLETS	5800KGS	5600KGS	15CBM

Authorized Signature

重量单（例）：

CERTIFICATE OF WEIGHT					
Buyers: RATEB KHADEM AL JAME SONS COMPANY. DAMASCUS, SYRIA TEL: +963118835835 FAX: +963118825510			Shipping Marks &Numbers: N/M		
Invoice Number: 2008-1259			Date: OCT.21,2008		
From: NINGBO PORT-CHINA			L/C No.: OLC 601/21/08/93		
To: LATTAKIA PORT SYRIA			Payment:		
Descriptions	Q'ty	PACKING	G.W.	N.W.	
ONE SET PVC PLASTIC INJECTION MOLDING MACHINES INCLUDING AUTO LOADER AND HOPPER DRYER FOR PCV POWDER MATERIAL SA1600/600 DETAILS AS PER PROFORMA INVOICE DATED 12/05/2008 L/C NUMBER: OLC 601/21/08/93 INTERNATIONAL BANK FOR TRADE AND FINANCE ISSUANCE DATE: 080828 SHIPPER: /28307208093014 NINGBO ...OCESSING ZONE NINGBO CHINA, ZIP CODE:315800 TEL: FAX:	1 SET	3 PALLETS	5800KGS	5600KGS	

Authorized Signature

提单（例）：

	NGBLTK10147
/28307208093014 MACHINERY CO LTD, EXPORT PROCESSING ZONE, NINGBO CHINA, ZIP CODE: 315800 TEL: FAX:	**GLOBAL LINES** OCEAN BILL OF LADING (For Combined Transport and Port to Port Shipment)

CONSIGNEE
TO THE ORDER OF THE INTERNATIONAL BANK FOR TRADE AND FINANCE

RECEIVED by the carrier the goods in apparent good order and condition except as otherwise noted the total number containers or other packages or units enumerated below for transportation form the place of receipt to the place of receipt, to the place of delivery subject to the terms and conditions hereof. One of the bills of lading must be surrendered duly endorsed in exchange for the goods, delivery order. Delivery of goods will only be made on payment of all freight and charges. On presentation of this document duly endorsed to the Carrier by or on behalf of the Holder of the Bill of Lading, the rights and liabilities arising in accordance with the terms and conditions hereof shall without prejudice to any rule of common law or statute rendering them binding on the Merchant become binding in all respects between the Carrier and the Holder of the Bill of Lading as though the contract evidenced hereby had been made between them.
IN WITNESS whereof the number of original Bill of Lading stated under have been signed, one of which being accomplished, the other(s) to be void.

NOTIFY PARTY
RATEB KHADEM AL JAME SONS COMPANY. DAMASCUS, SYRIA
TEL: +963118835835
FAX: +963118825510

PRE-CARRIAGE BY	PLACE OF RECEIPT	OVERSEA OFFICE OR DESTINATION PORT AGENT
	NINGBO	***ARABIAN CARGO GROUP - SYRIA LEVEL 1 - ARNOUS BLDG - SAEED KAHWAJI AVENUE - 29TH AYYAR STREET DAMASCUS - SYRIA TEL: 00963-11-2310020 FAX: 00963-
OCEAN VESSEL / VOYAGE NO. MSC COLOMBIA V. X844R	PORT OF LOADING NINGBO PORT-CHINA	
PORT OF DISCHARGE LATTAKIA PORT SYRIA	PLACE OF DELIVERY LATTAKIA PORT SYRIA	

MARKS & NUMBERS CONTAINER NUMBER, SEAL NUMBER	NUMBER AND KIND OF PACKAGES: DESCRIPTION OF GOODS	GROSS WEIGHT	MEASUREMENT
N/M	3 PALLETS	5800KGS	15CBM
	PLASTIC INJECTION MOLDING MACHINES INCLUDING AUTO LOADER AND HOPPER DRYER L/C NUMBER: OLC 601/21/08/93 INTERNATIONAL BANK FOR TRADE AND FINANCE ISSUANCE DATE: 080828 FREIGHT PAYBALE AT DISTENATION NAME AND ADDRESS OF THE SHIPPING COMPANY'S AGENT IN SYRIA: ***		
	ON BOARD 01		
MEDU3079980/5981899	SHIPPER'S LOAD COUNT & SEAL 1X20GP FCL CY-PO		

TOTAL NO. OF CONTAINER(S) OR PACKAGES (IN WORDS)	SAY THREE PALLETS ONLY				
Freight & Charges	PREPAID	COLLECT	NO. OF ORIGINAL THREE	FREIGHT PAYABLE AT	
FREIGHT COLLECT			PLACE OF ISSUE NINGBO	DATE OF ISSUE	
			SIGNED BY CHINA GLOBAL LINES LIMITED For and on behalf of CHINA GLOBAL LINES LIMITED 华洋航运有限公司		
Total Payment			AS AGENT FOR THE CARRIER GLOBAL LINES		

TERMS CONTINUES ON REVERSE SIDE HEREOF

产地证（例）：

	ORIGINAL	
1. Exporter: /28307208093014 MACHINERY CO LTD. EXPORT PROCESSING ZONE NINGBO, CHINA. ZIP CODE:315800 TEL: 8657486177242 FAX: 8657486221 8641725	Certificate No. **CCPIT 082286851** 08C3302A1261/00554 CERTIFICATE OF ORIGIN OF THE PEOPLE'S REPUBLIC OF CHINA	
2. Consignee: RATEB KHADEM AL JABE SONS COMPANY. DAMASCUS, SYRIA. TEL: +963118635835 FAX: +963118825510		
3. Means of transport and route: FROM NINGBO PORT-CHINA TO LATTAKIA PORT SYRIA BY VESSEL	5. For certifying authority use only. CHINA COUNCIL FOR THE PROMOTION OF INTERNATIONAL TRADE IS CHINA CHAMBER OF INTERNATIONAL COMMERCE	
4. Country/region of destination: SYRIAN ARAB REPUBLIC		

5. Marks and numbers	7. Number and kind of packages; description of goods	8. H.S.Code	9. Quantity G. WEIGHT	10. Number and date of invoices
N/M	ONE (1) SET OF PLASTIC INJECTION MOLDING MACHINES INCLUDING AUTO LOADER AND HOPPER DRYER WE HEREBY CERTIFY TO THE EFFECT THAT THE GOODS UNDER EXPORT ARE OF CHINESE ORIGIN. THE NAME OF FACTORY OR PRODUCER OF SUCH GOODS: MACHINERY CO. LTD. L/C NUMBER: OLC 601/21/08/93 INTERNATIONAL BANK FOR TRADE AND FINANCE ISSUANCE DATE: 080828 SHIPPER: /28307208093014 MACHINERY CO LTD. EXPORT PROCESSING ZONE NINGBO CHINA, ZIP CODE:315800 TEL: 8657486177242 FAX:8657486221 8641725	847710	5800KGS	2008-1259 OCT. 21, 2008

11. Declaration by the exporter: The undersigned hereby declares that the above details and statements are correct, that all the goods were produced in China and that they comply with the Rules of Origin of the People's Republic of China. NINGBO, CHINA OCT. 22, 2008 Place and date, signature and stamp of authorized signatory	12. Certification It is hereby certified that the declaration by the exporter is correct. (CHINA COUNCIL FOR THE PROMOTION OF INTERNATIONAL TRADE (NINGBO)) NINGBO, CHINA OCT. 22, 2008 Place and date, signature and stamp of certifying authority

熏蒸证明（例）：

中华人民共和国出入境检验检疫
ENTRY-EXIT INSPECTION AND QUARANTINE OF THE PEOPLE'S REPUBLIC OF CHINA

ORIGINAL

熏蒸／消毒证书
FUMIGATION/DISINFECTION CERTIFICATE

编号 No. 380021208003700

发货人名称及地址 Name and Address of Consignor	
收货人名称及地址 Name and Address of Consignee	IMPORTACIONES Y EXPORTACIONES PACIFIC LTDA.
品名 Description of Goods	WOODEN PALLET
产地 Place of Origin	NINGBO, CHINA
报检数量 Quantity Declared	2 PIECES
标记及号码 Mark & No.	N/M
启运地 Place of Despatch	NINGBO, CHINA
到达口岸 Port of Destination	VALPARAISO, CHILE
运输工具 Means of Conveyance	BY VESSEL

THE WOODEN PALLETS HAVE BEEN FUMIGATED BY METHYL BROMIDE 56G/M³ FOR 24HRS AT 16℃ FROM 6 TO 7 JUN, 2008.

＊　＊　＊　＊　＊　＊　＊

签证地点 Place of Issue: NINGBO
签证日期 Date of Issue: 8 OCT, 2008
授权签字人 Authorized Officer: WU YING
签名 Signature:

中华人民共和国出入境检验检疫机关及其官员或代表不承担签发本证书的任何责任。No financial liability with respect to this certificate shall attach to the entry-exit inspection and quarantine authorities of the P. R. of China or to any of its officers or representatives.

贸促会证明（例）：

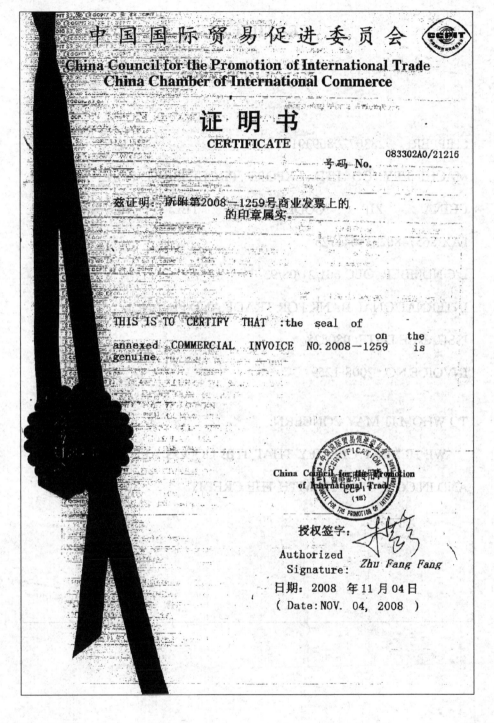

受益人证明（例）:

CERTIFICATE

DATE: OCT.21, 2008

SHIPPER: /28307208093014

MACHINERY CO LTD. EXPORT PROCESSING ZONE NINGBO CHINA, ZIP CODE:315800 TEL: 8657486177242

FAX: 86574862218641725

L/C NUMBER: OLC 601/21/08/93

INTERNATIONAL BANK FOR TRADE AND FINANCE

ISSUANCE DATE: 080828

INVOICE NO.: 2008-1259

TO WHOM IT MAY CONCERN:

　WE HEREBY CERTIFY THAT THE GOODS ARE BRAND NEW AND IN CONFORMITY WITH THE CREDIT.

船公司证明（例）：

SHIPPER: /28307208093014　　　　　　　　　　MACHINERY CO
LTD.EXPORT PROCESSING ZONE NINGBO CHINA, ZIP CODE:315800
TEL:　　　　　　FAX:8
L/C NUMBER: OLC 601/21/08/93
INTERNATIONAL BANK FOR TRADE AND FINANCE
ISSUANCE DATE: 080828
INVOICE NO.: 2008-1259

CERTIFICATE

DATE:2008-11-01

TO WHOM IT MAY CONCERN:

B/L NO.: NGBLTK10147

THE NAME OF THE VESSEL: MSC COLOMBIA V.X844R

　　WE HEREBY CERTIFY THAT THE CARRYING VESSEL IS SUBJECT TO INTERNATIONAL SAFETY MANAGEMENT CODE (ISM), CARRIES VALID SAFETY MANAGEMENT CERTIFICATE (SMC) AND DOCUMENT OF COMPLIANCE (DOC) FOR THE PURPOSE OF PRESENTING THEM TO THE PORT AUTHORITIES.

For and on behalf of
CHINA GLOBAL LINES LIMITED
华洋航运有限公司

　　　　　　　　　　　　　　　Authorized Signature(s)

受益人声明（例）：

DECLARATION

DATE: OCT.21,2008

SHIPPER: /28307208093014

MACHINERY CO LTD.EXPORT PROCESSING ZONE NINGBO CHINA, ZIP CODE:315800 TEL:

FAX:

L/C NUMBER: OLC 601/21/08/93

INTERNATIONAL BANK FOR TRADE AND FINANCE

ISSUANCE DATE: 080828

INVOICE NO.: 2008-1259

TO WHOM IT MAY CONCERN:

WE DECLARE UNDER OUR OWN RESPONSIBILITY THAT WE ARE NOT REPRESENTED FOR SYRIA AND THAT SYRIA IS NOT INCLUDED IN THE TERRITORY OF ANY OTHER AGENT WHO WOULD BENEFIT FROM ANY COMMISSION WHATEVER IN OUR PRODUCTS IMPORTED INTO SYRIA

Authorized Signature

相关知识

一、装运通知内容和缮制要点

装运通知（Shipping Advice），是发货人在货物装船并取得提单后，向买方或其指定的人发出的有关货物装运情况的说明。也称 Shipment Details，或 Shipment Declaration，或 Insurance Declaration。

在以 FOB 或 CFR 术语成交时，买方为方便向保险公司进行投保，往往要求装运通知。在以 CIF 或 CIP 价格成交时，收货人或买方要了解货物装运情况以便租订仓库、安排运输工具以做好接货的准备工作，或者筹措资金准备付款，此时也需要装运通知。

装运通知没有固定的格式，一般由发货人自行设计，主要内容包括：

（1）抬头：可以是买方，或者是买方指定的人或保险公司。若抬头为买方指定的保险公司，则应同时注明预保险单合同号（COVER NOTE）。

（2）日期：发送装运通知的日期，一般在货物装船后 3 天内。

（3）提单号及船名：与提单一致。

（4）预计开船日期和到达日期（ETD、ETA）：按船期表所列的日期。

（5）装运港、目的港、装运期：按合同或信用证的规定，一般与提单一致。

（6）商品描述部分：包括品名、唛头、数量、发票总值等。可以按商业发票的内容填写。

缮制装船通知应注意的事项有：

（1）CFR/CPT 交易条件下拍发装运通知的必要性。如漏发通知，则货物越过船舷后的风险仍由受益人承担。

（2）通知应按规定的方式、时间、内容、份数发出。通常以电报、电传、传真或电子邮件等方式发送。一般在装运后 3 天之内发出，若信用证或合同另有规定，还须按规定时间发出。常见的有以小时为准 Within 24/48 hours 和以天 within 2 days after shipment date 为准两种情形。信用证规定"Immediately after shipment"（装船后立即通知），应掌握在提单后三天之内。

（3）通知对象。应按信用证规定，具体讲可以是开证申请人、申请人的指定人或保险公司等。

（4）签署。一般可以不签署，如信用证要求"certified copy of shipping advice"，通常加盖受益人条形章。

（5）几个近似概念的区别。

- Shipping advice（装运通知）是由出口商（受益人）发给进口商（申请人）的。
- Shipping instructions 意思是"装运须知"，一般是进口商发给出口商的。
- Shipping note/ bill 指装货通知单/船货清单。
- Shipping order 简称 S/O，含义是装货单/关单/下货纸（是海关放行和命令船方将单据上载明的货物装船的文件）。
- Delivery note 是提货单/交货单/送货单的意思。

（6）L/C 中有关装运条款举例：

①Original fax from beneficiary to our applicant evidencing B/L number, name of ship, shipment date, quantity and value of goods.

②Shipment advice with full details including shipping marks, carton numbers, vessel's name,

B/L number, value and quantity of goods must be sent to us on the date of shipment.

二、受益人证明等证明类文件的内容和制作

常见的证明有：

（1）受益人（履行义务、完成工作）证明。

（2）船公司（有关运输方面的）证明。

（3）寄单证明。

（一）受益人证明

受益人证明（Beneficiary's Certificate），或称受益人声明（Beneficiary's Statement），可证明自己已经履行了合同义务，或者证明自己已按要求办理了某事，或证实某件事情，并达到了进口商的要求或进口国的有关规定等。

受益人证明没有固定格式，主要内容如下：

（1）受益人公司名称、地址。

（2）单据名称和出证日期。

（3）相关参考号码，如发票号码、信用证号码。

（4）证明内容（We hereby certify that…）。

（5）受益人公司签字盖章（SIGNATURE）。

信用证条款举例：

（1）Beneficiary's certificate certifies that the carrying steamer is not a blacklisted ship nor of Israeli nationality and she is not scheduled to call at any Israeli ports.

（2）Beneficiary's certificate certifies that shipped goods have kept the size with 400×400×200 (mm) tiles, dimensional tolerance + or －1 mm, diagonal tolerance + or －1 mm, thickness + or －1 mm.

（3）The following documents should be sent directly to applicant by registered airmail: 2 sets of typed and signed non-negotiable shipping documents including original Certificate of Origin. Beneficiary's certificate is required to certify that effect.

（4）Shipment samples should be sent to the nominees by registered airmail in compliance with the terms of the relative Letter of Credit. Beneficiary's certificate is required to certify that effect.

（二）船公司证明

船公司证明（Shipping Company's Certificate）系信用证受益人应开证申请人的要求，请船公司出具的不同认定内容的证明。

（1）黑名单证明。

（2）航程证明（Itinerary Certificate）。

（3）船长收据（Master's/Captain's Receipt）。

（4）集装箱船只证明。

（5）船龄以及船级证明。

（6）运费证明。

（三）寄单证明

1. 由出口公司或受益人出具的寄单证明

受益人按信用证规定将有关单据寄出后，根据信用证要求出具的说明寄单情况的单据。

一般包括所寄单据的名称、份数、寄出时间、寄送方式和寄送对象等。

2. 邮寄收据

有时信用证除要求受益人出具寄单证明外,还要求随附办理邮局或快递公司承办的收据,即邮寄收据。

如信用证条款:

ORIGINAL BENEFICIARY'S SIGNED LETTER/CERTIFICATE TOGETHER WITH THE COURIERS RECEIPT CERTIFYING THAT THE FULL SET OF ORIGINAL DOCUMENTS HAVE BEEN SENT TO XXX CO. BY AIRMAIL/DHL/SPEED POST 3 DAYS AFTER B/L DATE.

(四)其他证明

(1)寄样证明(Beneficiary's Certificate for Dispatch of Shipment Sample)。

(2)借记通知单(Debit Note)。

(3)扣佣通知书。

(4)包装、唛头方面的证明。

(5)出口地无领事证明等。

实训练习题

根据交易信息制作装船通知和受益人证明

```
BASIC HEADER F 01 BKCHCNBJA5XX 9828 707783
APPL. HEADER O 700 1917000731 NOSCCATTAXXX 3775 931472 0008010718 N
                    + BANK OF NOVA SCOTIA, TORONTO, CANADA
(BANK NO: 8015000)  + TORONTO, ONTARIO, CANADA


MT700 ------------------- ISSUE OF A DOCUMENTARY CREDIT -------------------

SEQUENCE OF TOTAL              27: 1/1
FORM OF DOCUMENTARY CREDIT     40A: IRREVOCABLE TRANSFERABLE
DOCUMENTARY CREDIT NUMBER      20: I01800/146791
DATE OF ISSUE                  31C: 000731
DATE AND PLACE OF EXPIRY       31D: 000915 CHINA
APPLICANT                      50: WENSCO FOODS LTD. ,
                                   1191 GREEN LAND STREET,
                                   WELL D. COQUITLAM, B. C. ,
                                   CANADA, V3K 5Z1
BENEFICIARY                    59: HUANGHAI CEREALS, OILS AND
                                   FOODSTUFFS IMP. AND EXP. CORP.
                                   NO. 7 HEPING ROAD
                                   QINGDAO, CHINA
CURRENCY CODE, AMOUNT          32B: USD10, 830.00
MAXIMUM CREDIT AMOUNT          39B: NOT EXCEEDING
```

AVAILABLE WITH…BY…	41D:	ANY BANK
		BY NEGOTIATION
DRAFTS AT…	42C:	DRAFTS AT 75 DAYS AFTER BILL OF LADING DAFT FOR 100 PERCENT OF INVOICE VALUE
DRAWEE	42D:	THE BANK OF NOVA SCOTIA, 650 WEST GEORGIA ST. , PO BOX 11502, VANCOUVER, B. C. , CANADA V6B 4P6
PARTIAL SHIPMENT	43P:	ALLOWED
TRANSHIPMENT	43T:	ALLOWED
LOADING/DISPATCH/TAKING IN CHARGE/FM	44A:	SHIPMENT FROM NINGBO, CHINA
FOR TRANSPORTATION TO…	44B:	TO VANCOUVER, B. C. , CANADA
LATEST DATE OF SHIPMENT	44C:	000831
DESCRIPTION OF GOODS/SERVICES	45A:	

EVIDENCING SHIPMENT OF
P. O. NO. 2027
950 CARTONS TROPIC ISLE CANNED MANDARIN ORANGES LS-WHOLE SEGMENTS 6/2. 84KG AT USD11. 40 PER CARTON.
FREE ON BOARD NINGBO, CHINA.

DOCUMENTS REQUIRED: 46A:
- SIGNED COMMERCIAL INVOICE IN TRIPLICATE.
- CANADA CUSTOMS INVOICE IN QUADRUPLICATE FULLY COMPLETED.
- IMPORT DECLARATION IN TRIPLICATE.
- CERTIFICATE OF ORIGIN FORM "A" IN TRIPLICATE.
- BENEFICIARY'S LETTER OF GUARANTEE STATING THEY WILL REIMBURSE LAA EXPENSES IN CASE OF REJECTION BY CANADIAN FOOD INSPECTION AGENCY IN TRIPLICATE.
- SHIPMENT ADVICE
- BENEFICIARY CERTIFICATE IN TRIPLICATE STATING
1. THE SHIPMENT DOES NOT INCLUDE NON – MANUFACTURED WOOD DUNNAGE, PALLETS, CRATING OR OTHER PACKAGING MATERIALS.
2. THE SHIPMENT IS COMPLETELY FREE OF WOOD BARK, VISIBLE PESTS AND SIGNS OF LIVING PESTS.
- FULL SET OF CLEAN "ON BOARD" OCEAN BILL OF LADING TO THE ORDER OF THE BANK OF NOVA SCOTIA MARKED "FREIGHT COLLECT" AND "NOTIFY WENSCO FOODS LTD. , 1191 GREEN LAND STREET, WELL D. COQUITLAM, B. C. , CANADA, V3K 5Z1. "

ADDITIONAL CONDITIONS 47A:
INSURANCE COVERED BY APPLICANT
THIS LETTER OF CREDIT IS TRANSFERABLE IF TRANSFERRED, THE DRAFT MUST BE ACCOMPANIED BY A LETTER BY THE BANK EFFECTING THE TRANSFER STATING THE NAME OF THE TRANSFEREE AND THAT THIS CREDIT HAS BEEN TRANSFERRED.

THE ADVISING BANK IS THE DESIGNATED TRANSFERRING BANK.
THIRD PARTY DOCUMENTS ARE ACCEPTABLE ONLY IF L|C IS TRANSFERRED.
AMENDMENT CHARGES (IF ANY) WILL BE FOR THE BENEFICIARY'S ACCOUNT IF THE CAUSE OF AMENDMENT OCCURRED FROM THE BENEFICIARY'S SIDE.
IT IS A CONDITION OF THIS LETTER OF CREDIT THAT PAYMENY WILL BE EFFECTED AT MATURITY BUT ONLY UPON RECEIPT OF WRITTEN NOTIFICATION FROM THE BUYER STATING THAT GOODS HAVE PASSED CANADIAND AUTHORITIES INSPECTION. THE REMITTING BANK|NEGOTIATING BANK MUST INDICATE ON THEIR LETTER TO SCOTIABANK THAT ALL DOCUMENTS MUST BE DELIVERED TO THE APPLICANT AGAINST A TRUE RECEIPT IN ORDER TO OBTAIN CLEARANCE OF MERCHANDISE TO SECURE INSPECTION BY CANADIAN AUTHORITIES.
PAYMENT/ACCEPTANCE OF DRAFTS WILL ONLY BE MADE AFTER RECEIPT OF WRITTEN ADVICE FROM THE APPLICANT STATION THAT THE MERCHANDISE HAS PASSED INSPECTION AND HAS BEEN RELEASED FOR SALE IN CANADA BY THE CANADIAN AUTHORITIES.
IF THE GOODS DO NOT PASS INSPECTION, THEN NOTICE TO THIS EFFECT MUST BE GIVEN IN WRITING BY THE CANADIAN AUTHORITIES WHO MUST PRESENT SAME TO SCOTIABANK UPON RECEIPT OF THE REJECTION NOTICE, THE NEGOTING BANK/REMITTING BANK WILL BE ADVISED ACCORDINGLY AND SCOTIABANK'S LIABILITY WILL BECOME NULL AND VOID.
PLEASE DIRECT ALL ENQUIRIES AND FORWARD DOCUMENTS IN ONE LOT (VIA COURIER) TO THE BANK OF NOVA SCOTIA, VANCOUVER INTERNATIONAL TRADE SERVICESK MALL LEVEL, 650 WEST GEORGIA STREET, VANCOUVER, B. C., CANADA V5B 4P6.
A DISCREPANCY HANDLING FEE OF USD45.00 WILL BE ASSESSED BY THE BANK OF NOVA SCOTIA ON EACH PRESENTATION OF DOCUMENTS NOT IN STRICT COMPLIANCE WITH THE TERMS AND CONDITIONS OF THE CREDIT.
THIS FEE IS FOR THE ACCOUNT OF THE BENEFICIARY AND WILL BE DEDUCTED FROM THE PROCEEDS WHEN PAYMENT IS EFFECTED, IN ADDITION TO ANY OUT OF POCKET EXPENSES INCURRED BY THE BANK OF NOVA SCOTIA IN THIS CONNECTION.
THIS IS THE OPERATIVE INSTRUMENT.
DRAFT (S) MUST INDICATE THE NUMBER AND DATE OF THIS CREDIT.
CHARGES   71B: ISSUING BANK CHARGES ARE FOR THE ACCOUNT OF THE APPLICANT. ALL OTHER BANKING CHARGES INCLUDING REIMBURSEMENT BANK CHARGES ARE FOR THE BENEFICIARY'S ACCOUNT
PERIOD FOR PRESENTATIONS 48: DOCUMENTS MUST BE PRESENTED FOR NEGOTIATION WITHIN 10 DAYS AFTER BILL OF LADING DATE, BUT WITHIN THE VALIDITY OF THIS CREDIT.
CONFIRMATION INSTRUCTION   49: WITHOUT
TRAILER
   MAC: BA00E6EA CHK: 9E5503EE1810
NNNN

参考资料:

(1) Commodity: 950 CARTONS TROPIC ISLE CANNED MANDARIN ORANGES LS-WHOLE SEGMENTS 6/2.84KG。

(2) Unit Price: AT USD11.40 PER CARTON。
(3) Trade terms: FOB NINGBO, CHINA。
(4) Container No. 00631。
(5) Shipped by S.S Beauty V23 B/L No. 200318。
(6) Invoice No. CMO234。

SHIPPING ADVICE

致:
TO:

Invoice No.

Date:

Sales Contract No.

装由 Shipped per S. S.	装船口岸 From	目的地 To	约于 On or about

唛头 Mark and Nos.	数量及品名 Quantities and Descriptions	总价 Amount

ISSUER	BENEFICIARY'S CERTIFICATE	
TO	INVOICE NO.	DATE

第二节 汇票

教学目标

最终目标：能根据贸易信息制作汇票。

促成目标：

1. 理解汇票的分类、作用、内容。
2. 熟悉《UCP600》中关于汇票的条款。
3. 能够制作汇票。

情景案例

机构：
外贸企业：宁波欧胜塑化有限公司（OCEAN PLASTIC & CHEMICAL PRODUCTS CO., LTD）。
人物：
小余：宁波欧胜塑化有限公司单证员。
张经理：宁波欧胜塑化有限公司业务经理。
背景资料：
（1）2016年11月6日，宁波欧胜塑化有限公司外贸业务部张经理与阿拉伯联合酋长国的公司 ABC TRADING CO., LLC 签订一份36 800支唇膏（LIP BALM）的出口合同，合同号为081106。
（2）2017年1月22日，小余在办公室制作用于议付的汇票一式两份。

汇票（例）：

```
凭                                              信用证
Drawn under _____                     L/C No. _____

日期
Dated _____ 支取 Payable with interest @ ____% 按____息____付款

号码          汇票金额                                                    20
No. _____  Exchange for _____ NING BO _____ 20___

见票              日后（本汇票之副本未付）付交                 金额
At _____ sight of this FIRST of Exchange (Second of Exchange
being unPaid) Pay to the order of                          the sum of
_____

款已收讫
Value received _____

此致:
To _____
```

BILL OF EXCHANGE

```
凭                                              信用证
Drawn under    HSBC BANK, DUBAI, UAE            L/C NO.  HSBC657708467464

日期
Dated   Dec. 8th, 2016    支取 Payable with interest @ .....%.....按.....息.....付款

号码          汇票金额                           宁波
NO  09OS002  Exchange for USD11,040.00          NINGBO  Jan. 22nd,  2017

见票            日后（本汇票之正本未付）付交
At   XXX _____ sight of this SECOND of Exchange (First of Exchange
being unpaid) Pay to the order of  SHANGHAI PUDONG DEVELOPMENT BANK, NINGBO  the sum of
SAY U.S. DOLLARS ELEVEN THOUSAND AND FORTY ONLY

款已收讫
Value received     36800 PCS OF LIP BALM

此致:
To    HSBC BANK, DUBAI, UAE               OCEAN PLASTIC & CHEMICAL
                                          PRODUCTS CO., LTD
```

相关知识

一、汇票定义和分类

《英国票据法》规定，汇票（Bills of Exchange or Draft）是一人向另一人签发的，要求

即期或定期或在可以确定的将来的时间，对某人或其指定人或持票人支付一定数额金钱的无条件的书面支付委托。

1. 汇票的种类
（1）按照付款时间不同分为即期汇票、远期汇票。
（2）按照是否记载权利人分为记名汇票、无记名汇票。
（3）按照汇票流通区域不同分为国内汇票、国际汇票。
（4）按照出票人的不同分为商业汇票、银行汇票。
（5）以汇票是否跟随单据分为跟单汇票、光票。

2. 汇票当事人及其权利责任
尚未进入流通领域的基本当事人：
（1）出票人（Drawer）。
（2）付款人（Drawee）。

3. 收款人（Payee）
进入流通领域后的当事人：
（1）背书人（Indorser）。
（2）被背书人（Indorsee）。
（3）参加承兑人（Acceptor for Honour）。
（4）保证人（Guarantor）。
（5）正当持票人（Holder in Due Course）。

二、汇票的制作要点

1. 汇票的基本要点
汇票制作没有规定的格式，一般的汇票有以下 10 个基本要点：
（1）"汇票"的字样。
（2）无条件支付的委托。
（3）一定金额。
（4）出票日期。
（5）出票地点。
（6）出票人签名。
（7）付款时间。
（8）付款地点。
（9）付款人姓名。
（10）收款人或其指定人。
如果是信用证项下，还需有：
（1）开证行名称。
（2）信用证号码。
（3）开证日期。

2. 注意事项
（1）汇票的付款人名称、地址是否正确。

（2）汇票上金额的大、小写必须一致。

（3）付款期限要符合信用证或合同（非信用证付款条件下）的规定。

（4）检查汇票金额是否超出信用证金额，如果信用证金额前有"大约"一词，则可按10%的增减幅度掌握。

（5）出票人、受款人、付款人都必须符合信用证或合同（非信用证付款条件下）的规定。

（6）币制名称应与信用证、发票上的一致。

（7）出票条款是否正确，如出票所根据的信用证或合同号码是否正确，是否按需要进行了背书。

（8）汇票是否由出票人进行了签字。

（9）汇票份数是否正确，如"只此一张"或"汇票一式二份，有第一汇票和第二汇票"。

实训练习题

请根据第一小节实训练习题信息，制作一份汇票

```
                        BILL OF EXCHANGE
凭                                                  信用证
Drawn under……………………………………………………………L/C NO.……………………
日期
Dated……………………………支取 Payable with interest @ …… % ……按……息……付款
号码        汇票金额              宁波
NO………Exchange for                   NINGBO…………20…………
见票              日后（本汇票之正本未付）付交
At …………………sight of this FIRST of Exchange (Second of Exchange
being unpaid) Pay to the order of            the sum of


款已收讫
Value received …………………………………………………………………………………
……………………………………………………………………………………………………
此致：
To ………………………………………………………………
   ……………………………………………………………………
```

第九章

寄单和交单议付

第一节　电汇方式下单据的寄送

教学目标

在电汇方式下，能根据贸易信息制作全套结汇单据。

情景案例

机构：
外贸企业：宁波保税区益友国际贸易有限公司。
人物：
小李：宁波保税区益友国际贸易有限公司单证员。
郑经理：宁波保税区益友国际贸易有限公司业务经理。
背景资料：
（1）2016年2月13日，宁波保税区益友国际贸易有限公司外贸业务部郑经理与墨西哥某公司签订一份400个标价机（PRICE LABELER）的出口合同。
（2）小李在办公室制作、补齐、整理客户清关用单据：发票、装箱单、航空运单等。

形式发票（例）：

NINGBO FREE TRADE ZONE YEAYOO IND'L & INT'L TRADING CO., LTD.

RM 709, LIUTING STAR BUSINESS MANSION, NO. 299-22, CANGSONG RD.,
NINGBO CHINA 315012
TEL: +86-574-87160701   FAX: +86-574-87160702

PROFORMA INVOICE

TO: Simarc
Geranio 272-A
Colonia Santa Maria Insurgentes
Codigo Postal: 06430
Delegación: Cuahutemoc
México, D.F.

NO.: VNO29006R
DATE: FEB 13 2009

PORT OF LOADING: NINGBO, CHINA   PORT OF DESTINATION: MEXICO

ITEM	NAME OF COMMODITY & SPECIFICATION	QUANTITY	UNIT PRICE	AMOUNT
			FOB NINGBO	
1	PRICE LABELER			
84-444006	8 DIGITS, RED	200 PC	@ USD 1.275	USD 255.000
84-444006	8 DIGITS, BLUE	200 PC	@ USD 1.275	USD 255.000
			SUB TOTAL:	USD 510.00
	AIR FREIGHT CHARGE FROM NINGBO TO MEXICO CITY			USD 1150.00
	TOTAL:			USD 1660.00
	MADE IN CHINA			

TOTAL SAY U.S. DOLLARS ONE THOUSAND SIX HUNDRED AND SIXTY ONLY.

宁波保税区益友国际贸易有限公司
FREE TRADE ZONE YEAYOO IND'L & INT'L TRADING CO.,LTD.

购销合同（例）：

工矿产品购销合同(编号 VNO29006) 合同签约地：宁波

供方：*******制品有限公司　　　　　(TEL: 0579-856***88　FAX: 0579-856***31)
需方：宁波保税区益友国际贸易有限公司　(TEL: 0574-87160701　FAX: 0574-87160702)

一、产品名称、规格及型号、数量、单价及总金额：

名称	客编号	工厂编号	数量	单价（含税含运费到宁波北仑仓库）	金额
标价机	84-444006	W-550 ES	1000个/30箱 500个红色，500个蓝色	3.200	3200.00
单色装入外箱，红色5箱，蓝色5箱			共10箱	总金额：3200.00	

总金额：人民币叁仟贰佰元整。(RMB3200.00)

二、交货时间、地点、方式：2009年3月5日前一次交清，货送上海指定外贸仓，交货前由需方提供详细进仓地址（方式；汽车运输）运费由供方负担。

　　三、包装要求：按工厂标准的MOTEX彩盒包装（跟VNO29001合同一样），其中W-550 ES（用新料做的）中的链条根据需方要求（工厂有模具的）；机器内装一国产墨水，另外配一个国产墨水；包装上无工厂信息及中文文字，用透明封箱带加封（及加封外箱四周），且外箱也须用白色打包带包装。

四、唛头：　　　　　　侧唛：ITEM NO.：84-444006
　　　　　　　　　　　　　DESC.：PRICE LABELLER
　　　　　　　　　　　　　COLOR：BLUE /RED （根据实际颜色）
　　　　　　　　　　　　　QTY.：　50 PCS
　　　　　　　　　　　　　G.W.：　　KGS
　　　　　　　　　　　　　N.W.：　　KGS
　　　　　　　　　　　　　MEAS.：　x　　x　　CM

五、质量要求：1 产品大小符合工厂规格，质量按供方标准产品样品。2.出货前请速寄出货样一式2份（出货样不要从大货中取出）

六、供方产品质量保证期：1. 外商收货半年内，如发现由于质量原因部分或全部产品无法使用，可以将无法使用的产品退回，由需方负责清关后退给供方。供方需将原货款返回需方，并由供方承担因退货引起的海运费、保险费、理关费、国内运输费等费用。2.外商收货之日以货物离开中国港口40天后计算。

七、结算方式及期限：需方在收到供方回签合同；验货合格后；在收到供方正确的增值税发票在出货时将全部货款支付与供方。

八、违约责任：按国家相关法律规定，由违约方承担相应责任。

九、解决合同纠纷的方式：友好协商，协商不成，交由宁波仲裁委员会仲裁。

十、其他约定事项

供方：(签章)　　　　　　　　　　　需方：(签章)宁波保税区益友国际贸易有限公司
地址：　　　　　　　　　　　　　　地址：宁波市苍松路299弄22号709室
代理人：　　　　　　　　　　　　　代理人：
电话：　　　　　　　　　　　　　　电话：0574-87160701
传真：　　　　　　　　　　　　　　传真：0574-87160702
日期：2009年　　月　　日　　　　　日期：2009年2月10日

托运单（例）：

宁波保税区益友国际贸易有限公司			
托运人 NINGBO FREE TRADE ZONE YEAYOO IND'L & INT'L TRADING CO., LTD. TEL:+86 0574-87160701			出口货物托运单
收货人 SIMARC, Geranio 272-A Colonia Santa Maria Insurgentes Codigo Postal: 06430 Delegación: Cuauhtemoc México, D.F.			上海今自物流 联系人一：王小姐 电话：021-35307393 传真：021-35307398
通知人 SAME AS CONSIGNEE			托运单号 YEA0900305 委托日期 2009-3-5 合同号码 VN029006 信用证号 运输方式 BY AIR 是否转运 NO 是否分批 NO
一程船名		起运港	SHANGHAI, CHINA	装船日期
二程船名		转运港		海运费USD FREIGHT PREPAID
正本提单	3	目的港	MEXICO CITY	包干费RMB 0
副本提单	3	ETD		ETA
标志和号码	货品名称 || 件数及包装	毛重	体积
1	PRICE LABELER 标府机 HS: 9611000090 || 10CTNS	220KGS	1.15CBM
SHIPPING MARKS N/M			特约事项 航班时间： 2009-3-7 箱型/数量： 墨西哥航空 进仓或拖卡：进仓 1. 我司货物现已OK，请安排订舱

宁波保税区益友国际贸易有限公司
地址：宁波市海曙区柞松路299弄22号柳汀星座商务楼709室
电话：+86-574-87161352　传真：+86-574-87160702
联系人：牟丽君

（托运人签章）

航空运单（例）：

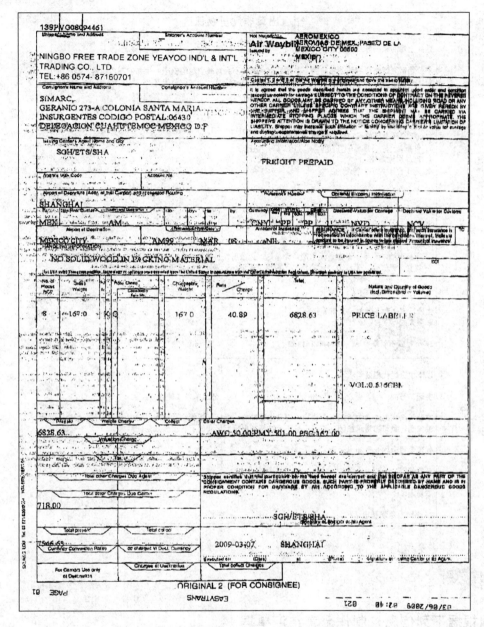

空运保函（例）：

空运出口非危货物保函

致：上海浦东国际机场货运站有限公司

本公司需通过航空运输下述货物，并保证下列货物不会对航空运输安全产生任何不良影响。特此声明无误。如有不符，我公司愿意承担因此引起的所有责任及一切法律后果。

1. 中文品名：标价机
   （需与海关报关单品名一致）
2. 英文品名：PRICE LABELER
   （需与航空运单或与其所附清单品名一致）
3. 件数：8 重量：176.0 目的港：MEX
4. 产品用途描述：
   用于打印数字，符号

5. 产品构成（制作材料及内含物质，需详细说明）：
   塑料制品，手动的标价机

本产品无油、无毒、无害、无电池，无马达，无放射性，无制冷剂，无氟利昂，无液体，无氧气发生装置，无气体，无压力，无酒精，无药物，无汞，无磁性，如有问题我司愿承担责任

生产厂家全称（须加盖公章）：
联系人：
24小时应急联系电话：0574-87161352   手机：13967833551

以下由空运代理公司填写：

主运单号：   分运单号（如有）：

本公司确认上述货主所托运之货物内容及描述准确，保证上述货物在空运过程中不会不利于航空运输安全。我司愿意承担因向浦东机场货运站不实申报所引起的所有责任及法律后果。

代理公司全称（须加盖公章）：
三字代码：
联系人：
24小时应急联系电话：   手机：

实训练习题

请根据下列信息，制作全套结汇单据

资料一：相关信息

(1) INVOICE NO：XD1234。
(2) PACKING：12 SETS TO ONE CARTON。
    G.W./N.W.：@8/7KG MEASUREMENT：@60X50X30（CM）。
(3) VESSEL NAME AND VOY. NO.：LONGSHEN V678。
    B/L ISSUED BY CHANGHAN SHIPPING AGENT 李运金。
(4) B/L NO.：COSCU06888。
(5) ON BOARD DATE：MAY 8，2008。

H. S. CODE: 6211339019。

资料二：外贸合同

SALES CONTRACT

(1) THE SELLERS:
OCEAN PLASTIC & CHEMICAL PRODUCTS CO., LTD

S/C NO. OPCP08008
DATE: MAR. 27, 2008

(2) ADDRESS: 1101 – 1105 SHANGDONG NATIONALS,
　　#1926 CANGHAI RD., NINGBO, 315041, CHINA
　　TEL: 0574 – ×××××××　FAX: 0574 – ×××××××
　　E – MAIL: Christina@163.com

(3) THE BUYERS: TONNY PRODUCTS PLC

(4) ADDRESS: BERSTOFSGADE 48, ROTTERDAM, THE NETHERLANDS
　　TEL: + (31) 74 12 37 08　FAX: + (31) 74 12 37 09
　　E – MAIL: chila@tvl.com.ntl

THE SELLERS AGREE TO SELL AND THE BUYERS AGREE TO BUY THE UNDERMENTIONED GOODS ACCORDING TO THE TERMS AND CONDITIONS AS STIPULATED BELOW

NAME OF COMMODITY & SPECIFICATION	QUANTITY	UNIT PRICE	TOTAL VALUE
JOGGING SUIT			CFRC3% AMSTERDAM
Art. No. KB5200	840 sets	EUR15.20	EUR12,768.00
Art. No. KP6300	600 sets	EUR12.50	EUR7,500.00
Art. No. KY5200	600 sets	EUR10.60	EUR6,360.00
TOTAL:	2,040 sets		EUR26,628.00

(5) PACKING:
PACKED IN CARTONS OF 12 SETS

(6) SHIPPING MARKS:
TONNY/XD06008/AMSTERDAM/NO. 1 – UP

(7) PORT OF SHIPMENT:
ANY CHINESE PORT

(8) PORT OF DESTINATION:
AMSTERDAM

(9) TIME OF SHIPMENT:
NOT LATER THAN MAY 31ST, 2008

(10) TERMS OF PAYMENT:
30% T/T IN ADVANCE, THE OTHERS 70% T/T AFTER SHIPMENT

(11) FORCE MAJEURE:
The Sellers shall not be held responsible if they, owing to Force Majeure causes, fail to make delivery within the time stipulated in the contract or can't deliver the goods. However, in such a case the Sellers shall inform the Buyers immediately by cable. The Sellers shall send to the Buyers by registered letter at the request of the Buyers a certificate attesting the existence of such a cause or causes issued by China Council for the Promotion of International Trade or by a competent Authority

（12） DISCREPANCY AND CLAIM：

In case discrepancy on the quality of the goods is found by the Buyers after arrival of the goods at the port of destination, claim may be lodged within 30 days after arrival of the goods at the port of destination. While for quantity discrepancy, claim may be lodged within 15 days after arrival of the goods at the port of destination, being supported by Inspection Certificate issued by a reputable public surveyor agreed upon by both parties. The Sellers shall, then consider the claim in the light of actual circumstances. For the losses due to natural cause or causes falling within the responsibilities of the ship-owners or the underwriters, the Sellers shall not consider any claim for compensation. In case the Letter of Credit does not reach the Sellers within the time stipulated in the Contract, or under FOB price terms Buyers do not send vessel to appointed ports or the Letter of Credit opened by the Buyers does not correspond to the Contract terms and the Buyers fail to amend thereafter its terms by telegraph within the time limit after receipt of notification by the Sellers, the Sellers shall have right to cancel the Contract or to delay the delivery of the goods and shall have also the right to lodge claims for compensation of losses.

（13） ARBITRATION：

All disputes in connection with the contract or the execution thereof, shall be settled amicably by negotiation. In case no settlement can be reached, the case under dispute may then be submitted to the "China International Economic and Trade Arbitration Commission" for arbitration. The arbitration shall take place in China and shall be executed in accordance with the provisional rules of Procedure of the said Commission and the decision made by the Commission shall be accepted as final and binding upon both parties for setting the disputes. The fees for arbitration shall be borne by the losing party unless otherwise awarded.

THE SELLERS：	THE BUYERS：
OCEAN PLASTIC & CHEMICAL	TONNY PRODUCTS PLC
PRODUCTS CO., LTD	ROTTERDAM THE NETHERLAND

第二节　托收方式下的结汇

教学目标

托收方式下能根据贸易信息制作全套结汇单据。

情景案例

机构：
外贸企业：宁波保税区益友国际贸易有限公司。
人物：
小李：宁波保税区益友国际贸易有限公司。
郑经理：宁波保税区益友国际贸易有限公司业务经理。
背景资料：
（1） 2016年6月14日宁波保税区益友国际贸易有限公司外贸业务部郑经理与波兰某公司签订一份9 600个起钉器（STAPLES REMOVER）的出口合同。
（2） 小李在办公室制作、补齐、整理客户清关用单据：发票、装箱单、提单、产地证等。

第九章 寄单和交单议付

托收委托书（例）：

To: Shanghai Pudong Development Bank — Offshore Banking Unit

Application number: _____ (For Bank use only) Date(day/month/year): _____

APPLICATION FOR EXPORT TRANSACTION

We present the following documents ("Documents") for:
- ✓ issuing or nominated bank's payment under the documentary credit below ("DC") without any financing (checking of documents is ○ required ○ not required)
- ○ your negotiation under the DC by way of advancing funds or agreeing to advance funds under the DC ○ your advance under ○ D/P ○ D/A
- ○ your purchase of a draft accepted by you under the DC ○ drawee's payment without financing under ○ D/P ○ D/A
- ○ your prepayment of a deferred payment undertaking incurred by you under the DC
- ○ your advance under the DC where the DC is not available with you

Financing under DC	Financing under DP/DA Bills
Currency and Amount:	Currency and Amount:
Finance Period: Interest Rate:	Finance Period: Interest Rate:

Drawer/Beneficiary (Full Name and Address): NINGBO FREE TRADE ZONE YEAYOO INDL & INT'L TRADING CO., LTD

Name of Contact Person (Mr/Mrs/Miss/Ms): MISS NOU
Contact Telephone Number: 0574-87160462 (Ext:)

Drawee/Applicant: TAURUS TRADE PAWEL DYMUS UL. KLAUDYNY 4-40 01-684 WARSZAWA

Facsimile Number: ___ Telephone Number: ___

Payment Terms (eg at sight, 30 days sight, etc): D/P at sight
Invoice Number: 12028026-2C
Account Number to be debited for all Bank Charges: OSA 1143 679445173
Bills of Lading/Air Waybills/Parcel Post No.: HKHKG4210812013

▼ Please mark number of documents attached

Draft		Insce. Policy/Cert.	
Commercial Invoice	3	Signed B/s Lading	3
Customs Invoice		Non-neg B/s Lading	3
Packing/Weight List	2	Parcel Post Receipt	
Survey Report		Air Waybill	
Other documents: FORM A 1+1C			

Bill Currency and Amount: USD 1200.00

Other instructions: ___

Proceeds Disposal
- ○ Deduct............from Pre-export Advance Number............
- ○ Credit our account number............under exchange contract(if applicable).
- ○ Apply proceeds to settle the drawing under the Back-to-Back DC.
- ○ Apply proceeds to settle the drawing under the D/P or D/A (...days) bills.
- ○ Others:

○ **LETTER OF CREDIT** Issuing Bank and DC Number: ___
Available with: ___ by: ___
A back-to-back DC (No. ___) has been issued by you against the support of this DC.

○ **DOCUMENTARY COLLECTION** Name and address of Collecting Bank: BANK ZACHODNI WBK SA 5-12TH FLOOR 61-894 POZNAN POLAND
or any bank nominated or designated by Shanghai Pudong Development Bank

INSTRUCTIONS to Collecting Bank (Please put a tick in the appropriate boxes)

A	Release Documents against PAYMENT ("D/P")	G	COLLECT charges from the DRAWEES
B	Release Documents against ACCEPTANCE ("D/A")	H	DEDUCT charges from the PROCEEDS
C	ACCEPTANCE/PAYMENT may be postponed until arrival of carrying vessel	I	Collect interest@......% p.a. from drawees from date of......until date of......
D	Any communication between the Collecting Bank and Shanghai Pudong Development Bank ☐ by telecommunication ☐ by airmail		
E	PROTEST for Non-acceptance and/or Non-payment	J	WAIVE — Interest, expenses and/or collection charges if refused
F	DO NOT PROTEST	K	DO NOT WAIVE

(NOTE: If no instructions are given regarding protest the Bank will assume that protest is NOT required)

宁波保税区益友国际贸易有限公司
NINGBO FREE TRADE ZONE YEAYOO INDL & INTL TRADING CO., LTD.   S.V.

Authorised Signature(s) and Chop

THIS APPLICATION IS SUBJECT TO THE TERMS AND CONDITIONS PRINTED OVERLEAF.

For Bank Use Only

Amount:	Interest Rate:	DC	○ Net Restricted	○ Confirmed	○ Lost/Fraudulent Status
Period:	Date of Proceed Granted	Repayment Date	○ Restricted	○ Without Recourse	
Other instructions:		Approval by	1st Check by	2nd Check by	

发票（例）：

NINGBO FREE TRADE ZONE YEAYOO IND'L & INT'L TRADING CO., LTD

RM 709, LIUTING STAR BUSINESS MANSION, NO. 299-22 CANGSONG RD.,
NINGBO CHINA 315012
TEL: +86-574-87160701   FAX: +86-574-87160702

COMMERCIAL INVOICE

TO: Taurus Trade Pawel Dymus
Ul. Klaudyny 4/40
01-684 Warszawa
POLAND

NO.: VNO28026-2C
DATE: JUN 30 2008

PORT OF LOADING: NINGBO, CHINA   PORT OF DESTINATION: GDYNIA, POLAND

ITEM	DESC. & SPECIFICATION	QUANTITY	UNIT PRICE	AMOUNT
1 STR9055	STAPLES REMOVER	9,600 PC	CFR GDYNIA @ USD 0.125	USD 1,200.00
	TOTAL:			USD 1,200.00

TOTAL SAY U.S. DOLLARS ONE THOUSAND TWO HUNDRED ONLY.

宁波保税区益友国际贸易有限公司
NINGBO FREE TRADE ZONE YEAYOO IND'L & INT'L TRADING CO.,LTD.

装箱单

NINGBO FREE TRADE ZONE YEAYOO IND'L & INT'L TRADING CO., LTD.

RM 709, LIUTING STAR BUSINESS MANSION, NO. 299/22, CANGSONG RD.,
NINGBO CHINA 315012
TEL: +86-574-87160701, 87160901 FAX: +86-574-87160702

PACKING LIST

TO:

NO.: VNO28026-2C
DATE: JUN 30 2008

PORT OF LOADING: NINGBO, CHINA   PORT OF DESTINATION: GDYNIA, POLAND

ITEM	DESC.	QTY.	PACKING		MEAS.	G.W.	N.W.	
			INNER	MASTER CTNS				
1 STR9055	STAPLES REMOVER	9600 PC	480	20	@42*26.5*30/0.67	@14/280	@12/240	42
	TOTAL:			20	0.67CBM	280KG	240KG	

TOTAL SAY TWENTY CARTONS ONLY.

SHIPPING MARKS:
TAURUS - TRADE
ROZSZYWACA Z BIOKADA (480SZT)
STR9055
GDYNIA
C/NO:1-20

宁波保税区益友国际贸易有限公司
NINGBO FREE TRADE ZONE YEAYOO IND'L & INT'L TRADING CO.,LTD.

提单（例）：

产地证（例）：

ORIGINAL	
1. Goods consigned from: (Exporter's business name, address, country) NINGBO FREE TRADE ZONE YEAYOO IND'L & INT'L TRADING CO., LTD. RM 799 LIFTING STAR BUSINESS MANSION NO.299-2 CANGSONG ROAD NINGBO CHINA	Reference No. G08380003750008 **GENERALIZED SYSTEM OF PREFERENCES** **CERTIFICATE OF ORIGIN** (Combined declaration and certificate) **FORM A** Issued in THE PEOPLE'S REPUBLIC OF CHINA (country) See Notes overleaf.
2. Goods consigned to (Consignee's name, address, country) TAURUS TRADE PAWEL ONYKS UL. RUNODNY 1-10 01-844 WARSZAWA	
3. Means of transport and route (as far as known) FROM NINGBO, CHINA TO GDYNIA, POLAND BY SEA	4. For official use

5. Item number	6. Marks and numbers of packages	7. Number and kind of packages; description of goods	8. Origin criterion (see Notes overleaf)	9. Gross weight or other quantity	10. Number and date of invoices
		TWENTY (20) CTNS OF STAPLES REMOVER TAURUS TRADE ROGZYNACA-Z-BRIGADA (BROSZT) SERVICE GDYNIA CTNS 1-20	P	9600KGS	VY028026-20 JUN. 30. 2008

11. Certification It is hereby certified, on the basis of control carried out, that the declaration by the exporter is correct. NINGBO CHINA, JUL. 01. 2008 Place and date, signature and stamp of certifying authority	12. Declaration by the exporter The undersigned hereby declares that the above details and statements are correct; that all the goods were produced in **CHINA** (country) and that they comply with the origin requirements specified for those goods in the Generalized System of Preferences for goods exported to NINGBO Place and date, signature of authorized signatory

S 66358392

托运单（例）：

宁波保税区益友国际贸易有限公司		
托运人 NINGBO FREE TRADE ZONE YI AYOO IND'L & INT'L TRADING CO., LTD. TEL:+86 0574-87160701	出口货物托运单	
收货人 TO ORDER	环球国际货运七部 联系人一：俞经理 /小徐 电话：87327113 传真：87302127	
通知人 TAURUS TRADE PAWEL DYMUS UL.KLAUDYNY 4-40 01-684 WARSZAWA, POLAND	托运单号	YEA080623
^	委托日期	2008-6-23
^	合同号码	VN028026-2C
^	信用证号	
^	运输方式	BY SEA
^	是否转运	NO
^	是否分批	NO

手写：D/P at sight

一程船名 ／ 起运港 NINGBO, CHINA ／ 装船日期
二程船名 ／ 转运港 ／ 海运费USD 0
正本提单 3 ／ 目的港 GDYNIA, POLAND ／ 包干费RMB 0
副本提单 3 ／ ETD ／ ETA

标志和号码	货品名称	件数及包装	毛重	体积
1	STAPLES REMOVER	20CTNS	280KGS	0.67CBM

SHIPPING MARKS
TAURS TRADE
DESC.:
ITEM NO.:
GDYNIA
C/NO:1-UP

特约事项
船期：
箱型/数量：拼箱
进仓或拖卡：进仓

宁波保税区益友国际贸易有限公司
地址：宁波市海曙区苍松路299弄2号柳汀星座商务楼709室
电话：+86-574-87161352　传真：+86-574-87160702
联系人：牟丽君

（托运人签章）

通关单（例）：

中华人民共和国出入境检验检疫
出境货物通关单

编号：310300208287163000

1. 发货人 浙江天时国际经济技术合作有限公司 ZHEJIANG TEAMS INTERNATIONAL ECONOMIC & TECHNICAL COOPERATION CO.,LTD.		5. 标记及号码 IMPORTER:COOL MARKETING PRODUKT:KREDKI DO TWARZY QUANTITY:4040 PCS NR OF CARTON:4 CTN SIZE OF CARTON:34*32*40 CM WEIGHT OF CARTON:13.5/11.5 KG
2. 收货人 *** COOL MARKETING COMPANY		
3. 合同/信用证号 VN028066C /***	4. 输往国家或地区 波兰	
6. 运输工具名称及号码 飞机 ***	7. 发货日期 2008.12.03	8. 集装箱规格及数量 ***
9. 货物名称及规格 蜡笔 *** *** （以下空白）	10. H.S.编码 9609900000 *** *** （以下空白）	11. 申报总值 *596美元 *** *** （以下空白）	12. 数/重量、包装数量及种类 *4040套 *46千克 *4纸箱 （以下空白）

13. 证明

上述货物业经检验检疫，请海关予以放行。

本通关单有效期至 二〇〇九 年 一 月 四 日

签字： 日期：2008

14. 备注

I 7078669 　　①货物通关　　印刷流水号：17078669　　[2-2(2000.1.1)]

报关单

中华人民共和国海关出口货物报关单

JG02

预录入编号:		海关编号:	
出口口岸 NINGBO	备案号	出口日期	申报日期
经营单位 3302260298	运输方式 BY SEA	运输工具名称	提运单号
发货单位 浙江天时国际经济技术合作有限公司	贸易方式 GENERAL	征免性质	结汇方式 T/T
许可证号	运抵国(地区) 波兰	指运港 格丁尼亚	境内货源地 宁波
批准文号 4093936	成交方式 CFR	运费	保费	杂费
合同协议号	件数 20 CTNS	包装种类	毛重(公斤) 280.00	净重(公斤) 240.00
集装箱号	随附单据		生产厂家
标记唛码及备注			

项号	商品编号	商品名称、规格型号	数量及单位	最终目的国(地区)	单价	总价	币制	征免
1	82032000	SRAPLES REMOVER 起钉器	9600 PCS 台	波兰	0.1121	1076.00	USD	

税费征收情况

录入员	录入单位	兹声明以上申报无讹并承担法律责任	海关审单批注及放行日期(签章)
报关员			审单 审价
单位地址		申报单位	征税 统计
邮编	电话	填制日期	查验 放行

实训练习题

请根据下列托收方式下的货物明细单，制作全套结汇单据

<table>
<tr><td colspan="7" align="center">出口货物明细单</td></tr>
<tr><td colspan="7">出口商名称地址：ZHEJIANG MACINERY & EQUIPMENT IMP&EXP CORP.
　　　　　　　　NO. 23，XIAOWEN STREET，NINGBO　CHINA</td></tr>
<tr><td colspan="7">进口商名称地址：HONGYU COMPANY
　　　　　　　　RM. 201，MINTAI BUILDING　SINGAPORE</td></tr>
<tr><td colspan="7">合同号码：CQMYG000851　　　　　发票号码：YSDSS09652</td></tr>
<tr><td colspan="7">签约日期：2008年7月1日　　发票日期：2008年10月8日　　装运日期：2008年10月10日</td></tr>
<tr><td colspan="7">起运地：宁波　　　　　　　目的地：SINGAPORE　　　　　提单日期：2008年10月10日</td></tr>
<tr><td colspan="7">贸易性质：一般　　　　　　贸易条件：CIF　　　　　　　付款方式：D/P SIGHT</td></tr>
</table>

货物名称规格	数量（SET）	包装（CASE）	尺码（CM）	毛重（KG）	净重（KG）	单价（USD）	总值（USD）
DIESEL ENGINE							
DE801	20	CASE	86×70×66	110	98	275	5500
DE802	20	CASE	86×70×66	110	98	284	5680
DE803	15	CASE	92×120×84	154	120	454	6810
DE804	15	CASE	88×160×70	188	146	720	10800
	70			562	462		28790

运输标志：HONGYU / SINGAPORE / C/NO. 1 – UP

包装：每台装一个木箱

提单收货人：TO ORDER OF SHIPPER　　提单被通知人：按进口商填

保险代理人：TAIPING INSURANCE CO.
　　　　　　BLDG. 210 QUEEN STREET SINGAPORE

代收行：THE SINGAPORE COMMERCIAL　BANK

分批装运：不准　　　转运：不准

运费：预付　USD22/运费吨　计费标准："M"

船名：CHANGQING V. 8　　提单号码：7425　　保险单号码：8725014

险别：ALL AND WAR RISK　　加成：10%　　费率：0.14%

第三节　信用证方式下交单议付

教学目标

信用证方式下能根据贸易信息制作全套结汇单据。

情景案例

> **机构：**
> 外贸企业：宁波保税区益友国际贸易有限公司。
> **人物：**
> 小李：宁波保税区益友国际贸易有限公司。
> 郑经理：宁波保税区益友国际贸易有限公司业务经理。
> **背景资料：**
> （1）2007年9月19日，宁波保税区益友国际贸易有限公司外贸业务部郑经理与波兰某公司签订一份圆珠笔（BALL PEN）的出口合同。
> （2）小李在办公室制作、补齐、整理客户清关用单据：发票、装箱单、提单、普惠制产地证书、客户装船授权函等。

信用证（例）：

上海浦东发展银行
SHANGHAI PUDONG DEVELOPMENT BANK

LETTER OF CREDIT ADVICE

OUR REF : EX940107003777
DATED : 2007-9-24

TO: NINGBO FREE TRADE ZONE YEAYOO IND'L & INT'L TRADING CO.,LTD
致：宁波保税区益友国际贸易有限公司

ISSUING BANK: BANCO DE SABADELL, S.A.
开证行   08201 SABADELL

RECEIVED VIA:
转递行/转证行

L/C NO :   5228314148300
信用证编号

L/C AMOUNT: USD11751.40
信用证金额

WE HAVE PLEASURE IN ADVISING YOU THAT WE HAVE RECEIVED FROM THE ABOVE BANK THE CAPTIONED CREDIT, IN FULL DETAILS, CONTENTS OF WHICH ARE AS PER THE ATTACHED. PLEASE NOTE THAT UNLESS OTHERWISE STAMPED ON THE ATTACHED CREDIT, THIS CREDIT DOES NOT BEAR OUR CONFIRMATION NOR INVOLVE ANY UNDERTAKING(S) ON OUR PART. THIS ADVICE AND THE ATTACHED (AND ANY SUBSEQUENT AMENDMENT) MUST ACCOMPANY ALL PRESENTATIONS. IN THE CASE OF MESSAGES RECEIVED BY CABLE OR TELEX, WE ACCEPT NO RESPONSIBILITY OR LIABILITY FOR ANY ERRORS, OMISSION OR DELAYS IN THE TRANSMISSION OF THE CABLE OR TELEX.
IF YOU FIND ANY TERMS IN THIS CREDIT YOU ARE UNABLE TO COMPLY WITH OR ANY ERRORS IN YOUR NAME AND/OR ADDRESS, PLEASE COMMUNICATE (DIRECT WITH YOUR) BUYERS IMMEDIATELY WITH A VIEW TO ARRANGING ANY DEFINED AMENDMENTS AND THUS AVOID DIFFICULTIES WHICH WOULD OTHERWISE ARISE WHEN DOCUMENTS ARE PRESENTED.

我行荣幸的通知贵公司，兹收到来自上述银行的全电信用证，信用证内容附后。
提请贵公司注意，除非我行在随附的信用证上盖章注明，否则我行对该证不加具保兑，也不承担任何责任。
此信用证通知及随附的信用证，包括今后可能有的信用证修改，在所有交单中都应一并提交。若收到的信息以电报或电传方式发送，则我行对电报和电传传递过程中发生的任何错误、遗漏和延迟都不负任何责任。
请仔细阅读随附的信用证，若您发现有无法执行的条款或您的名称、地址有错误，请迅速与买方取得直接联系，安排其进行修改，以避免将来在交单时可能遇到的困难。

FOR SHANGHAI PUDONG DEVELOPMENT BANK
上海浦东发展银行

This Letter of Credit is subject to UCP LATEST VERSION

SHANGHAI PUDONG DEVELOPMENT BANK NINGBO BRANCH NO 21 JIANGXIA STREET NINGBO P.R.C CHINA P.C 315000
TEL.NO.:0574-87268062 FAX NO.:0574-87268808 TLX:370105 SWIFT BIC:SPDBCNSH342

```
Eximbills Enterpriste Incoming Swift
===============================================
Message Type:700
Send Bank:BSABESBBXXX
          BANCO DE SABADELL, S.A.
          08201 SABADELL
Recv Bank:SPDBCNSH342
          SHANGHAI PUDONG DEVELOPMENT BANK
          315000 NINGBO
User Name:11000664           Print Times:1
Print Date:2007-09-24 15:28:59      MIR:070921BSABESBBAXXX3861010266
```

:27:[Sequence of Total]
    1/1
:40A:[Form of Documentary Credit]
    IRREVOCABLE
:20:[Documentary Credit Number]
    5228314148300
:31C:[Date of Issue]
    070921
:40E:[Applicable Rules]
    UCP LATEST VERSION
:31D:[Date and Place of Expiry]
    080109 VALENCIA (SPAIN)
:50:[Applicant]
    WELLSEASON, S.L.
    CTRA. ADEMUZ, KM. 15, 700
    46184 SAN ANTONIO DE BENAGEBER(VALE
    SPAIN
:59:[Beneficiary]
    /ACC. 940 114 580 000 00 575
    NINGBO FREE TRADE ZONE YEAYOU IND'L
    AND INT'L TRADING CO., LTD. RM799,
    LIUTING STAR BUSINESS MANSION, N.299
    , 22, CANGSONG RD., NINGBO, CHINA 315012
:32B:[Currency Code, Amount]
    USD11751.4
:39A:[Percentage Credit Amount Tolerance]
    00/00
:41A:[Available With...By...]
    BSABESBBXXX
    BY PAYMENT
:43P:[Partial Shipments]
    NOT ALLOWED
:43T:[Transshipment]
    ALLOWED
:44A:[Take in Charge/Dispatch FM/Place of RCPT]
    NINGBO
:44B:[Final Desti/Trans To/Place of Delivery]
    VALENCIA PORT, SPAIN
:44D:[Shipment Period]
    NOT BEFORE DECEMBER 10TH 2007 AND NOT LATER THAN DECEMBER 25TH
    2007.
:45A:[Description of Goods and/or Services]
    DELIVERY TERMS FOB NINGBO (INCOTERMS 2000)
    COVERING:
    4042 DISPLAYS OF 24 PINBALL AS PER OUR ORDER N.317 AS PER
    PROFORMA INVOICE N. VN027055 AND VN027055F.
:46A:[Document Required]
    SIGNED COMMERCIAL INVOICE IN THREE FOLD.
    . PACKING LIST IN THREE FOLD DETAILED BY CONTAINER.
    . CERTIFICATE OF ORIGIN GSP FORM A IN ONE ORIGINAL AND ONE COPY
    ISSUED BY CHINA AUTHORITY. NOT LATER THAN B/L DATE, OTHERWISE
    STATING CLAUSE ISSUED RETROSPECTIVELY.
    . FULL SET OF OCEAN CLEAN ON BOARD BILL OF LADING, ISSUED BY
    CASA CHINA(NINGBO OFFICE) IS ACCEPTABLE, MARKED FREIGHT COLLECT, TO
    THE ORDER AND BLANK ENDORSED AND NOTIFY WELLSEASON S.L. CTRA
    ADEMUZ KM.15, 46184 SAN ANTONIO DE BENAGEBER VALENCIA SPAIN.
    . COPY OR PHOTOCOPY AUTHORIZATION LETTER FOR PRODUCTION THAT WILL
    BE PROVIDED BY WELLSEASON, S.L. AFTER RECEIPT OF THE SAMPLES.

:47A:[Additional Conditions]
    + PLS. DO NOT SEND ANY DRAFT
    THIRD PARTY DOCUMENTS SHOWING DIFFERENT ROUTING, INVOICE NUMBER
    AND DATE ARE ACCEPTABLE.
    + GSP FORM 'A' CERTIFICATE SHOWING THIRD PARTY EXPORTER, SHIPPING
    ROUTE, DIFFER FROM B/L, INVOICE NO. AND DATE DIFFER ACCEPTABLE.
    + THE VALIDITY OF THIS L/C IS CONDITIONED TO THE REMITTANCE FROM
    THE BENEFICIARY OF 1 SAMPLE OF EACH DESIGN AND REFERENCE FOR THE
    APPROVAL OF THE APPLICANT BEFORE TO START THE MASS PRODUCTION.
    AND ALSO IS CONDITIONED TO THE SENDING OF 5 DISPLAYS OF EACH
    REFERENCE BY AIR DELIVERY AS ADVANCED PRODUCTION BEFORE THE
    SHIPMENT. BENEFICIARY'S CERTIFICAT TO THIS EFFECT IS REQUIRED.
    + A CHARGE OF EUR 95.00 (IN THE CURRENCY OF THE CREDIT) WILL BE
    DEDUCTED FOR EACH PRESENTATION BEARING DISCREPANCIES.
:71B:[Charges]
    ALL BANKING CHARGES
    OUTSIDE THE ISSUING BANK,
    INCLUDING REIMBURSEMENT CHARGES
    ARE FOR BENEFICIARY'S ACCOUNT.
:48:[Period for Presentation]
    DOCUMENTS TO BE PRESENTED NOT
    LATER THAN 15 DAYS FROM SHIPMENT
    DATE, BUT WITHIN L/C VALIDITY.
:49:[Confirmation Instructions]
    WITHOUT
:78:[Instructions to the Paying Bank]
    UPON RECEPTION OF DOCUMENTS STRICTLY IN ACCORDANCE WITH CREDIT
    TERMS WE SHALL CREDIT YOU AS PER YOUR INSTRUCTIONS.
:72:[Sender to Receiver Information]
    PLEASE ADVISE URGENTLY TO BEN.
    AT 21 JIANG XIA STREET, NINGBO
    BRANCH.
:999:[null]
    {M9901070755324|0|940}
        }{5:{MAC:E5D14E8E}{CHK:28B8DAAF7985}}{S:{SAC:}{COP:P}}

发票（例）：

NINGBO FREE TRADE ZONE YEAYOO
IND'L & INT'L TRADING CO., LTD.
RM 709, LIUTING STAR BUSINESS MANSION, N. 299.22, CANGSONG RD.,
NINGBO, CHINA 315012
TEL: +86-574-87160701   FAX: +86-574-87160702

COMMERCIAL INVOICE

TO: WELLSEASON S.L

NO.: VNO27055
DATE: DEC 20 2007
L/C NO.: 5228314148300

PORT OF LOADING: NINGBO | PORT OF DESTINATION: VALENCIA PORT, SPAIN

ITEM	NAME OF COMMODITY & SPECIFICATION	QUANTITY	UNIT PRICE	AMOUNT
			FOB NINGBO PORT	
1 043179#	BALL PEN OUR REF. BAP8909 DISPLAY 24 BOLIGRAFOS CON CAJA BETTY DUN-14 CARTON -- DUN-14 INNER BOX -- EAN-13 PIECE -- 8414778431799	2021 BOX	@ USD 2.462	USD 4975.70
045205#	DISPLAY 24 BOLIGRAFOS BETTY BOOP DUN-14 CARTON -- DUN-14 INNER BOX -- EAN-13 PIECE -- 8414778452053	2021 BOX	@ USD 2.462	USD 4975.70
		TOTAL:		USD 9951.40

TOTAL SAY U.S. DOLLARS NINE THOUSAND NINE HUNDRED FIFTY ONE AND CENTS FORTY ONLY.

MARKS: DELIVERY TERMS: FOB NINGBO (INCOTERMS 2000)
COVERING
4042 DISPLAYS OF 24 PENBALL AS PER OUR ORDER N. 317 AS PER PROFORMA INVOICE N. VNO27055 AND VNO27055F.

装箱单（例）：

NINGBO FREE TRADE ZONE YEAYOO
IND'L & INT'L TRADING CO., LTD.
RM 709, LIUTING STAR BUSINESS MANSION, N. 299.22, CANGSONG RD.,
NINGBO, CHINA 315012
TEL: +86-574-87160701   FAX: +86-574-87160702

PACKING LIST

TO:

NO.: VNO27055
DATE: DEC 20 2007
L/C NO.: 5228314148300

PORT OF LOADING: NINGBO | PORT OF DESTINATION: VALENCIA PORT, SPAIN

ITEM	DESC.	QTY./UNIT	PACKING			MEAS.(CBM)	G.W.(KG)	N.W.(KG)
			INNER	MASTER	CTNS			
1 043179#	BALL PEN OUR REF. BAP8909 DISPLAY 24 BOLIGRAFOS CON CAJA BETTY DUN-14 CARTON -- DUN-14 INNER BOX -- EAN-13 PIECE -- 8414778431799	2016 BOX 5 BOX	18BOXES TO BE SHIPPED BY AIR FREIGHT	36BOXES	56	@63.5X50.5X33.6/6.03	@17/952	@15/840
045205#	DISPLAY 24 BOLIGRAFOS BETTY BOOP DUN-14 CARTON -- DUN-14 INNER BOX -- EAN-13 PIECE -- 8414778452053	2016 BOX 5 BOX	18BOXES TO BE SHIPPED BY AIR FREIGHT	36BOXES	56	@63.5X50.5X33.6/6.03	@17/952	@15/840
		TOTAL:			112	12.06CBM	1904KGS	1680KGS

TOTAL SAY ONE HUNDRED AND TWELVE CARTONS ONLY.

Remarks:
SHIPPING MARKS:
M.I.S.A.
VALENCIA
Referencia:
Cantidades: PCS
Peso neto: Kgs
Peso bruto: Kgs
Medidas: cmsX cmsX cms
C/NO:
MADE IN CHINA

宁波保税区益友国际贸易有限公司
NINGBO FREE TRADE ZONE YEAYOO IND'L & INT'L TRADING CO.,LTD.

提单（例）：

Shipper	Country or Origin	Bill of Lading No
NINGBO FREE TRADE ZONE YEAYOO IND'L AND INT'L TRADING CO.,LTD.RM709 LIUTING STAR BUSINESS MANSION, N.299.22,CANGSONG RD,NINGBO, CHINA 315012		NBYVLC-217460A
	F/Agent Name & Ref. SPACE CARGO VALENCIA CALLE MENORCA ,17-ENTRESUELO 46023 VALENCIA	Shipper's Ref
Consignee(If 'To Order' so indicate) TO THE ORDER	TEL:34-96-3303306 /FAX: 34-96-3310904	
	CASA CHINA CASA CHINA LIMITED (As Carrier)	
Notify Party(No claim shall attach for failure to notify) WELLSEASON S.L. CTRA.ADEMUZ KM.15, 46184 SAN ANTONIO DE BENAGEBER VALENCIA SPAIN.		

Place of Receipt	Port of Loading NINGBO		
Vessel V.V801R MSC TOMOKO	Port of Discharge VALENCIA	Place of Delivery VALENCIA	No.of original Bills of Loading THREE (3)

Marks & Numbers	No.of Pkgs. or Shipping Units	Description of Goods & Pkgs.	Gross Weight KGS	Measurements CBM
SHIPPER'S LOAD, COUNT & SEAL. SAID TO CONTAIN : CRXU4383919/6134305 40'(112CTNS/1904KGS/12.060CBM) DETAIL AS PER ATTACHED LIST	112 CTNS	DETAIL AS PER ATTACHED LIST	1904.000	12.060
Total	112 CTNS	Temperature Control Instructions: PART OF ONE (1X40') CONTAINER ONLY.	SHIPPED ON BOARD : 25/12/2007	

ORIGINAL

Excess Value Declaration: Refer to Clause 6(4)(B)+(C) on reverse side

Freight Details, Charges etc:
CFS/CY
FREIGHT COLLECT

RECEIVED by the Carrier the Goods as specified above in apparent good order and condition unless otherwise stated, to be transported to such place as agreed, authorised or permitted herein and subject to all the terms and conditions appearing on the front and reverse of this Bill of Lading to which the Merchant agrees by accepting this Bill of Lading, any local privileges and customs notwithstanding.

The particulars given above as stated by the shipper and the weight, measure, quantity, condition, contents and value of the Goods are unknown to the Carrier.

In WITNESS where of one(1) original Bill of Lading has been signed if not otherwise stated above, the same being accomplished the other(s), if any ,to be void.If required by the Carrier one (1) original Bill of Lading must be surrendered duly endorsed in exchange for the Goods or delivery order.

SHANGHAI 25/12/2007
Place and date of issue
Signed on behalf of the Carrier:

AS CARRIER

by

提单附件（例）：

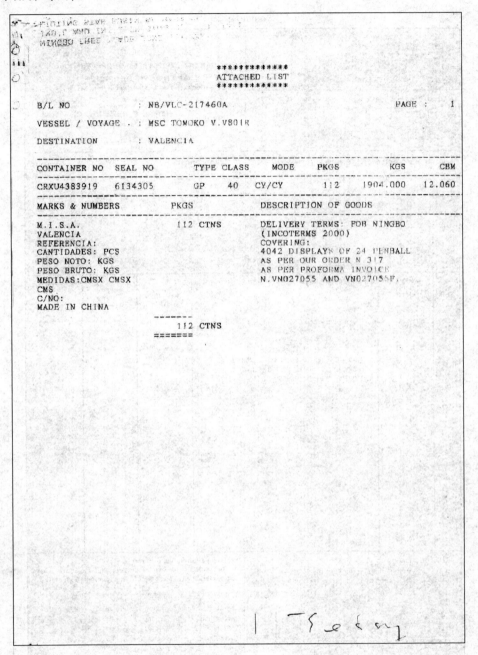

FORM A（例）：

	ORIGINAL	
1. Goods consigned from (Exporter's business name, address, country) NINGBO FREE TRADE ZONE YEAYOO IND'L AND INT'L TRADING CO., LTD. RM708, CONTIX STAR BUSINESS MANSION, NO.999-21 QINGSHI RD, NINGBO, CHINA 315012		Reference No. C073800107800028 **GENERALIZED SYSTEM OF PREFERENCES** **CERTIFICATE OF ORIGIN** (Combined declaration and certificate) **FORM A** Issued in THE PEOPLE'S REPUBLIC OF CHINA (country) See Notes overleaf
2. Goods consigned to (Consignee's name, address, country) WELLSEASON, S.L. CTRA. ADEMUZ, KM 15, 700 46184 SAN ANTONIO DE BENAGEBER (VALENCIA) SPAIN		
3. Means of transport and route (as far as known) FROM NINGBO TO VALENCIA PORT, SPAIN BY SEA		4. For official use

5. Item number	6. Marks and numbers of packages	7. Number and kind of packages; description of goods	8. Origin criterion (see Notes overleaf)	9. Gross weight or other quantity	10. Number and date of invoices
		ONE HUNDRED AND TWELVE (112) CTNS OF BALL PEN FOB NINGBO (INCOTERMS 2000) 4042 DISPLAYS OF 24 PENBALL AS PER OUR ORDER N.317 AS PER PROFORMA INVOICE N. VN027055 AND VN027055F. D.U.S.A VALENCIA REFERENCIA: CANTIDADES: PCS PESO NETO: KGS PESO BRUTO: KGS MEDIDAS: CMSX CMSX CMS C/NO: MADE IN CHINA	"P"	4042BOXES	VN027055 DEC. 20, 2007

11. Certification It is hereby certified, on the basis of control carried out, that the declaration by the exporter is correct. [seal] NINGBO, CHINA, DEC. 20, 2007 Place and date, signature and stamp of certifying authority	12. Declaration by the exporter The undersigned hereby declares that the above details and statements are correct; that all the goods were produced in CHINA (country) and that they comply with the origin requirements specified for those goods in the Generalized System of Preferences for goods exported to SPAIN (importing country) NINGBO, CHINA, DEC. 20, 2007 Place and date, signature of authorized signatory

S 66358385

确认函（例）：

THE AUTHORIZATION LETTER FOR THE PRODUCTION

We WELLSEASON. S.L. Acknowledge the remittance from the beneficiary of 1 sample of each design and reference for approval of us before to start the mass production. And also is conditioned to the sending of 5 displays each reference by air delivery as advanced production before the shipment. Have been sent to us by

Our Supplier: NINGBO FREE TRADE ZONE YEAYOO IND'L & INT'L TRADING CO., LTD.

Production of the items enclosed in our ORDER No 317

According with the Proforma invoice no: VNO27055 and VNO27055F

Items subject to the L/C number: 5228314148300

We acknowledge the receipt of the above mentioned samples and give our authorization and consent to the mass production of this order and his shipment.

Yours Sincerely,
Benaguacil 18 December de 2007.

授权函（例）：

20/12 '07 JUE 13:21 FAX   ☒001

Wellseason, S.L.

TO: NINGBO FREE TRADE ZONE YEAYOO IND'L & INT'L TRADING CO., LTD

ATTN: Mr Vion   DATE: 18 December / 07

Dear Mr Vion,

We WELLSEASON, S.L. ISSUE THIS LETTER TO CERTIFY THAT WE KNOW AND GIVE OUR AUTHORIZATION TO SHIP ON BOARD THE FOLLOWING ORDER:

- OUR SUPPLIER: NINGBO FREE TRADE ZONE YEAYOO IND'L & INT'L TRADING CO., LTD

- SHIPMENT OF OUR ORDER: 317

- ACCORDING WITH PROFORMA INVOICE: VNO27055 and VNO27055F

- FORWARDER COMPANY: CASA CHINA LTD.

- PORT OF CHARGE: NINGBO

- L/C NUMBER IS: 5228314148300

If you need any further information, please do not hesitate to contact us.
Best regards,

MARIAN DOLZ

实训练习题

请根据下列某信用证业务资料（一/二/三），制作全套结汇单据

资料一：信用证如下

```
MT700 ------------------------------ ISSUE OF A DOCUMENTARY CREDIT ------------------------------
SEQUENCE OF TOTAL                    27: 1/1
FORM OF DOCUMENTARY CREDIT           40A: IRREVOCABLE
DOCUMENTARY CREDIT NUMBER            20: XT173
DATE OF ISSUE                        31C: 080510
DATE AND PLACE OF EXPIRY             31D: DATE 080630 PLACE CHINA
APPLICANT                            50: YIYANG TRADING CORPORATION
                                         88 MARAHALL AVE
                                         DONCASTER VIC 3108 CANADA
ISSUING BANK                         52A: NATIONAL PARIS BANK
                                         24 MARSHALL VEDONCASTER
                                         MONTREAL, CANADA
BENEFICIARY                          59: NINGBO IMPORT & EXPORT TRADE CORPORATION
                                         1321 ZHONGSHAN ROAD, NINGBO, CHINA
CURRENCY CODE, AMOUNT                32B: CURRENCY USD AMOUNT 32,800.00
AVAILABLE WITH...BY...               41D: ANY BANK
                                         BY NEGOTIATION
DRAFTS AT...                         42C: SIGHT
DRAWEE                               42A: NATIONAL PARIS BANK
PARTIAL SHIPMENT                     43P: PROHIBITED
TRANSSHIPMENT                        43T: PROHIBITED
LOADING/DISPATCH/TAKING
IN CHARGE/FM                         44A: NINGBO
FOR TRANSPORTATION TO...             44B: MONTREAL, CANADA
LATEST DATE OF SHIPMENT              44C: 080620
DESCRIPTION OF GOODS/SERVICES        45A:
    CHINESE GREEN TEA AS PER S/C No. TXT264 CIF MONTREAL
DOCUMENTS REQUIRED:                  46A:
    + SIGNED COMMERCIAL INVOICE IN 2 ORIGINALS AND 4 COPIES.
    + PACKING LIST IN 1 ORIGINAL AND 4 COPIES.
    + CERTIFICATE OF ORIGIN GSP CHINA FORM A, ISSUED BY THE CHAMBER OF COMMERCIAL
      OR OTHER AUTHORITY DULY ENTITLED FOR THIS PURPOSE.
    + FULL SET OF NEGOTIABLE INSURANCE POLICY OR CERTIFICATE AND BLANK ENDORSED
      FOR 110 PERCENT OF THE INVOICE VALUE COVERING ALL RISKS
```

+ FULL SET OF B/L (3 ORIGINALS AND 5 COPIES) CLEAN ON BOARD, MADE OUT TO ORDER OF SHIPPER AND BLANK ENDORSED AND MARKED "FREIGHT PREPAID" AND NOTIFY APPLICANT.

+ ONE FULL SET OF NON-NEGOTIABLE SHIPPING DOCUMENTS MUST BE SENT TO THE APPLICANT BY AIR COURIER WITHIN 3 DAYS AFTER SHIPMENT AND BENEFICIARY'S CERTIFICATE TO THIS EFFECT IS REQUIRED.

+ COPY OF TELEX/FAX ADVICE, ADDRESSED TO APPLICANT BY BENEFICIARY WITHIN THREE DAYS AFTER SHIPMENT DATE BEARING THE FOLLOWING DETAILS: DATE OF SHIPMENT, NUMBER OF B/L, NAME OF SHIPPING COMPANY, AND VESSEL, QUANTITY, WEIGHT AND DESCRIPTION OF SHIPPED GOODS, SHIPPING MARKS AND NUMBERS, NUMBER OF CONTAINER, PORT OF LOADING AND E. T. D. , PORT OF DESTINATION AND E. T. A.

CHARGES 71B: ALL BANKING CHARGES OUTSIDE CANADA ARE FOR BENEFICIARY'S ACCOUNT

PERIOD FOR PRESENTATION   48: DOCUMENTS MUST BE PRESENTED WITHIN 15 DAYS AFTER THE DATE OF SHIPMENT BUT WITHIN THE VALIDITY OF THE CREDIT.

CONFIRMATION INSTRUCTION   49: WITHOUT

SENDER TO RECEIVER INFO   72: THIS LC IS SUBJECT TO UCP ICC PUB. NO. 600. THIS IS OPERATIVE INSTRUMENT AND NO MAIL CONFIRMATION WILL FOLLOW.

资料二：其他信息

（1）INVOICE NO.：TX0522
（2）INVOICE DATE：JUN. 01, 2008
（3）PACKING

	G. W/kg	N. W/kg	MEAS/（m³）
ART NO. 005	7/CTN	5/CTN	0.2/CTN
ART NO. 006	6/CTN	5/CTN	0.2/CTN
ART NO. 007	6/CTN	5/CTN	0.2/CTN

PACKED IN 20′ CONTAINER（集装箱号：GATU0506118）

（4）H. S. CODE：5802.3090
（5）POLICY NO. ：XH043101984
（6）FREIGHT FEE：USD815
（7）INSURANCE FEE：USD984
（8）REFERENCE NO. ：20080819
（9）B/L NO. ：HJSHB142939
（10）B/L DATE：JUN. 10, 2008
（11）VESSEL：NANGXING V. 086

资料三：外贸合同

宁波进出口贸易公司
NINGBO IMPORT & EXPORT TRADE CORPORATION
SALES CONFIRMATION
1321 ZHONGSHAN ROAD, NINGBO, CHINA
Tele：0574-65788877
Fax：0574-65788876

TO：YIYANG TRADING CORPORATION　　　　　　S/C NO：TXT264
　　88 MARAHALL AVE　　　　　　　　　　　　DATE：MAY. 01, 2008
　　DONCASTER VIC 3108, CANADA

We hereby confirm having sold to you the following goods on terms and conditions as stated below

MARKS & No.	DESCRIPTIONS OF GOODS	QUANTITY	U/ PRICE	AMOUNT
YIYANG MONTREAL C/No. 1-66	CHINESE GREEN TEA ART No. 005 ART No. 006 ART No. 007 Packed in 66 cartons	100kg 110kg 120kg	CIF MONTREAL USD 110.00 USD 100.00 USD 90.00	USD 11,000.00 USD 11,000.00 USD 10,800.00

PACKING：PACKED IN 66 CARTONS OF 5 KILOGRAMS EACH
LOADING PORT：NINGBO
DESTINATION：MONTREAL
PARTIAL SHIPMENT：PROHIBITED
TRANSHIPMENT：PROHIBITED
PAYMENT：L/C AT SIGHT
INSURANCE：FOR 110 PERCENT OF THE INVOICE VALUE COVERING ALL RISKS,
TIME OF SHIPMENT, LATEST DATE OF SHIPMENT 080620

THE BUYER：　　　　　　　　　　　　THE SELLER：
YIYANG TRADING CORPORATION　　　　NINGBO IMPORT & EXPORT TRADE CORPORATION

第四节　审单

教学目标

最终目标：能审核单据、处理不符点单据。

促成目标：

1. 能审核单据、处理不符点单据。
2. 熟悉《UCP600》中关于寄单、审单、交单议付的条款。
3. 熟悉审单方法和技巧。
4. 熟悉不符点单据的处理方法。

情景案例

机构：
工贸企业：宁波机械有限公司。
贸促会（CCPIT）。
中国太平洋财产保险股份有限公司。
货运代理：宁波市海润国际货运代理有限公司。
承运人（船公司）：中海集装箱运输浙江有限公司。
银行：中国银行宁波北仑分行。

人物：
小白：宁波机械有限公司单证员。
贾经理：宁波机械有限公司业务经理。

背景资料：
（1）2007年9月18日，宁波机械有限公司外贸业务部贾经理与阿联酋某公司签订了一份注塑机的出口合同，CIF JEBEL ALI, UAE。11月22日收到信用证。
（2）2008年1月30日—2月8日，小白在办公室制作、补齐、整理客户清关用单据。制作：商业发票、装箱单等；整理：产地证书、保险单、提单等。

中国银行股份有限公司
BANK OF CHINA LIMITED

NINGBO BRANCH, BEILUN SUB-BRANCH
BL05
ADDRESS: NO. 245 HUASHAN ROAD, BEILUN,
NINGBO, CHINA

TELEX: 37014 BOCBL
FAX:0574-86896653
TEL: 0574-86896653

信用证通知书
NOTIFICATION OF DOCUMENTARY CREDIT

2007-11-22

TO 致: 6052600 CO.LTD. NINGBO CHINA	如需垂询或协助请引我编号→ AD92A0? PLEASE QUOTE OUR REF. NO. 如有查询或需协助,欢迎致电86896653, 注意:贵司交单议付请附客户交单委托书并扼要填写, 如需押汇请附押汇申请书 顺祝!
ISSUING BANK 开证行 8001373 HSBC BANK MIDDLE EAST (THE BRITISH BANK OF THE MIDDLE EAST) DUBAI	TRANSMITTED TO US THROUGH 转递行 REF NO.

L/C NO. 信用证号 DPCDEI074569	DATED 开证日期 2007-11-19	AMOUNT 金额	EXPIRY PLACE 有 LOCAL
EXPIRY DATE 效期 2008-01-10	TENOR 期限 0 DAYS	CHARGE 未付费用	CHARGE BY 费用 BENE
RECEIVED VIA 来证方式 SWIFT	AVAILABLE 是否生效 VALID	TEST/SIGN 印押是否相符 YES	CONFIRM 我行是 REFUSE

DEAR SIRS, 迳启者:
WE HAVE PLEASURE IN ADVISING YOU THAT WE HAVE RECEIVED FROM THE A/M BANK A(N) LETTER CREDIT. CONTENTS OF WHICH ARE AS PER ATTACHED SHEET(S).
THIS ADVICE AND THE ATTACHED SHEET(S) MUST ACCOMPANY THE RELATIVE DOCUMENTS WHEN PRESENTED FOR NEGOTIATION.
兹通知贵司,我行收自上述银行信用证一份,现随附通知。贵司交单时,请将本通知书及信用证
一并提示。

REMARK 备注:
PLEASE NOTE THAT THIS ADVICE DOES NOT CONSTITUTE OUR CONFIRMATION OF THE ABOVE L/C N DOES IT CONVEY ANY ENGAGEMENT OR OBLIGATION ON OUR PART.

THIS L/C CONSISTS OF   SHEET(S), INCLUDING THE COVERING LETTER AND ATTACHMENTS(S)
本信用证连同面函及附件共   纸。

IF YOU FIND ANY TERMS AND CONDITIONS IN THE L/C WHICH YOU ARE UNABLE TO COMPLY WITH AND OR AN ERROR(S), IT IS SUGGESTED THAT YOU CONTACT APPLICANT DIRECTLY FOR NECESSARY AMENDMENT(S TO AVOID ANY DIFFICULTIES WHICH MAY ARISE WHEN DOCUMENTS ARE PRESENED.
如本信用证中有无法办到的条款或/或错误,请迳与开证申请人联系,进行必要的修改,以排 时可能发生的问题。

THIS L/C IS ADVISED SUBJECT TO the applicable UCP rules (issued by the ICC) as stipulated in the credit.
本信用证之通知系遵循信用证中提及的国际商会跟单信用证统一惯例。

YOURS FAITHFULLY,
FOR BANK OF CHINA

```
NOV22 11:27:58                          LOGICAL TERMINAL HI71
                ISSUE OF A DOCUMENTARY CREDIT    PAGE 00001
                                                 FUNC ZJNBBPRQ
                                                 UMR 33274692
     ACK  PTS7651 AUTH OK, KEY DIGEST, BKCHCNBJ BBMEABAD RECORD
BASIC HEADER       F  01 BKCHCNBJA92A 1580 607822
APPLICATION HEADER O 700 1644 071121 BBMEABADAXXX 7142 796873 071121 2044 N
                             *HSBC BANK MIDDLE EAST LIMITED
                             *DUBAI
USER HEADER        SERVICE CODE    103:
                   BANK. PRIORITY  113:
                   MSG USER REF.   108: 073250307581
                   INFO. FROM CI   115:
SEQUENCE OF TOTAL  *27  : 1 / 1
FORM OF DOC. CREDIT *40 A : IRREVOCABLE
DOC. CREDIT NUMBER *20  : DPCDBI074569.
DATE OF ISSUE      31 C : 071119
APPLICABLE RULES   *40 E : UCP LATEST VERSION

EXPIRY             *31 D : DATE 080110 PLACE CHINA
APPLICANT          *50   : RAWASY AL KHALEEJ PLASTIC IND.
                           P O BOX 28089
                           SHARJAH
                           U.A.E
BENEFICIARY        *59   :


AMOUNT             *32 B :       CURRENCY USD AMOUNT 55,500.00
MAX. CREDIT AMOUNT 39 B : NOT EXCEEDING
AVAILABLE WITH/BY  *41 D : BANK OF CHINA LTD
                           NINGBO BRANCH NINGBO
                           NINGBO BRANCH
                           139 YAOXING JIE
                           BY NEGOTIATION
DRAFTS AT ...      42 C : REF FIELD 47A CLAUSE 12.
DRAWEE             42 D : ISSUING BANK
PARTIAL SHIPMENTS  43 P : NOT ALLOWED
TRANSHIPMENT       43 T : ALLOWED
PORT OF LOADING    44 E :
                           NINGBO PORT, CHINA
PORT OF DISCHARGE  44 F :
                           JEBEL ALI PORT, DUBAI, UNITED ARAB EMIRATES
LATEST DATE OF SHIP. 44 C : 071225
DESCRIPT. OF GOODS 45 A :
                           CIF JEBEL ALI PORT, DUBAI, UAE
                           PLASTIC INJECTION MOLDING MACHINE.
                           ALL OTHER DETAILS AS PER PROFORMA INVOICE NO. 2007/01 DATED
                           18SEP2007.
DOCUMENTS REQUIRED 46 A :
                           1. SIGNED COMMERCIAL INVOICE IN QUADRUPLICATE MENTIONING:
                           A) RELEVANT HARMONISED SYSTEM COMMODITY CODE NUMBER(S)
                           APPLICABLE TO THE PRODUCTS SHIPPED UNDER THIS CREDIT.
                           B) NAME AND ADDRESS OF THE MANUFACTURERS/PRODUCERS/EXPORTERS.
                           CERTIFYING:
                           C) THAT THE GOODS SHIPPED ARE GUARANTEED FOR A PERIOD OF 14
                           MONTHS FROM THE DATE OF B/L.
                           2. FULL SET OF 3/3 ORGINALS AND 2 NON NEGOTIABLE COPIES OF
                           CLEAN 'ON BOARD' OCEAN/MARINE BILLS OF LADING MADE OUT TO THE
                           ORDER OF SHIPPER, ENDORSED IN BLANK, MARKED 'FREIGHT PREPAID' AND
                           NOTIFY APPLICANT AND HSBC BANK  MIDDLE EASTLTD, P O BOX 66,
                           DUBAI, UAE QUOTING THIS DOCUMENTARY CREDIT NUMBER.
                           3. A CERTIFICATE OF ORIGIN STATING THAT THE GOODS ARE OF CHINA
                           ORIGIN AND THE FULL NAME AND ADDRESS OF THE MANUFACTUER/PRODUCER
                           AND EXPORTER SIGNED BY THE CHINA COUNCIL FOR THE PROMOTION OF
```

```
                                         LOGICAL TERMINAL HI71
                    ISSUE OF A DOCUMENTARY CREDIT     PAGE 00001
                                                      FUNC ZJNBBPRQ
                                                      UMR  33274692
S.WIACF. PUS7651 AUTH OK, KEY DIGEST, BKCHCNBJ BBMBABAD RECORD
BASIC HEADER       F  01 BKCHCNBJA92A 1580 607822
APPLICATION HEADER O 700 1644 071121 BBMBABADAXXX 7142 796873 071121 2044 N
                              *HSBC BANK MIDDLE EAST LIMITED
                              *DUBAI
USER HEADER        SERVICE CODE    103:
                   BANK. PRIORITY  113:
                   MSG USER REF.   103: 073250307581
                   INFO. FROM CI   115:
SEQUENCE OF TOTAL  *27  : 1 / 1
FORM OF DOC. CREDIT *40 A : IRREVOCABLE
DOC. CREDIT NUMBER  *20  : DPCDBI074569.
DATE OF ISSUE        31 C : 071119
APPLICABLE RULES   *40 E : UCP LATEST VERSION
EXPIRY             *31 D : DATE 080110 PLACE CHINA
APPLICANT          *50   : RAWASY AL KHALEEJ PLASTIC IND.
                           P O BOX 28089
                           SHARJAH
                           U A E
BENEFICIARY        *59   :

AMOUNT             *32 B :        CURRENCY USD AMOUNT 55,500.00
MAX. CREDIT AMOUNT  39 B : NOT EXCEEDING
AVAILABLE WITH/BY  *41 D : BANK OF CHINA LTD
                           NINGBO BRANCH NINGBO
                           NINGBO BRANCH
                           139 YAOXING JIE
                           BY NEGOTIATION
DRAFTS AT ...       42 C : REF FIELD 47A CLAUSE 12.
DRAWEE              42 D : ISSUING BANK
PARTIAL SHIPMENTS   43 P : NOT ALLOWED
TRANSHIPMENT        43 T : ALLOWED
PORT OF LOADING     44 E :
                           NINGBO PORT, CHINA
PORT OF DISCHARGE   44 F :
                           JEBEL ALI PORT, DUBAI, UNITED ARAB EMIRATES
LATEST DATE OF SHIP. 44 C : 071225
DESCRIPT. OF GOODS  45 A :
                           CIF JEBEL ALI PORT, DUBAI, UAE
                           PLASTIC INJECTION MOLDING MACHINE.
                           ALL OTHER DETAILS AS PER PROFORMA INVOICE NO. 2007/01 DATED
                           18SEP2007.
DOCUMENTS REQUIRED  46 A :
                           1. SIGNED COMMERCIAL INVOICE IN QUADRUPLICATE MENTIONING:
                           A) RELEVANT HARMONISED SYSTEM COMMODITY CODE NUMBER(S)
                           APPLICABLE TO THE PRODUCTS SHIPPED UNDER THIS CREDIT.
                           B) NAME AND ADDRESS OF THE MANUFACTURERS/PRODUCERS/EXPORTERS.
                           CERTIFYING:
                           C) THAT THE GOODS SHIPPED ARE GUARANTEED FOR A PERIOD OF 14
                           MONTHS FROM THE DATE OF B/L.
                           2. FULL SET OF 3/3 ORGINALS AND 2 NON NEGOTIABLE COPIES OF
                           CLEAN 'ON BOARD' OCEAN/MARINE BILLS OF LADING MADE OUT TO THE
                           ORDER OF SHIPPER, ENDORSED IN BLANK, MARKED 'FREIGHT PREPAID' AND
                           NOTIFY APPLICANT AND HSBC BANK MIDDLE EASTLTD, P O BOX 66,
                           DUBAI, UAE QUOTING THIS DOCUMENTARY CREDIT NUMBER.
                           3. A CERTIFICATE OF ORIGIN STATING THAT THE GOODS ARE OF CHINA
                           ORIGIN AND THE FULL NAME AND ADDRESS OF THE MANUFACTUER/PRODUCER
                           AND EXPORTER SIGNED BY THE CHINA COUNCIL FOR THE PROMOTION OF
```

ISSUE OF A DOCUMENTARY CREDIT

NEGOTIATE ANY BILL DRAWN UNDER THIS CREDIT UNDER RESERVE OR AGAINST AN INDEMNITY, ALL DISCREPANCIES MUST BE ADVISED BY TELEX TO THE OPENING BANK FOR ACCEPTANCE OR REFUSAL AND REIMBURSEMENT CLAIMED ONLY AFTER ACCEPTANCE OF DISCREPANCIES BY THE OPENING BANK.

8. UNDER NO CIRCUMSTANCES MAY A BANK LISTED IN THE ARAB-ISRAELI BOYCOTT BLACKLIST BE PERMITTED TO NEGOTIATE DOCUMENTS UNDER THIS DOCUMENTARY CREDIT.

9. IN ACCORDANCE WITH THE PROVISIONS OF ARTICLE 16 C III OF UCP600, IF WE GIVE NOTICE OF REFUSAL OF DOCUMENTS PRESENTED UNDER THIS CREDIT WE SHALL HOWEVER RETAIN THE RIGHT TO ACCEPT A WAIVER OF DISCREPANCIES FROM THE APPLICANT AND, SUBJECT TO SUCH WAIVER BEING ACCEPTABLE TO US, TO RELEASE DOCUMENTS AGAINST THAT WAIVER WITHOUT REFERENCE TO THE PRESENTER PROVIDED THAT NO WRITTEN INSTRUCTIONS TO THE CONTRARY HAVE BEEN RECIEVED BY US FROM THE PRESENTER BEFORE THE RELEASE OF THE DOCUMENTS. ANY SUCH RELEASE PRIOR TO RECEIPT OF CONTRARY INSTRUCTIONS SHALL NOT CONSTITUTE A FAILURE ON OUR PART TO HOLD THE DOCUMENTS AT THE PRESENTER'S RISK AND DISPOSAL, AND WE WILL HAVE NO LIABILITY TO THE PRESENTER IN RESPECT OF ANY SUCH RELEASE.

10. ALL PARTIES SHOULD NOTE THAT BECAUSE OF SANCTIONS IMPOSED WE AND OTHER PARTIES MAY BE UNABLE IN RELATION TO THIS DOCUMENTARY CREDIT TO PROCESS OR ENGAGE IN TRANSACTIONS INVOLVING A SANCTIONS BREACH. THE SANCTIONS HAVE BEEN IMPOSED BY UN, EU, US AND OTHER AUTHORITIES WHICH MAY REQUIRE INFORMATION DISCLOSURE. WE AND OTHER PARTIES SHALL NOT BE LIABLE FOR ANY LOSS, DAMAGE OR DELAY ARISING IN CONNECTION WITH THE ABOVE MATTERS. PLEASE CONTACT US IF CLARIFICATION IS REQUIRED.

11. BENEFICIARY'S CONTACT DETAILS:
TEL:
FAX:

12. PAYMENT TERMS
A) 20 PCT OF THE DC VALUE (   ) PAYABLE IN ADVANCE AGAINST PRESENTATION OF A SIMPLE RECEIPT AS SPECIFIED UNDER FIELD 46A CLAUSE NO. 7
B) 20 PCT OF THE DC VALUE WILL BE PAID AFTER 90 DAYS FROM B/L DATE
C) 20 PCT OF THE DC VALUE WILL BE PAID AFTER 180 DAYS FROM B/L DATE.
D) 20 PCT OF THE DC VALUE WILL BE PAID AFTER 270 DAYS FROM B/L DATE.
E) 20 PCT OF THE DC VALUE WILL BE PAID AFTER 360 DAYS FROM B/L DATE.
CLAUSE 12-B), C), D) AND E) WILL BE PAID AS SPECIFIED ABOVE UPON PRESSENTATION OF THE SHIPPING DOCUMENTS AS SPECIFIED UNDER FIELD 46A CLAUSE NO: 1 TO 6.

13. REIMBURSEMENTS UNDER THIS CREDIT ARE SUBJECT TO THE UNIFORM RULES FOR BANK TO BANK REIMBURSEMENTS UNDER DOCUMENTARY CREDITS, ICC PUBLICATION NO 525.

15. YOU MAY ADD CONFIRMATION TO THIS CREDIT IF REQUESTED BY THE BENEFICIARY. IN CASE CONFIRMATION IS ADDED DRAFTS MUST BE DRAWN ON THE CONFIRMING BANK. CONFIRMATION CHARGES ARE ON ACCOUNT OF THE BENEFICIARY (THIS CLAUSE OVERRIDES FIELD 49 OF THIS DC).

DETAILS OF CHARGES 71 B : ALL CHGS OUTSIDE COUNTRY OF ISSUE
FOR ACCOUNT OF BENEFICIARY/EXPORTER
CONFIRMATION CHARGES ARE FOR
ACCOUNT OF BENEFICIARY/EXPORTER

```
MT-0700                ISSUE OF A DOCUMENTARY CREDIT            PAGE 00004
                                                                FUNC ZJNBBPRQ
                                                                UMR  33274692
PRESENTATION PERIOD     48  : WITHIN 14 DAYS AFTER THE DATE OF
                              SHIPMENT BUT WITHIN THE VALIDITY OF
                              THE CREDIT
CONFIRMATION           *49  : CONFIRM
REIMBURSING BANK       53 D : HSBC BANK USA NA
                              REIMBURSEMENT NEWARK
                              500 STANTON CHRISTIANA ROAD & OPS 1
                              NEWARK DE 19713-2107 U S A
INSTRUCTIONS            78
                              1. PROVIDED DOCUMENTS CONFORM TO THE TERMS OF THIS DOCUMENTARY
                              CREDIT, UPON MATURIY, PLS CLAIM REIMBURSEMENT (LESS
                              RIEMBURSEMENT CHGS) TO THE DEBIT OF OUR ACCOUNT: 000 04527 6
                              SWT: MRMDUS33 WITH THE NOMINATED REIMBURSING BANK UNDER SWIFT
                              ADVISE TO US.
                              2. THE AMOUNT OF EACH NEGOTIATION MUST BE ENDORSED ON THE REVERSE
                              OF THIS CREDIT AND THE NEGOTIATING BANK'S COVERING SCHEDULE TO
                              CERTIFY THE SAME.
SEND. TO REC. INFO.     72  : ALL DOCUMENTS SHOULD BE DESPATCHED
                              IN ONE LOT BY COURIER TO, HSBC BANK
                              MIDDLE EAST LTD, TRADE SERVICES,
                              IMPORT DEPT, P O BOX 66, DUBAI,
                              UNITED ARAB EMIRATES.
TRAILER                       ORDER IS <MAC:> <PAC:> <ENC:> <CHK:> <TNG:> <PDE:>
                              MAC: BB504FA4
                              CHK: 19D681938E8D
```

```
2008-1-30 10:20                                    NO.996   P.1
                                            Jan. 30 2008 09:24AM P.

TO:
FROM:
DATE: 1-30
                         海 运 托 单
SAP 号码: 2007-1560 (请在发票中显示此号码,谢谢!)
请按如下托单的内容配    船,运费预付,需熏蒸证书
```

1. Shipper	...CO LTD, EXPORT PROCESSING ZONE, NINGBO CHINA. ZIP CODE: 315800
2. Consignee	TO THE ORDER OF ... MACHINERY CO LTD
3. Notify Party	RAWASY AL KHALEEJ PLASTIC IND. P.O. BOX 28089 SHARJAH UAE HSBC BANK MIDDLE EAST LTD, P O BOX 66, DUBAI, UAE
4. Port of Loading	NINGBO PORT, CHINA
5. Port of Discharge	JEBEL ALI PORT, DUBAI, UNITED ARAB EMIRATES
6. 唛头	RAWASYPLAS
6. 货名	PLASTIC INJECTION MOLDING MACHINE CREDIT NUMBER: DPCDEIQ74569 THE NAME, ADDRESS AND TELEPHONE NUMBER OF THE CARRYING VESSEL'S AGENT IN THE COUNTRY OF DESTINATION:
7. 件数	2 PALLETS
8. 毛重/净重	11700KGS/11500KGS
9. 体积	30CBM
10. 提单	正本3副
12. 集装箱配置	40'GP
13. 装箱时间	尽快,货已好!
14. 转船/分批出运	
15. 特别注明内容	内上车拉箱
以下由货代填写并请回传真	谢谢!
确认装箱时间	1.31
确认开船日期	2.4
确认海运费	
确认人民币费用	
确认船公司名称	CSCL
确认预计到港日期	

F: 2350
L: 732L

第九章 寄单和交单议付

HRS 宁波市海润国际货运代理有限公司		集装箱号 Container No.	CCLU 4350842	集装箱规格 Type of Container: 40'GP
装 箱 单 CONTAINER LOAD PLAN		铅封号 Seal No.	1082265	

船名 Ocean Vessel	航次 Voy No.	装货港 Port of Loading	中转港 Port of Transit:	ABU EA
XIN XIA MEN	V.0053W	NINGBO	卸货港 Port of Discharging:	DUBAI

提单号码 B/L No.	标志和号码 Marks & Numbers	件数及包装种类 No. & Kind of Pkgs.	货名 Description of Goods	重量(公斤) Weight Kg	尺码(立方米) Measurement Cu.M	备注 Remarks
8NGBJEA3AP995 ZHZ 200801N293		RAWA5%PLAS2PALLETS	PLASTIC INJECTION MOLDING MACHINE 070701202062 07070202071 附件箱 2 油 2桶 DT0130螺丝 8 口箱12 DT0180螺丝 10 口箱14 样本 1箱	11700KGS	30CBM	8个×1
		总件数 Total Number of Packages 重量及尺码总计 Total Weight & Measurement		2	15500KGS	30CBM 冷藏温度 ℃

驾驶员签收及车号	装箱人签名	装箱日期	总毛重 Gross Weight

装箱人名称/地址/电话:		特殊要求	
电话: 传真:		2PTS 11700 30	

备注: 如未按要求服务,请在装箱单上注明或投诉。

中华人民共和国海关出口加工区出境货物备案清单

现场验放报关单
主页

预录入编号：618749201　　海关编号：311120080618749201

出口口岸	北仑海关 (3104)	备案号：H31117006023	出口日期	申报日期 2008-02-01
经营单位 3302530004		运输方式 江海运输	运输工具名称 XINXIAMEN/0053W	提运单号 BNGBJEA3A1995
发货单位 3302530004		贸易方式 区内加工货物(5015)	征免性质 ()	结汇方式 信用证(L/C)
许可证号		运抵国(地区) 阿联酋(138)	指运港 迪拜(1543)	宁波出口加工区(33025)
批准文号		成交方式 CIF	运费 502/2350/3	保费 502/73.26/3 杂费 0/0/0
合同协议号 2007-1560		件数 2	包装种类 托盘	毛重(公斤) 11700　净重(公斤) 11500
集装箱号 CCLU4350842 A 1 (2)		随附单据		生产厂家

标记唛码及备注
31112C082107001343 FOB USD53076.74
报关员：31000709

项号	商品编号	商品名称、规格型号	数量及单位	最终目的国(地区)	单价	总价	币制	征免
1 [581]	8477101090 0707012020622	注塑机	1 台	阿联酋(138)	24500	用途：加工返销	美元	全免
2 [582]	8477101090 0707020020711	注塑机	1 台	阿联酋(138)	31000	用途：加工返销	美元	全免

税费征收情况

录入员 王盈莹	录入单位 宁波保税区依迪计算机服务有限公司	兹声明以上申报无讹并承担法律责任 该单已审结 出口报关 审结时间：2008-2- 申报单位（签章） 宁波保税区瑞成报关有限公司 报关专用章 2008-2-1 填制日期 宁波(5)	海关审单批注及放行日期（签章） 审单 征税 查验
报关员 俞荣 单位地址 邮编 315010 电话 13805864234			

宁波海关监制

出口产品明细表

出口单位		合同评审号	0703362(2007-1560)		
		信用证号	DPCDEI074569		
		信用证金额			
客户名称	RAWASY AL KHALEEJ PLASTIC IND.P O BOX 28089 SHARJAH UAE	合同金额			
		合同付款方式	20%为定金，余款分四次付清，一年期信用证。		
开证行	HSBC BANK MIDDLE EAST(THE BRITISH BANK OF THE MIDDLE EAST)DUBAI	价格条款	C&F		
发票抬头		箱型	40″GP	箱量	1
提单收货人	TO ORDER	目的港/国家	DUBAI/U.A.E		
		最终目的地	U.A.E		
		装运期限	080118	有效期限	080118
		可否转运		可否分批	
提单通知人	SAME AS APPLICANT	运费	预付	目的地到付	
		其他单据要求			

机器型号	数量	预付款数	报关发票金额	客户发票金额
	1	20%为定金		
	1			

业务员姓名		制表日期	080116
备注			

COMMERCIAL INVOICE

Buyers:	Shipping Marks &Numbers:
RAWASY AL KHALEEJ PLASTIC IND. P O BOX 28089 SHARJAH U A E	RAWASYPLAS

Invoice Number:	2007-1560	Date:	Jan.30,2008
From:	NINGBO PORT, CHINA	L/C No.:	DPCDEI074569
To:	JEBEL ALI PORT, DUBAI, UNITED ARAB EMIRATES	Payment:	

Descriptions	Q'ty	Unit Price	Amount
		CIF JEBEL ALI PORT, DUBAI, UAE	
PLASTIC INJECTION MOLDING MACHINE	1 SET 1 SET 2 SETS		
ALL OTHER DETAILS AS PER PROFORMA INVOICE NO. 2007/01 DATED 18SEP2007. A) RELEVANT HARMONISED SYSTEM COMMODITY CODE NUMBER(S) APPLICABLE TO THE PRODUCTS SHIPPED UNDER THIS CREDIT:847710 B)NAME AND ADDRESS OF THE MANUFACTURERS/PRODUCERS/EXPORTERS: CO., LTD. EXPORT PROCESSING ZONE NINGBO CHINA WE HEREBY CERTIFYING: C) THAT THE GOODS SHIPPED ARE GUARANTEED FOR A PERIOD OF 14 MONTHS FROM THE DATE OF B/L.			

PACKING LIST

Buyers: RAWASY AL KHALEEJ PLASTIC IND. P O BOX 28089 SHARJAH U A E		Shipping Marks & Numbers: RAWASYPLAS	
Invoice Number:	2007-1560	Date:	Jan.30,2008
From:	NINGBO PORT, CHINA	L/C No.:	DPCDEI074569
To:	JEBEL ALI PORT, DUBAI, UNITED ARAB EMIRATES	Payment:	

Descriptions	Q'ty	PACKING	G.W.	N.W.	DIMENSION
PLASTIC INJECTION MOLDING MACHINE					
	1 SET	1 PALLET	4700KGS	4600KGS	12CBM
	1 SET	1 PALLET	7000KGS	6900KGS	18CBM
	2 SETS	2 PALLETS	11700KGS	11500KGS	30CBM
ALL OTHER DETAILS AS PER PROFORMA INVOICE NO. 2007/01 DATED 18SEP2007.					

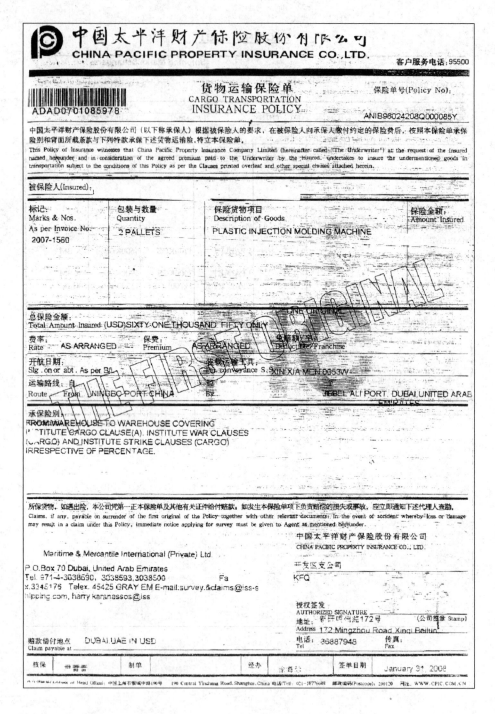

ORIGINAL	
1. Exporter:	Certificate No. **CCPIT 074144691** 08C3303A1261/00046
2. Consignee: RAWASI AL KHALEEJ PLASTIC IND. P.O. BOX 28089 SHARJAH U.A.E	**CERTIFICATE OF ORIGIN** **OF** **THE PEOPLE'S REPUBLIC OF CHINA**
3. Means of transport and route: FROM NINGBO PORT CHINA TO JEBEL ALI PORT, DUBAI, UNITED ARAB EMIRATES BY SEA	5. For certifying authority use only CHINA COUNCIL FOR THE PROMOTION OF INTERNATIONAL TRADE IS CHINA CHAMBER OF INTERNATIONAL COMMERCE
4. Country / region of destination: UNITED ARAB EMIRATES	

6. Marks and numbers	7. Number and kind of packages; description of goods	8. H.S.Code	9. Quantity G. WEIGHT	10. Number and date of invoices
RAWASYPLAS	TWO (2) PALLETS OF PLASTIC INJECTION MOLDING MACHINE WE HEREBY STATE THAT THE GOODS ARE OF CHINA ORIGIN. THE FULL NAME AND ADDRESS OF THE MANUFACTURER/PRODUCER AND EXPORTER: LTD. EXPORT PROCESSING ZONE NINGBO CHINA	847710	11700KGS	2007-1560 JAN. 30, 2008

11. Declaration by the exporter. The undersigned hereby declares that the above details and statements are correct, that all the goods were produced in China and that they comply with the Rules of Origin of the People's Republic of China. NINGBO, CHINA JAN. 31, 2008 Place and date, signature and stamp of authorized signatory	12. Certification It is hereby certified that the declaration by the exporter is correct. NINGBO, CHINA JAN. 31, 2008 Place and date, signature and stamp of certifying authority

			B/L NO. 3NGBJEA3AP995
			HRC

中海集装箱运输(香港)有限公司
CHINA SHIPPING CONTAINER LINES (HONG KONG) CO., LTD.

Cable : CSHKAC   Telex : 87986   CSHKAHX

Port-to-Port or Combined Transport
BILL OF LADING

1. Shipper

2. To the order of shipper

RECEIVED in external apparent good order and condition, except otherwise noted. The total number of containers or other packages or units shown in this Bill of Lading receipt, is said by the shipper to contain the goods described above, which description the carrier has no reasonable means of checking and is not part of the Bill of Lading. One original Bill of Lading should be surrendered, except clause 22 paragraph 5, in exchange for delivery of the shipment. Signed by the consignee or duly endorsed by the holder in due course. Whereupon the other original(s) issued shall be void. In accepting this Bill of Lading, the Merchants agree to be bound by all the terms on the face and back hereof as if each had personally signed this Bill of Lading.
WHEN the Place of Receipt of the Goods is an inland point and is so named herein, any notation of "ON BOARD" "SHIPPED ON BOARD" or words to like effect on this Bill of Lading shall be deemed to mean on board the truck, trail car, air craft or other inland conveyance (as the case may be), performing carriage from the Place of Receipt of the Goods to the Port of Loading.
SEE clause 4 on the back of this Bill of Lading (Terms continued on the back hereof Read Carefully).

3. Notify Party (Carrier not to be responsible for failure to notify)
RAWASY AL KHALEEJ PLASTIC IND.
P.O.BOX 28089 SHARJAH U A E
HSBC BANK MIDDLE EAST LTD.P O BOX 66,DUBAI,UAE

4. Pre-carriage by*

5. Place of Receipt*

6. Ocean Vessel   Voy.No.
XIN XIA MEN   0053 W

7. Port of Loading
NINGBO PORT CHINA   **ORIGINAL**

8. Place of discharge
JEBEL ALI PORT,DUBAI,UNITED ARAB EMIRATES

9. Place of Delivery*
JEBEL ALI PORT,DUBAI,UNITED ARAB EMIRATES

10. Final Destination (for the merchant's reference only)

11. Marks & Nos.	12. No. of containers or P'kgs.	13. Kind of Packages : Description of Goods	14. Gross Weight kgs	15. Measurement
RAWASYPLAS	2	SHIPPER'S LOAD, COUNT & SEAL SAID TO CONTAIN PALLETS PLASTIC INJECTION MOLDING MACHINE THE DOCUMENTARY CREDIT NUMBER:DPCDEI074569 THE NAME,ADDRESS AND TELEPHONE NUMBER OF THE CARRYING VESSEL'S AGENT IN THE COUNTRY OF DESTINATION:CHINA SHIPPING (UAE) AGENCY L.L.C P.O.BOX 62578, DUBAI 2/F SHARAF TRAVEL BLDG, NEXT TO RAMADA HOTEL,BUR DUBAI UNITED ARAB EMIRATES TEL NO: +971 4 352 6633 FAX NO: +971 4 352 6622 E-MAIL: DUBAI@CNSHIPPINGUAE.COM	11700 KGS	30 CBM
			1X40'GP CY-CY FREIGHT PREPAID CCLU4330342/082265/40'G	

Description of Contents for Shipper's Use Only (CARRIER NOT RESPONSIBLE)

17. TOTAL NO. CONTAINERS OR PACKAGES (IN WORDS)
SAY TWO(2) PALLETS ONLY.

18. FREIGHT & CHARGES	19. Revenue Tons	20. Rate	21. Per	22. Prepaid	23. Collect
CHINA SHIPPING (UAE) AGENCY L.L.C. P.O. Box 62578, Dubai 2/F Sharaf Travel Bldg, Next to Ramada Hotel, Bur Dubai United Arab Emirates Tel No: +971 4 352 6633 Fax No: +971 4 352 6622 EMAIL: dubai@cnshippinguae.com	ON BOARD CSCL(ZHEJIANG)			(73) GENERAL MANAGER AS AGENT FOR THE CARRIER	

24. Ex. Rate	25. Prepaid at	26. Payable at	27. Place and date of issue NINGBO FEB 08,2008
	28. Total prepaid in	29. No. of Original B/L THREE	Signed for the Carrier

DATE FEB 08,2008

BY ....

NO. 700503354

CHINA SHIPPING CONTAINER LINES (HONG KONG) CO., LTD. STANDARD FORM 9701
* Applicable Only When Document Use as a Combined Transport Bill of Lading

相关知识

一、审单方法和不符点单据的处理

（一）审单原则

1. 严格一致

所谓严格一致的原则，是指在单据和信用证条款之间，一个字与一个字、一个字母与一个字母的相符，即使是拼写错误，也会构成单证不一致。单据就像是信用证的"镜子影像"。

2. 实质一致

所谓实质一致的原则，是允许单据有差异，只要差异不损害申请人，或不背离"合理、公平、善意"的概念即可。

（二）审单工作方法

1. 横审法

"横审"是根据信用证的条款逐字逐句地审核各种单据的内容，做到"单证一致"。

2. 纵审法

"纵审"是以商业发票为中心，与其他单据相对照，要求单据与单据之间所共有的项目相互一致，即"单单一致"。

（三）信用证项下的不符点

1. 信用证项下的不符点

不符点（Discrepancy）是指信用证项下受益人所提交的单据表面出现的一处或多处不符合信用证的条款或条件的错误。

当单据出现不符点后，信用证的开证行就可以免除付款的责任。

2. 指定银行对单据不符的处理

（1）将所有单据退还给提交人更改，以便在信用证有效期内和最迟交单期内再次交单。

（2）仅仅退还不符单据。让提交人更改，以便在信用证有效期内和最迟交单期内再次交单。

（3）在交单人授权下将信用证项下的不符单据以等待批准方式寄送给开证行，要求他审查和批准接受单据或拒绝接受单据。

（4）将所有单据退还交单人，请他采取直接行动寄单给开证行。

（5）如果交单人准许，以电报、电传或电讯发至开证行，要求凭不符单据授权付款、承兑或议付。

（6）从收益人或他的银行出具赔偿担保信，凭以议付、付款或承兑，该信保证如果开证行拒绝接受不符单据和拒绝偿付，则任何议付、付款、承兑金额连同利息和有关费用将被担保信出具人偿还。

（7）根据实际经验，并征得收益人同意，办理"保留权利"的付款、承兑或议付，即如果开证行凭不符单据而拒绝偿付，则银行保留对收益人的追索权。

（8）寄单托收。

3. 开证行对单据不符的处理

《UCP600》第十六条提到不符单据、放弃及通知：

a. 当按照指定行事的指定银行、保兑行（如有的话）或者开证行确定交单不符时，可以拒绝承付或议付。

b. 当开证行确定交单不符时，可以自行决定联系申请人放弃不符点；然而这并不能延长第十四条 b 款所指的期限。

c. 当按照指定行事的指定银行、保兑行（如有的话）或开证行决定拒绝承付或议付时，必须给予交单人一份单独的拒付通知。

该通知必须声明：

i. 银行拒绝承付或议付；及

ii. 银行拒绝承付或者议付所依据的每一个不符点；及

iii. a）银行留存单据听候交单人的进一步指示；或者

iii. b）开证行留存单据直到其从申请人处接到放弃不符点的通知并同意接受该放弃，或者其同意接受对不符点的放弃之前从交单人处收到其进一步指示；或者

iii. c）银行将退回单据；或者

iii. d）银行将按之前从交单人处获得的指示处理。

d. 第十六条 c 款要求的通知必须以电讯方式，如不可能，则以其他快捷方式，在不迟于自交单之翌日起第五个银行工作日结束前发出。

e. 按照指定行事的指定银行、保兑行（如有的话）或开证行在按照第十六条 c 款 iii 项 a）或 b）发出了通知后，可以在任何时候将单据退还交单人。

f. 如果开证行或保兑行未能按照本条行事，则无权宣称交单不符。

g. 开证行在拒绝承付或保兑行拒绝承付或者议付，并且按照本条发出了拒付通知后，有权要求返还已偿付的款项及利息。

实训练习题

假如你是个银行工作人员，2009年11月11日收下某出口企业一套信用证项下单据，请根据信用证内容审单，至少找出五个不符点。

信 用 证 通 知 书
ADVICE OF A LETTER OF CREDIT

致TO:
贝发集团股份有限公司
BEIFA GROUP CO LTD

日期DATE: 8 SEPTEMBER 2009
我行编号OUR REF: 83009110020439

信用证编号(L/C No): M923539

开证日期(Issuing Date): 7 SEPTEMBER 2009

信用证金额(Amount): USD 138,595.02

信用证效期(Date of Expiry): 14 NOVEMBER 2009

最后装船期(Latest Shipment Date): 30 OCTOBER 2009

开证行(Issuing Bank): BANCO SANTANDER, S.A. INSTITUCIONDE BANCA MULTIPLE, GROUPFINANCIERO SANTANDER, S.A.

兹通知信用证一份，内容见附件。
WE HAVE PLEASURE IN ADVISING YOU A DOCUMENTARY CREDIT WHICH IS ATTACHED TO THIS ADVISING LETTER.

如贵公司发现本信用证有无法办到的条款和条件，或发现信用证存在错误，请直接与开证申请人联系，进行必要的修改，以避免在交单时产生困难。
IF YOU FIND ANY TERMS AND CONDITIONS IN THE L/C WHICH ARE UNABLE TO COMPLY WITH, OR IF YOU FIND ANY ERROR(S), IT IS SUGGESTED THAT YOU CONTACT THE APPLICANT DIRECTLY FOR NECESSARY AMENDMENT(S) SO AS TO AVOID ANY DIFFICULTIES WHICH MAY ARISE WHEN DOCUMENTS ARE PRESENTED.

本通知不构成我行其他任何责任和义务。
OUR ADVICE OF THE ABOVE L/C CONVEYS NO FURTHER ENGAGEMENT OR OBLIGATION ON OUR PART.

本信用证的通知依照国际商会《跟单信用证统一惯例》（2007年修订版）第600号出版物。
THIS ADVICE IS SUBJECT TO UNIFORM CUSTOMS AND PRACTICE FOR DOCUMENTARY CREDITS. (2007 REVISION) ICC PUBLICATION NO.600.

中国建设银行股份有限公司
CHINA CONSTRUCTION BANK CORPORATION

AUTHORIZED SIGNATURE

```
MT700
SENDER:
BMSXMXMM
BANCO SANTANDER,S.A. INSTITUCION
DE BANCA MULTIPLE,GROUP
FINANCIERO SANTANDER,S.A.
RECEIVER:
PCBCCNBJNPX
CHINA CONSTRUCTION BANK
NINGBO BR. INTL DEPT.
L/C ARRIVAL DATE: 8 SEPTEMBER 2009
27:  SEQUENCE OF TOTAL
     1/1
40A: FORM OF L/C (Y/N/T)
     IRREVOCABLE
20:  DOCUMENT CREDIT NO
     M923539
31C: DATE OF ISSUE
     090907
40E: APPLICABLE RULES
     UCP LATEST VERSION
31D: DATE AND PLACE OF EXPIRE
     091114CHINA
50:  APPLICANT
     OFFICE DEPOT DE MEXICO, SA DE CV
     JUAN SALVADOR AGRAZ NO. 101
     COL. SANTA FE DEL. CUAJIMALPA
     DE MORELOS, MEXICO. D.F.
59:  BENEFICIARY
     BEIFA GROUP CO LTD
     NO 298 JIANGNAN EAST ROAD BEILUN
     NINGBO 315801 CHINA
     TEL 86 574 8618 6680
32B: CURRENCY CODE,AMOUNT
     USD138595,02
39A: PERCENTAGE CREDIT AMOUNT
     05/05
41A: AVAILABLE WITH..BY
     PCBCCNBJNPX
     BY DEF PAYMENT
42P: DEFFERED PAYMENT DETAILS
     60 DAYS AFTER PRESENTATION
43P: PARTIAL SHIPMENT
     ALLOWED
43T: TRANSSHIPMENT
     ALLOWED/PERMITIDOS
44E: PORT OF LOADING
                2/4           OUR REF. 830091I0020439
```

```
        NINGBO CHINA
44F: PORT OF DISCHARGE
        MANZANILLO COL. MEXICO OR LAZARO CARDENAS MICH. MEXICO
44B: PLACE OF FINAL DESTIN.
        MEXICO CITY
44C: LATEST DATE OF SHIPMENT
        091030
45A: DESCRIPTION OF GOODS
        + WRITING INSTRUMENT
46A: DOCUMENTS REQUIRED
        + 1 ORIGINAL AND 3 COPIES OF COMMERCIAL INVOICE DATED AND
        SHOWING INCOTERM FOB AND RFC ODM950324V2A
        + 1 ORIGINAL AND 4 COPIES OF FCR CONSIGNED AND NOTIFY TO: OFFICE
        DEPOT DE MEXICO S.A. DE C.V.  ODM950324V2A, JUAN SALVADOR AGRAZ
        NO. 101 COL. SANTA FE DELEGACION CUAJIMALPA DE MORELOS C.P.
        05300 MEXICO D.F. TEL 52 46 40 00 FAX 52 46 40 00 EXT 3000.
        MARKED FREIGHT COLLECT.
        + 1 ORIGINAL AND 3 COPIES OF PACKING LIST
        + 1 ORIGINAL AND 3 COPIES OF CERTIFICATE OF ORIGIN ISSUED BY THE
        GOVERNMENT OF THE ORIGIN COUNTRY PRODUCT.
        + 1 ORIGINAL AND 3 COPIES OF CERTIFICATE OF QUALITY
        + 1 ORIGINAL OF BENEFICIARY'S LETTER INDICATING THIS SHIPMENT
        HAS NO SOLID WOOD PACKING MATERIAL AND CETIFYING THAT COPIES OF
        ALL THE REQUIRED DOCUMENTS WERE SENT TO OFFICE DEPOT DE MEXICO
        SA DE CV IN ATTENTION TO JOSE LUIS MARTINEZ CORONEL BY SPECIAL
        COURIER SERVICE SHIPMENTS.
47A: ADDITIONAL CONDITIONS
        + BENEFICIARY MUST PRESENT AN EXTRA PHOTOCOPY OF ALL DOCUMENTS
        REQUIRED IN THIS L/C FOR BANCO SANTANDER (MEXICO) S.A. FILE.
        + CERTIFICATE OF ORIGIN SHOWING DIFFERENT INVOICE NBR IS
        ACCEPTABLE
        + IN CASE OF FORWARDER CARGO RECEIPT IS PRESENTED WE WILL
        CONSIDER CARGO RECEIVED DATE OF DOCUMENT AS SHIPMENT DATE AND
        DOCUMENTS PRESENTATION. IN CASE OF SEVERAL FCR PRESENTED, WE
        WILL CONSIDER THE FIRST DATE FOR DOCUMENTS PRESENTATION.
        FCR MUST SHOW LOADING POINT, DISCHARGE POINT, AND FINAL
        DESTINATION.
        + THE LATEST SHIP DATE MUST BE BASED ON CARGO RECEIVED DATE ON
        FCR
71B: CHARGES
        ISSUING BANK CHARGES TO BE PAID BY:
        APPLICANT
        FOREIGN BANK CHARGES TO BE PAID BY:
        BENEFICIARY
48:  PERIOD FOR PRESENTATION
        DOCUMENTS MUST BE PRESENTED
```

```
     WITHIN 15 DAYS AFTER ISSUANCE
     OF THE TRANSPORT DOCUMENT BUT
     WITHIN THE VALIDITY OF THIS CREDIT
49:  CONFIRMATION INSTRUCTION
     MAY ADD
78:  INSTR TO PAY/ACCEP/NEG
     UPON RECEIPT IN OUR COUNTERS DOCUMENTS IN GOOD ORDER AND
     COMPLIED WITH ALL TERMS AND CONDITIONS WE WILL REMIT FUNDS AS
     PER
     YOUR DOC REMITTANCE INSTRUCTIONS AT MATURITY DATE.
72:  SENDER TO RECEIVER INF
     PLS ACKNOW RECEIPT QUOTING YR REF.
     NBR. SEND DOCS BY COURIER TO/BANCO
     SANTANDER S.A. VASCO DE QUIROGA NO
     3900 TORRE A, PISO 17,COL.SANTA FE
     C.P.05300 MEXICO D.F./ IN 1 LOT
     ATTN. L/C DEPT./EFE.
```

OUR REF. 83009110020439

COMMERCIAL INVOICE

THE SELLER: BEIFA GROUP CO., LTD.
ADDRESS: NO.298 Jiangnan East Road, Beilun, Ningbo, 315801, China
TELEPHONE: 86-574-86155924 86155933 86186888(OPERATOR)
FAX NUMBER: 86-574-86155295
EMAIL ADD: service@beifa.com
URL: http://www.beifa.com
TO: OFFICE DEPOT DE MEXICO SA DE CV AV JUAN SALVADOR AGRAZ NO.101 COL.CUAJIMALPA C.P.05300 MEXICO DF
FROM: NINGBO, CHINA TO: MANZANILLO COL. MEXICO
LC NO.: M923539

INVOICE NO.: F0337-09080022/46
DATE: 2009-10-15

PO#	SKU#	DESCRIPTION OF GOODS	FOB	QUANTI	TOTAL AMOUNT
		INCOTERM FOB AND RFC ODM950324V2A WRITING INSTRUMENT: ERASER, BALL PEN, MECHANICAL PENCIL, GEL INK PEN, ROLLER PEN, BOARD MARKER, HIGHLIGHTER PEN, MARKER PEN, BALL PEN REFILL, BRUSH, LEAD REFILLS			
BEIFA91030	30048	PAQUETE CON 6 ROOLER BALL COL SURTIDOS	$ 0.690	4,032	$ 2,782.08
BEIFA91030	30049	PAQUETE CON 3 RESALTADORES	$ 0.570	3,312	$ 1,887.84
BEIFA91030	30054	PAQUETE CON 4 MARCADORES PARA PIZARRON BLANCO	$ 0.580	20,736	$ 12,026.88
BEIFA91030	30058	PAQUETE DE 4 MARCADORES PERMANENTES PUNTO FINO	$ 0.370	5,040	$ 1,864.80
BEIFA91030	30060	PAQUETE DE 2 MARCADORES PERMANENTES PUNTO FINO	$ 0.210	6,192	$ 1,300.32
BEIFA91030	30064	JUEGO DE 3 LAPICEROS Y DOS MINAS DE REPUESTO	$ 0.650	3,168	$ 2,059.20
BEIFA91030	32520	PLUMA 4 EN 1 CON REPUESTOS	$ 1.300	3,024	$ 3,931.20
BEIFA91030	32524	PAQUETE DE 12 BOLIGRAFOS NEGROS	$ 0.330	6,480	$ 2,138.40
BEIFA91030	35727	Boligrafo con grip caja con 12 pzas color negro	$ 0.529	1,296	$ 685.58
BEIFA91030	35728	Boligrafo con grip caja con 12 pzas color azul	$ 0.529	864	$ 457.06
BEIFA91030	35729	Marcador Permanente caja con 12 pzas negro PUNTA CINCEL	$ 3.150	2,304	$ 7,257.60
BEIFA91030	35730	Boligrafo 4 en 1 blister con 3	$ 0.350	1,728	$ 604.80
BEIFA91030	35732	Boligrafo Retractil con grip b/5	$ 0.400	2,592	$ 1,036.80
BEIFA91030	35733	Caja de marcadores para pzarron punto cincel con grip 12	$ 3.150	2,232	$ 7,030.80
BEIFA91030	35742	PAQUETE CON 4 MARCADORES PARA PIZARRON BLANCO PUNTA REDONDA	$ 0.930	864	$ 803.52
BEIFA91030	35762	PAQUETE CON 4 MARCADORES PARA PIZARRON BLANCO PUNTA CINCEL	$ 0.980	5,040	$ 4,939.20
BEIFA91030	41285	MARCATEXTOS PUNTA CINCEL COLORES SURTIDOS	$ 0.370	5,664	$ 2,095.68
BEIFA91030	41287	MARCADORES PARA PIZARRON COLORES SURTIDOS	$ 3.087	672	$ 2,074.46
BEIFA91030	41356	BORRADOR PARA PIZARRON BLANCO	$ 0.450	4,032	$ 1,814.40
BEIFA91030	41360	BOLIGRAFO RETRACTIL PUNTO MEDIANO TINTA NEGRA CAJA CON 12	$ 1.220	1,008	$ 1,229.76
BEIFA91030	41378	GOMAS BLANCAS 3PK	$ 0.130	4,860	$ 631.80
BEIFA91030	43793	BOLIGRAFO DE GEL CON PUNTO EXTRAFINO COLORES SURTIDOS	$ 0.760	1,584	$ 1,203.84
BEIFA91030	43795	BOLIGRAFO DE GEL CON PUNTO EXTRAFINO COLOR NEGRO	$ 0.760	1,296	$ 984.96
BEIFA91030	43796	BOLIGRAFO DE GEL PUNTO EXTRAFINO COLOR NEGRO	$ 0.630	2,592	$ 1,632.96
BEIFA91030	43797	BOLIGRAFO DE GEL PUNTO MEDIANO COLOR SURTIDOS FLOURESCENTES	$ 0.630	2,592	$ 1,632.96
BEIFA91030	43800	PLUMA PARA MOSTRADOR	$ 0.570	3,456	$ 1,969.92
BEIFA91030	43808	BOLIGRAFO RETRACTIL GREEN TRIANGULAR TINTA NEGRA COLORES VIVOS	$ 0.630	864	$ 544.32
BEIFA90228	42692	GOMAS BLANCAS MODELO OD30 2PK	$ 0.121	8,160	$ 987.36
TOTAL				105,684	$ 67,608.50

MARKS & NOS
OFFICE DEPOT MEXICO
Vendor Part#:
UPC#:
PO#:
RFC#: ODM-950324-V2A
SKU#:
Carton Dimension: XX CM
Country of Origin: China
Carton#: xx of xx
G.W.: XX KGS
N.T.: XX KGS

BEIFA GROUP CO., LTD.

(页 3 / 5 - This print header can be changed using the printHeader HTML tag - see the viewONE HTML manual for further information)

PACKING LIST

THE SELLER: BEIFA GROUP
ADDRESS: NO. 298 Jiangnan East Road, Beilun, Ningbo, 315801, China
TELEPHONE: 86-574-86186589 86155933 86186888 (OPERATOR)
FAX NUMBER: 86-574-86155285
EMAIL ADD: service@beifa.com
URL: http://www.beifa.com
TO: OFFICE DEPOT DE MEXICO SA DE CV AV JUAN SALVADOR AGRAZ NO. 101 COL. CUAJIMALPA C.P. 05300 MEXICO DF

INVOICE NO.: F0337-09080022/46
DATE: 2009-10-15

PO#	SKU#	DESCRIPTION OF GOODS	QUANTITY	CTNS	N.W.	G.W.
		INCOTERM FOB AND RFC ODM950324V2A				
		WRITING INSTRUMENT: ERASER, BALL PEN, MECHANICAL PENCIL, GEL INK PEN, ROLLER PEN, BOARD MARKER, HIGHLIGHTER PEN, MARKER PEN, BALL PEN REFILL, BRUSH, LEAD REFILLS				
BEIFA91030	30048	PAQUETE CON 6 ROOLER BALL COL SURTIDOS	4,032	28	350	406
BEIFA91030	30049	PAQUETE CON 5 RESALTADORES	3,312	23	241.5	287.5
BEIFA91030	30054	PAQUETE CON 4 MARCADORES PARA PIZARRON BLANCO	20,736	144	1756.8	1900.8
BEIFA91030	30058	PAQUETE DE 4 MARCADORES PERMANENTES PUNTO FINO	5,040	35	262.5	332.5
BEIFA91030	30060	PAQUETE DE 2 MARCADORES PERMANENTES PUNTO FINO	6,192	43	172	238
BEIFA91030	30064	JUEGO DE 3 LAPICEROS Y DOS MINAS DE REPUESTO	3,168	22	158.4	187
BEIFA91030	32520	PLUMA 4 EN 1 CON REPUESTOS	3,024	63	207.9	283.5
BEIFA91030	32524	PAQUETE DE 12 BOLIGRAFOS NEGROS	6,480	45	517.5	567
BEIFA91030	35727	Boligrafo con grip caja con 12 pzas color negro	1,296	9	108	117.9
BEIFA91030	35728	Boligrafo con grip caja con 12 pzas color azul	864	6	72	78.6
BEIFA91030	35729	Marcador Permanente caja con 12 pzas negro PUNTA CINCEL	2,304	32	704	744.32
BEIFA91030	35730	Boligrafo 4 en 1 blister con 3	1,728	12	78	90
BEIFA91030	35732	Boligrafo Retractil con grip b/5	2,592	18	144	162
BEIFA91030	35733	Caja de marcadores para pizarron punta cincel con grip 12	2,232	31	682	721.06
BEIFA91030	35742	PAQUETE CON 4 MARCADORES PARA PIZARRON BLANCO PUNTA REDONDA	864	6	63	69
BEIFA91030	35762	PAQUETE CON 4 MARCADORES PARA PIZARRON BLANCO PUNTA CINCEL	5,040	70	511	581
BEIFA91030	41285	MARCATEXTOS PUNTA CINCEL COLORES SURTIDOS	5,664	59	377.6	483.8
BEIFA91030	41287	MARCADORES PARA PIZARRON COLORES SURTIDOS	672	14	245	273
BEIFA91030	41356	BORRADOR PARA PIZARRON BLANCO	4,032	112	246.4	358.4
BEIFA91030	41360	BOLIGRAFO RETRACTIL PUNTO MEDIANO TINTA NEGRA CAJA CON 12	1,008	14	91	112
BEIFA91030	41378	GOMAS BLANCAS 3PK	4,860	18	216	234
BEIFA91030	43793	BOLIGRAFO DE GEL CON PUNTO EXTRAFINO COLORES SURTIDOS	1,584	11	121	137.5
BEIFA91030	43795	BOLIGRAFO DE GEL CON PUNTO EXTRAFINO COLOR NEGRO				
BEIFA91030	43796	BOLIGRAFO DE GEL PUNTO EXTRAFINO COLOR NEGRO	2,592	18	171	198
BEIFA91030	43797	BOLIGRAFO DE GEL PUNTO MEDIANO COLOR SURTIDOS FLUORESCENTES	2,592	18	171	198
BEIFA91030	43800	PLUMA PARA MOSTRADOR	3,456	24	187.2	211.2
BEIFA91030	43808	BOLIGRAFO RETRACTIL GREEN TRIANGULAR TINTA NEGRA COLORES VIVOS	864	12	57.6	69.6
BEIFA90228	42692	GOMAS BLANCAS MODELO OD30 2PK				408
TOTAL			105,684	930	8385.4	9562.58

MARKS & NOS
OFFICE DEPOT MEXICO
Vendor Part#:
UPC#:
PO#:
RFC#: ODM-950324-V2A
SKU#:
Carton Dimension: XX CM
Country of Origin: China
Carton#: xx of xx
G.W.: XX KGS
N.T.: XX KGS

```
SHIPPER
BEIFA GROUP CO.,LTD
NO.298 JIANGNAN EAST ROAD
BEILUN NINGBO 315801 CHINA
TEL 86 574 86186680
```

KUEHNE NAGEL

FORWARDER'S CERTIFICATE OF RECEIPT

```
**** PLEASE QUOTE IN YOUR REPLY ****
KN REFERENCE        4359-0358-910.031
NINGBO                     28/10/2009
```

```
CONSIGNEE
OFFICE DEPOT DE MEXICO,S.A.DE C.V.
ODM950324V2A,JUAN SALVADOR AGRAZ
NO.101 COL.SANTA FE DELEGACION
CUAJIMALPA DE MORELOS C.P.05300,
MEXICO D.F.TEL:52464000 *
```

```
NOTIFY PARTY 2
* FAX:52464000 EXT:3000
**.MEXICO
```

```
NOTIFY PARTY
OFFICE DEPOT DE MEXICO,S.A.DE C.V.
ODM950324V2A,JUAN SALVADOR AGRAZ
NO.101 COL.SANTA FE DELEGACION
CUAJIMALPA DE MORELOS C.P.05300,
MEXICO D.F.TEL:52464000 *
```

```
FINAL AGENT
KUEHNE & NAGEL, S.A. DE C.V.
CALLE 28 NO. 90-A, COL. FEDERAL
MEXICO, D.F. 15700, MEXICO
RFC:K&N030814796
```

```
OCEAN VESSEL . . . : CAP GILBERT
PORT OF LOADING . : NINGBO
PORT OF DISCHARGE : MANZANILLO
PLACE OF DELIVERY :
TERMS OF DELIVERY : FOB NINGBO
INSURANCE . . . . : NOT ARR'GED BY KN
```

```
PRE CARRIAGE BY . :
VOYAGE . . . . . : 944E
ETS . . . . . . . : 28/10/2009
ETA . . . . . . . : 16/11/2009
MOVEMENT . . . . : CFS/CY
LOADED IN CONT. . : CADU4007408
```

MARKS & NOS	QTY PCS	DESCRIPTION OF GOODS	GRSS WT KGS	CBM
TOTAL	930	AS PER ATTACHED	9582.18	45.730

```
WE CERTIFY HAVING ASSUMED CONTROL OF THE ABOVE MENTIONED CONSIGNMENT IN
EXTERNAL APPARENT GOOD ORDER AND CONDITION, WITH IRREVOCABLE INSTRUCTIONS
FOR SHIPMENT.
FORWARDING INSTRUCTIONS CAN ONLY BE CANCELLED OR ALTERED AFTER SURRENDER
OF THE ORIGINAL CERTIFICATE TO US, AND PROVIDED WE ARE STILL IN A POSITION
TO COMPLY WITH SUCH CANCELLATION OR ALTERATION. THE GOODS AND INSTRUCTIONS
ARE ACCEPTED AND DEALT WITH SUBJECT TO OUR STANDARD TRADING CONDITIONS.

PLACE AND DATE OF ISSUE AS SHOWN ABOVE.FREIGHT COLLECT
NUMBER OF ORIGINALS ISSUED : 1/1  ON BOARD DATE:28/10/2009
```

KUEHNE & NAGEL LIMITED

```
(页 5 / 5 - This print header can be changed using the printHeader HTML tag - see the viewONE HTML manual for further information)

ATTACHMENT FOR                              FORWARDER'S CERTIFICATE OF RECEIPT
                                            **** PLEASE QUOTE IN YOUR REPLY ****
                                            FCR NO:        4359-0358-910.031
                                            NINGBO                 28/10/2009

MARKS & NOS         QTY   PCS   DESCRIPTION OF GOODS    GRSS WT KGS      CBM
OFFICE DEPOT        930   CARTON(S)  MERCHANDISE AS PER     9582.18    45.730
MEXICO                          FOLLOWING
VENDOR PART#:                   PURCHASE ORDERS:
UPC#:                           PO#BEIFA91030
PO#:                            ERASER
RFC#:                           BALL PEN
ODM-950324-V2A                  MECHANICAL PENCIL
SKU#:                           GEL INK PEN
CARTON DIMENSION:               ROLLER PEN
XX CM                           BOARD MARKER
COUNTRY OF ORIGIN               HIGHLIGHTER PEN
:CHINA                          MARKER PEN
CARTON#:XX OF XX                BRUSH
G.W.:XX KGS
N.T.:XX KGS                     CARGO RECEIVED DATE:
                                20.OCT.2009

                                LOADED IN CONTAINER:
                                CADU4007408/2451219/40G
         TOTAL      930                                     9582.18    45.730
```

ORIGINAL

1. Exporter	Certificate No.
BEIFA GROUP CO., LTD NO. 298 JIANGNAN EAST ROAD BEILUN NINGBO 315801 CHINA PHONE 86574 86186680	CCPIT 083196787 09C3302B0039/00000 **CERTIFICATE OF ORIGIN** **OF** **THE PEOPLE'S REPUBLIC OF CHINA**
2. Consignee OFFICE DEPOT DE MEXICO S.A. DE C.V. ODM950324-V2A, JUAN SALVADOR AGRAZ NO. 101 COL. SANTA FE DELEGACION CUAJIMALPA DE MORELOS C.P. 05300, MEXICO D.F. PHONE 52 46 40 00 FAX 52 46 40 00 EXT 3000	
3. Means of transport and route FROM NINGBO, CHINA TO MANZANILLO COL, MEXICO BY SEA	5. For certifying authority use only
4. Country / region of destination MEXICO	

6. Marks and numbers	7. Number and kind of packages; description of goods	8. H.S.Code	9. Quantity	10. Number and date of invoices
	NINE HUNDRED AND THIRTY (930) CTNS OF WRITING INSTRUMENT(ERASER, BALL PEN, MECHANICAL PENCIL, GEL IK PEN, ROLLER PEN, BOARD MARKER, HIGHLIGHTER PEN, MARKER PEN, BRUSH)AS PER PO NO.:BEIFA9T030 ************* OFFICE DEPOT MEXICO Vendor Part#: UPC#: PO#: RECL: ODM 950324-V2A SKU#: Carton Dimension: XX CM Country of Origin: China Carton#: xx of xx G.W.: XX KGS N.W.: XX KGS	96.08	105684PIEZAS	F0337 00080022 10 OCT.15, 2009

11. Declaration by the exporter The undersigned hereby declares that the above details and statements are correct; that all the goods were produced in China and that they comply with the Rules of Origin of the People's Republic of China. BEIFA GROUP CO., LTD NO. 298 JIANGNAN EAST ROAD BEILUN NINGBO PHONE 86574 86186680 NINGBO, CHINA NOV.2, 2009 Place and date, signature and stamp of authorized signatory	12. Certification It is hereby certified that the declaration by the exporter is correct. (中国国际贸易促进委员会 签证证明专用章 (甬) CHINA COUNCIL FOR THE PROMOTION OF INTERNATIONAL TRADE NING BO) Place and date, signature and stamp of certifying authority

Office DEPOT
Taking Care of Business

Quality Certificate

Vendor Name: BEIFA GROUP CO.,LTD
Factory Name: BEIFA GROUP CO.,LTD
Date: 2009-10-22

Shipment's Information:

PO#	Sku Mex	Description	Quantity
BEIFA91030	30054	PAQUETE CON 4 MARCADORES PARA PIZARRON BLANCO	20,736
BEIFA91030	32520	PLUMA 4 EN 1 CON REPUESTOS	3,024
BEIFA91030	32524	PAQUETE DE 12 BOLIGRAFOS NEGROS	8,480
BEIFA91030	35727	Boligrafo con grip caja con 12 pzas color negro	1,296
BEIFA91030	35728	Boligrafo con grip caja con 12 pzas color azul	864
BEIFA91030	35729	Marcador Permamente caja con 12 pzas negro PUNTA CINCEL	2,304
BEIFA91030	35730	Boligrafo 4 en 1 blister con 3	1,728
BEIFA91030	35732	Boligrafo Retractil con grip b/5	2,592
BEIFA91030	35733	Caja de marcadores para pizarron punta cincel con grip 12	2,232
BEIFA91030	35742	PAQUETE CON 4 MARCADORES PARA PIZARRON BLANCO PUNTA REDONDA	864
BEIFA91030	35762	PAQUETE CON 4 MARCADORES PARA PIZARRON BLANCO PUNTA CINCEL	5,040
BEIFA91030	41360	BOLIGRAFO RETRACTIL PUNTO MEDIANO TINTA NEGRA CAJA CON 12	1,008
BEIFA91030	41378	GOMAS BLANCAS 3PK	4,860
BEIFA91030	41356	BORRADOR PARA PIZARRON BLANCO	4,032
BEIFA91030	30046	PAQUETE CON 6 ROOLER BALL COL SURTIDOS	4,032
BEIFA91030	30049	PAQUETE CON 5 RESALTADORES	3,312
BEIFA91030	30058	PAQUETE DE 4 MARCADORES PERMANENTES PUNTO FINO	5,040
BEIFA91030	30060	PAQUETE DE 2 MARCADORES PERMANENTES PUNTO FINO	6,192
BEIFA91030	30064	JUEGO DE 3 LAPICEROS Y DOS MINAS DE REPUESTO	3,188
BEIFA91030	41285	MARCATEXTOS PUNTA CINCEL COLORES SURTIDOS	5,684

BEIFA91030	41287	MARCADORES PARA PIZARRON COLORES SURTIDOS	672
BEIFA91030	43793	BOLIGRAFO DE GEL CON PUNTO EXTRAFINO COLORES SURTIDOS	1,584
BEIFA91030	43795	BOLIGRAFO DE GEL CON PUNTO EXTRAFINO COLOR NEGRO	1,296
BEIFA91030	43796	BOLIGRAFO DE GEL PUNTO EXTRAFINO COLOR NEGRO	2,592
BEIFA91030	43797	BOLIGRAFO DE GEL PUNTO MEDIANO COLOR SURTIDOS FLOURESCENTES	2,592
BEIFA91030	43800	PLUMA PARA MOSTRADOR	3,456
BEIFA91030	43808	BOLIGRAFO RETRACTIL GREEN TRIANGULAR TINTA NEGRA COLORES VIVOS	864
BEIFA91030	42692	GOMAS BLANCAS MODELO OD30 2PK	8,160

This is to authorize release of shipment as listed above, under Invoice No. **F0337-09080022/46**, to Office Depot Mexico, based on inspection report # ODM-BeiFa90930-0910, dated: **2009-10-15**, by Factory.

This certificate does NOT relieve vendor / factory's responsibility to supply quality products to Office Depot Mexico.

Authorized Signature
(by Office Depot Global Sourcing QA):

Date: OCT/22/09

INV NO: F0337-09080022/46
DATE: 2009-11-06
L/C NO: M923539

BENEFICIARYS LETTER

THIS SHIPMENT NO SOLID WOOD PACKING MATERIAL AND CERTIFYING THAT COPIES OF ALL THE DOCUMENTS REQUIRED IN THIS L/C WERE SENT TO OFFICE DEPOT DE MEXICO, S.A. DE C.V. IN ATTENTION TO JOSE LUIS MARTINEZ CORONEL BY SPECIAL COURIER SERVICE.

BEIFA GROUP CO., LTD.

第十章

跨境电商单据

第一节 快递面单和"三单合一"

教学目标

最终目标：能根据交易信息填制跨境电商单据。
促成目标：
1. 了解跨境电商基本原理。
2. 熟悉常见快递面单格式。
3. 了解"三单合一"。

情景案例

机构：
外贸企业：宁波欧胜塑化有限公司（OCEAN PLASTIC & CHEMICAL PRODUCTS CO., LTD）。
国际快递公司：TNT。
人物：
小陈：宁波欧胜塑化有限公司跨境电商专员。
小许：TNT公司收件员。
背景资料：
（1）2016年6月6日晚，宁波欧胜塑化有限公司跨境电商业务部业务员小陈在速卖通平台上接到一份3盒唇膏（LIP BALM）的订单，客户已经付款。
（2）小陈打包货物，写好快递面单，准备发货（见图1、图2）。
（3）6月7日上午，小陈通知快递公司小许上门取件。

图1 快递面单

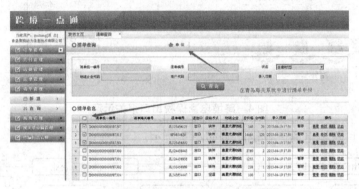

图2 跨境电商出口企业服务平台界面

跨境电商相关流程如图3和图4所示。

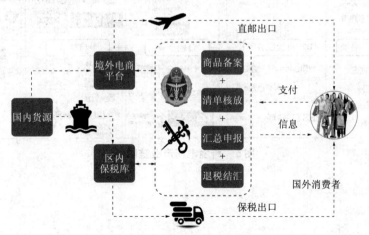

图3 跨境电商出口流程示意

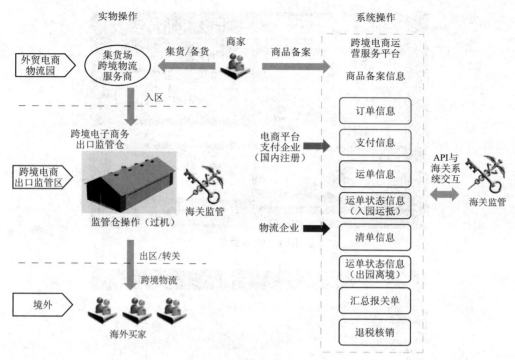

图 4 跨境电商保税出口报关示意

2016 中国出口跨境电商产业链图谱如图 5 所示。

图 5 跨境电商产业链图谱

相关知识

一、跨境电子商务的特点

跨境电子商务是基于网络发展起来的。网络空间相对于物理空间来说是一个新空间，是一个由网址和密码组成的虚拟但客观存在的世界。网络空间独特的价值标准和行为模式深刻地影响着跨境电子商务，使其不同于传统的交易方式而呈现出自己的特点。

跨境电子商务具有如下特征。

（一）全球性（Global Forum）

网络是一个没有边界的媒介体，具有全球性和非中心化的特征。依附于网络发生的跨境电子商务也因此具有了全球性和非中心化的特性。电子商务与传统的交易方式相比，其重要特点在于电子商务是一种无边界交易，丧失了传统交易所具有的地理因素。互联网用户不需要考虑跨越国界就可以把产品尤其是高附加值产品和服务提交到市场。网络的全球性特征带来的积极影响是信息的最大程度的共享，消极影响是用户必须面临因文化、政治和法律的不同而产生的风险。任何人只要具备了一定的技术手段，在任何时候、任何地方都可以让信息进入网络，相互联系进行交易。美国财政部在其财政报告中指出，对基于全球化的网络建立起来的电子商务活动进行课税是困难重重的，因为：电子商务是基于虚拟的电脑空间展开的，丧失了传统交易方式下的地理因素；电子商务中的制造商容易隐匿其住所而消费者对制造商的住所是漠不关心的。比如，一家很小的爱尔兰在线公司，通过一个可供世界各地的消费者点击观看的网页，就可以通过互联网销售其产品和服务，很难界定这一交易究竟是在哪个国家内发生的。

（二）无形性（Intangible）

网络的发展使数字化产品和服务的传输盛行。而数字化传输是通过不同类型的媒介，例如数据、声音和图像在全球化网络环境中集中而进行的，这些媒介在网络中是以计算机数据代码的形式出现的，因而是无形的。以一个 e-mail 信息的传输为例，这一信息首先要被服务器分解为数以百万计的数据包，然后按照 TCP/IP 协议，通过不同的网络路径传输到一个目的地服务器并重新组织转发给接收人，整个过程是在网络中瞬间完成的。电子商务是数字化传输活动的一种特殊形式，其无形性使税务机关很难控制和检查销售商的交易活动，税务机关面对的交易记录都是体现为数据代码的形式，使税务核查员无法准确地计算销售所得和利润所得，从而给税收带来困难。

数字化产品和服务基于数字传输活动的特性也必然具有无形性，传统交易以实物交易为主，而在电子商务中，无形产品却可以替代实物成为交易的对象。以书籍为例，传统的纸质书籍，其排版、印刷、销售和购买被看作产品的生产、销售。然而在电子商务交易中，消费者只要购买网上的数据权便可以使用书中的知识和信息。

（三）匿名性（Anonymous）

由于跨境电子商务具有非中心化和全球性的特性，因此很难识别电子商务用户的身份和其所处的地理位置。在线交易的消费者往往不显示自己的真实身份和自己的地理位置，重要的是这丝毫不影响交易的进行，网络的匿名性也允许消费者这样做。在虚拟社会里，隐匿身份的便利迅即导致自由与责任的不对称。人们在这里可以享受最大的自由，却只承担最小的责任，甚至干脆逃避责任。

电子商务交易的匿名性导致了逃避税现象的恶化，网络的发展降低了避税成本，使电子商务避税更轻松易行。电子商务交易的匿名性使应纳税人利用避税地联机金融机构规避税收监管成为可能。电子货币的广泛使用，以及国际互联网所提供的某些避税地联机银行对客户的"完全税收保护"，使纳税人可将其源于世界各国的投资所得直接汇入避税地联机银行，规避了应纳所得税。美国国内收入服务处（IRS）在其规模最大的一次审计调查中发现，大量的居民纳税人通过离岸避税地的金融机构隐藏了大量的应税收入。而美国政府估计大约三万亿美元的资金因受避税地联机银行的"完全税收保护"而被藏匿在避税地。

（四）即时性（Instantaneous）

对于网络而言，传输的速度和地理距离无关。传统交易模式，信息交流方式如信函、电报、传真等，在信息的发送与接收间，存在着长短不同的时间差。而电子商务中的信息交流，无论实际时空距离远近，一方发送信息与另一方接收信息几乎是同时的，就如同生活中面对面交谈。某些数字化产品（如音像制品、软件等）的交易，还可以即时清结，订货、付款、交货都可以在瞬间完成。

电子商务交易的即时性提高了人们交往和交易的效率，免去了传统交易中的中介环节，但也隐藏了法律危机。

（五）无纸化（Paperless）

电子商务主要采取无纸化操作的方式，这是以电子商务形式进行交易的主要特征。在电子商务中，电子计算机通信记录取代了一系列的纸面交易文件。由于电子信息以比特的形式存在和传送，整个信息发送和接收过程实现了无纸化。无纸化带来的积极影响是使信息传递摆脱了纸张的限制，但由于传统法律的许多规范是以规范"有纸交易"为出发点的，因此，无纸化带来了一定程度上法律的混乱。

电子商务以数字合同、数字时间截取了传统贸易中的书面合同、结算票据，削弱了税务当局获取跨国纳税人经营状况和财务信息的能力，且电子商务所采用的其他保密措施也将增加税务机关掌握纳税人财务信息的难度。在某些交易无据可查的情形下，跨国纳税人的申报额将会大大降低，应纳税所得额和所征税款都将少于实际所达到的数量，从而引起征税国国际税收流失。例如，世界各国普遍开征的传统税种之一的印花税，其课税对象是交易各方提供的书面凭证，课税环节为各种法律合同、凭证的书立或做成，而在网络交易无纸化的情况下，物质形态的合同、凭证形式已不复存在，因而印花税的合同、凭证贴花（即完成印花税的缴纳行为）便无从下手。

（六）快速演进（Rapidly Evolving）

基于互联网的电子商务活动处在瞬息万变的过程中，短短的几十年中，电子交易经历了从 EDI 到电子商务零售业的兴起的过程，而数字化产品和服务更是花样出新，不断地改变着人类的生活。

跨境电子商务具有不同于传统贸易方式的诸多特点，而传统的监管制度是在传统的贸易方式下产生的，必然会在电子商务贸易中漏洞百出。网络深刻地影响着人类社会，也给相应的法律规范带来了前所未有的冲击与挑战。

二、跨境电子商务模式

我国跨境电子商务主要分为企业对企业（即 B2B）和企业对消费者（即 B2C）的贸易模式。在 B2B 模式下，企业运用电子商务以广告和信息发布为主，成交和通关流程基本在线下完成，本质上仍属传统贸易，已纳入海关一般贸易统计。在 B2C 模式下，我国企业直接面对国外消费者，以销售个人消费品为主，物流方面主要采用航空小包、邮寄、快递等方式，其报关主体是邮政或快递公司，目前大多未纳入海关登记。

跨境电子商务还可分为出口跨境电子商务和进口跨境电子商务。

三、快递面单

快递面单是指快递行业在运送货物的过程中用以记录发件人、收件人以及产品重量、价格等相关信息的单据。目前快递行业多用条码快递单，以保证快递行业的连续数据输出，便于管理。

目前快递面单所用纸张一般为多联无碳复写纸等，加工工艺中主要用到连码、跳码等可变码的印刷，多为3联以上，特别是 EMS 等用的快递单多为5联或6联。快递面单可分为普通条码单和背胶条码单，普通条码单需配合快递袋使用，背胶条码单最后一联可撕开贴在货物上，使用更加方便，常规尺寸有 217mm×127mm、230mm×140mm、230mm×127mm、240mm×150mm 等。目前快递运单生产行业中所用的最先进的系统是柯达万印喷码系统，具有加工效率高、精密度高和稳定性高等优势。

四、三单合一

"三单"指在跨境电子商务通关服务平台上，电子商务企业提供的报关单、支付企业提供的支付清单、物流企业提供的物流运单。根据海关总署的规定，对于通过保税仓入境的物品过往海关时需要"三单合一"，即支付单、订单、物流单三单要一致匹配。支付单由有支付资质的企业推送给海关，订单和物流单由跨境电子商务平台或提供保税仓仓储物流服务的第三方公司推送给海关，海关核对三单信息，没有问题后再放行。

实训练习题

请根据交易信息制作快递面单

卖方信息：OCEAN PLASTIC & CHEMICAL PRODUCTS CO., LTD

买家信息：Robinson 先生

国：U.S.A.　　　州：New Jersey　　　城市：Parsippany

地址：1515 Route Ten　　　邮政编码：07054-4596　　　电话：800-755-4444

货物信息：唇膏40支

包装：1个纸箱，净重3kg，毛重4kg，15cm×15cm×15cm